GETTING COLLEGE READY

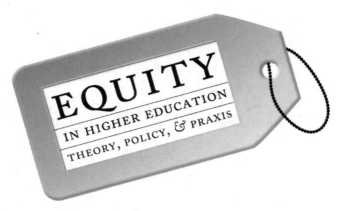

EQUITY
IN HIGHER EDUCATION
THEORY, POLICY, & PRAXIS

Virginia Stead, H.B.A., B.Ed., M.Ed., Ed.D.
GENERAL EDITOR

VOL. 3

The Equity in Higher Education Theory, Policy, & Praxis series
is part of the Peter Lang Education list.
Every volume is peer reviewed and meets
the highest quality standards for content and production.

PETER LANG
New York • Bern • Frankfurt • Berlin
Brussels • Vienna • Oxford • Warsaw

Julie Minikel-Lacocque

GETTING COLLEGE READY

Latin@ Student Experiences
of Race, Access, and Belonging at
Predominantly White Universities

PETER LANG
New York • Bern • Frankfurt • Berlin
Brussels • Vienna • Oxford • Warsaw

Library of Congress Cataloging-in-Publication Data
Minikel-Lacocque, Julie.
Getting college ready: Latin@ student experiences of race, access, and belonging
at predominantly White universities / Julie Minikel-Lacocque.
pages cm. — (Equity in higher education theory, policy, & praxis; v. 3)
Includes bibliographical references and index.
1. Hispanic American college students. 2. Hispanic American college students—
Social conditions. 3. Hispanic Americans—Education (Higher)—Social aspects.
4. College student orientation—United States. 5. College attendance—United States.
6. Universities and colleges—United States—Sociological aspects.
7. Discrimination in higher education—United States.
8. Educational equalization—United States. I. Title.
LC2670.6.M6   378.1'982968073—dc23   2015000939
ISBN 978-1-4331-2765-6 (hardcover)
ISBN 978-1-4331-2764-9 (paperback)
ISBN 978-1-4539-1538-7 (e-book)
ISSN 2330-4502 (print)
ISSN 2330-4510 (online)

Bibliographic information published by **Die Deutsche Nationalbibliothek.**
Die Deutsche Nationalbibliothek lists this publication in the "Deutsche
Nationalbibliografie"; detailed bibliographic data are available
on the Internet at http://dnb.d-nb.de/.

Author photo by Amelia John

© 2015 Peter Lang Publishing, Inc., New York
29 Broadway, 18th floor, New York, NY 10006
www.peterlang.com

Printed in the United States of America

To the six students who
graciously allowed me into their lives
and taught me much.
Mil gracias.

TABLE OF CONTENTS

ACKNOWLEDGMENTS

First and foremost, my deepest gratitude goes to Antonio, Crystal, Engracia, Jasmine, Mario, and Moriah. I also wish to thank the various CMU staff and faculty members who allowed me into their offices and classrooms, agreeing to speak with me in the name of improving college access and success for underrepresented students.

Maggie Hawkins guided me through years of preparation for this project. Through my apprenticeship with her and her caring support, whole worlds were opened up to me. Her insight and critique on various drafts of this project were invaluable. Simone Schweber generously served as my "ideas consultant" during multiple phases of this project. I especially thank her for the hours spent together in her office as she helped me work through the sometimes thorny nature of in-depth, qualitative research. It was through these conversations and her faith in me as a scholar that I learned how to conduct humane, compassionate research.

I wish to thank others who read chapters and offered their keen insight: Paula McAvoy, Derria Byrd, Robin Fox, Gloria Ladson-Billings, Stacey Lee, Ruth López Turley, René Antróp-González, Amato Nocera, Marci Alexander, and Tom Blau. For providing meals and play dates and sharing in my excitement along the way, I thank Dawn Blau and Jean Haughwout. My appreciation also goes to the friends and family members who listened with a supportive ear as I talked about this research and understood my absence, physical or figurative, due to my absorption in this project.

Heartfelt appreciation goes to my parents, Maria and Jim, for providing unwavering support, reading drafts along the way, and helping with childcare so I could squeeze in those all-important "writing days." My unending gratitude to Maria, my mother, whose passion for writing sparked my own, and, who, with love, patience, and exceptionally hard work, helped me learn to write so many years ago. Thank you to my sisters, who have always encouraged me, have read and engaged with my work, and have taught me much.

Thank you to Katy Heyning and the College of Education and Professional Studies at the University of Wisconsin-Whitewater, whose generous support and guidance made this book possible. I also thank my wonderful students at UW-Whitewater for their excitement and curiosity about this book. And I deeply thank the editor of this series, Virginia Stead, for her kind responsiveness and sharp editing.

And finally, and most certainly not least, my profound gratitude goes to my life partner and number one support, David. I could not have done this without his unrelenting encouragement, expert parenting abilities, and sharp intellect that was always at the ready for numerous consultations. My thanks and love go to my children, Benjamin and Adah, for their curiosity, sense of justice, and for their understanding of the time I needed to dedicate to this project. Thank you.

INTRODUCTION

When I left home for college on that August morning in 1991, I was ready. My parents, both college educated, sat quietly in front of me, navigating our trip through the picturesque midwestern landscape sprawled before us. The giddy excitement that pulsed through me was only somewhat tempered by the knowledge that within a matter of hours I would face an emotional goodbye to them. Mostly, I was ready. Ready to take on the next chapter of my life, this time-honored last stage on the road to becoming a full-fledged adult. I was ready to explore, to experiment, to "find myself." I was confident in the preparation my suburban public education had provided me, and I was ready to take on something more challenging. I never once doubted my parents' ability to pay my tuition, and I planned on looking for a part-time campus job in a few weeks. I was ready to leave my friends and family, all of whom were either college graduates or current students themselves. Significantly, I am also White. I embarked on this adventure knowing that my peers in college would be from similar backgrounds, not only educationally and socioeconomically but also racially. I was not afraid of standing out or being mistreated because of how I looked.

My small liberal arts college, importantly, was also ready for me. It boasted a long history of educating mostly middle- and upper-class Whites, and it was one of the few colleges of its age that opened its doors to men *and* women since its inception. It was known for its academic rigor, its enriching campus-sponsored activities and programs, and its robust social life. It was, in all ways, ready for a well-educated, middle-class, White feminist student who was prepared to take on the many challenges it would offer.

This book, however, is not about the luxury of such a seamless transition to college. This book is about the experiences of six Latin@ college students, most of whom are the first in their families to attend college, as they transition to a prestigious, predominantly White state flagship university in the Midwest, which I call Central Midwestern University (CMU).[1] Over the course of a year, I got to know these young men and women as they shared their lives with me. In what follows, I share their voices and experiences as I understood them as well as the lessons gleaned from my time with them—lessons that demand we examine the ways in which we conceive of "college readiness."

The Changing Face of College in the United States: A Reality?

At its inception in the late 1780s, U.S. higher education was solely for the elite white male (for a thorough history of higher education in the United States, see Thelin, 2004). Roughly 50 years later, women's colleges were founded, followed by various coeducational institutions. Federal policies such as the Morrill Land Grant Act of 1862 and the GI Bill of 1944 were aimed, in part, at increasing access to higher education, thus effectively diversifying campuses. This series of changes on U.S. campuses has continued today, less as a result of federal policies directed at higher education and more due to social change. Today, greater attention is paid, for example, on many campuses to accessibility for those students with physical disabilities; most campuses have recognized the need to create a safe atmosphere for LGBTQ students; various types of support exist for first-generation students, students from a low SES, and for Students of Color; and, finally, campuses across the United States are publicly engaged in efforts to recruit students and faculty from underrepresented groups.

Indeed, efforts to make campuses more diverse are made highly visible; most universities showcase their commitment to diversity on their website's homepage and in recruiting materials. These public displays of inclusion can mask an unfavorable reality, however. One prominent public university's website, for example, recently displayed a photograph of fans at a sporting event. It was discovered, however, that the university used computer software to alter a photograph of a group of White fans at the sporting event to include images of students of color, thus giving the appearance of a more diverse crowd. Indeed, a closer look reveals a disconnect between rhetoric and reality; despite these advertised efforts, most public four-year universities remain predominantly White.

The College Student Population Today

Attaining a college education is often equated with "moving up in the world," and with good reason. College graduates not only have access to more desirable jobs and enjoy the higher status associated with a college degree, but they also have a significantly higher earning potential than their non-college-educated peers (Barrow & Rouse, 2005). A post-secondary education, however, is not equally accessible to all sectors of the U.S. population, which is becoming increasingly diverse: Between 2000 and 2010, 63% of the growth in the population aged 18 to 24 years was People of Color (U.S. Census Bureau, as reported in Orfield, Marin, & Horn, 2005, p. 61). Additionally, nearly half of U.S. public high school graduates came from lower-income families in 2006 (Orfield et al., 2009, p. 61). Thus, more than ever, the pool of potential college students is highly diverse both racially and socioeconomically.

Unfortunately, the reality of an increasingly diverse population has decidedly not translated into our college campuses becoming more diverse. A brief stroll through a sampling of campuses across the U.S. reveals that far too many of our institutions of higher education—even those that are public and therefore ostensibly accessible to a wider portion of the population—are predominantly White. Indeed, differences in college-going and -completion rates along socioeconomic and racial divides are staggeringly large: In 2000, the gap in college-going rates between low- and high-income traditionally aged college students was nearly 30%, and today these discrepancies continue to grow (College Board, 2002, as reported in Orfield et al., 2005, p. 62). With regard to race, in 2010, 30.3% of Whites aged 25 and over had a bachelor's degree or higher, compared to 19.8% of African-Americans and only 13.9% of Latinos (Statistical Abstract of the United States: 2012, p. 151). In addition, the first-generation college students are "relatively rare" at the nation's selective institutions of higher education (Espenshade & Radford, 2009, p. 23).

The State of Affairs at Flagship Campuses in the United States

Flagship universities in the United States are commonly conceived of as the largest, most prominent public research-focused university in a given state, designed to offer an affordable, top-notch education to its citizens. As Tobin (2009) explains, American flagship universities "were created to meet the social and economic needs of the states that chartered them, to serve as a great equalizer and preserver of an open, upwardly mobile society..." (p. 240). Most flagship universities are also land-grant institutions, a category brought about by the Morrill Land Grant Act of 1862. The Morrill Act created a partnership between the federal and state governments and "granted" states land on which the state was mandated to provide accessible, affordable higher education focused on "useful arts" to its citizens. However, the perceived legacy of the Morrill Act is contested, and some scholars argue that the effects of the act "have been misunderstood or exaggerated" and point out that many "land-grant" institutions already existed before the Morrill Act, and, what's more, were already engaged in efforts to offer "practical" fields of study (Thelin, 2004, p. 76–77).

Despite the commonly understood mission of flagships to be the "people's universities," these institutions also face criticism for their lack of diversity. In fact, the lack of diversity seems to be *more* pronounced at the country's flagship universities, and the problem is worsening. At flagships, the percentage of students from families in the top income quartile has been steadily rising since 1982; and, at the same time, the percentage of students from low-income families at flagships has been declining (Tobin, 2009). Rising tuition costs and increased selectivity at many flagships over the last few decades have combined to decrease access to these institutions (Bowen, Chingos, & McPherson, 2009). In addition, at the majority of flagships, the percentage of students with parents who have college degrees is increasing, as is the percentage of students with parents holding graduate degrees (Tobin, 2009). What's more, although both the number and proportion of Pell Grant recipients has risen overall, the percentage of these students at flagship universities has declined (Tobin, 2009). Bowen and colleagues (2009) put this state of affairs in plain terms: "...flagships are far from 'representative'; the students at these prestigious universities are, by any measure, a special group" (p. 15).

U.S. Latin@s in Higher Education

Nested within the larger context of the widening achievement gap in the U.S. with regard to post secondary education, as well as the lack of diversity on our campuses, is the condition of college access and persistence for U.S. Latin@s. Indeed, the word "crisis" was recently used to describe the educational context for U.S. Latin@s, who are at once the least educated and the fastest-growing group within the United States (Gándara & Contreras, 2009). Specifically, in 2006, Latin@s made up 19% of the school-age population in the United States; in 2025, one in four or 25% of K-12 students in the country will be Latin@ (Gándara & Contreras, 2009, p. 304–05). In terms of college completion, Latin@s are lagging behind other racial groups, as seen above. And, in 2005, when the students in the study presented here finished their junior year in high school, only 50% of U.S. Latin@ high school students graduated. Additionally, compared to 73% of White high school graduates, 54% of Latin@ graduates went directly to college; the majority of this 54%, however, attended two-year institutions. Significantly, a mere seven percent of bachelor's degrees were given to Latin@s (U.S. Department of Education, 2007 & 2006.). What's more, although there has been "substantial growth" in post-secondary degree completion for other groups, Latin@ degree completion has "remained stagnant" (Gándara & Contreras, 2009, p. 24).

Given these statistics, it is crucial that we learn more about the college experiences of those Latin@ students who *do* enroll in selective institutions—perhaps specifically selective, *public* institutions that are ostensibly charged with offering accessible, high-quality programs—most of which are predominantly White. However, despite the influential body of research on Latin@ students' experiences in K–12 schooling (e.g., Valenzuela, 1999; Valdés, 1996; Valdés, 2001; and Flores-González, 2002; Gándara & Contreras, 2009), in-depth qualitative research that explores the lives of Latin@ students as they transition to college is relatively scarce.

The Study

Over the course of one year, I got to know Antonio, Crystal, Engracia, Jasmine, Mario, and Moriah as I studied their transitions to Central Midwestern University (CMU). CMU is located in Collegeville, a mid-sized, liberal-leaning city and is the state's flagship university. CMU's website boasts that it has "long been recognized" as a national leader in terms of "achievement and prestige." One need not spend more than a matter of minutes on the sprawling, attractive campus, however, to notice the stark lack of diversity: CMU's student body is 88% White, 5.4% Asian American, 3.2% Hispanic, 2.8% African American, and only .8% Native American. Thus, the students in this study represent a distinct minority on CMU's campus. Specifically, these students self-identify as Latino, Latina, Hispanic, Mexican-American, Chicano, and/or Puerto Rican; all of the students told me they use more than one term to self-identify.

I met these young men and women during the summer just after they graduated high school. It was then that I began interviewing them about their experiences in their K-12 schooling, college preparation, and expectations of college generally and of CMU specifically. I continued to interview them, get to know them, attend classes with them, and spend time with them in various ways, ranging from serving as a tutor to providing transportation when needed. In addition to my individual interviews with the students, I gathered the students and conducted one group interview, or "focus group," toward the end of their first year at CMU. I also did follow-up interviews three years later. Finally, I interviewed CMU staff members who were charged with supporting underrepresented students at CMU.

As part of my research and analytical process, I consistently shared my interpretations with the student-participants and asked for feedback. I also gave the student-participants a draft of anything I wrote that included them, and I discussed my work with each of them. I did not move forward with any written interpretations of the research until I had given each student-participant the chance to read and approve what I had written. Importantly, however, there was great variety in the students' level of involvement in this process: For example, one student consistently asked me when I would have something ready for her to read, and another welcomed the process but told me he was too busy to read what I had written. The others fell somewhere between these two extremes. None of the students, however, had suggestions for substantial changes; rather, they reflected on what they had read when we met for interviews or emailed me their brief comments.

Framing the Study: Critical Race Theory

Various educational researchers have taken up Critical Race Theory (CRT) to, in part, refute ideologies regarding schooling that treat racial minorities as "other" and deficient. (See, as examples, Ladson-Billings & Tate, 1995;

Ladson-Billings, 1998; Ladson-Billings & Donnor, 2005; Solórzano & Yosso, 2000; Solórzano, Villalpando & Oseguera, 2005; Yosso, Smith, Ceja, & Solórzano, 2009; Yosso 2005, 2006.) CRT theorists Ladson-Billings and Tate (1995) insist that theories about race must be analyzed explicitly within educational research—in addition to class- and gender-based theories—if we are to sufficiently address inequality in the United States. In essence, the use of CRT in education foregrounds racial inequalities in schooling, challenges the ways in which schooling and race are conceived of within academia, centers the experiences of People of Color, and calls for a focus on social justice.

The following six summative themes, identified by Matsuda, Lawrence, Delgado, and Crenshaw (1993), have come to define CRT and are commonly cited by CRT scholars:

1. Critical Race Theory recognizes that racism is endemic to American life.
2. Critical Race Theory expresses scepticism toward dominant legal claims of neutrality, objectivity, colorblindness, and meritocracy.
3. Critical Race Theory challenges ahistoricism and insists on a contextual/historical analysis of the law.... Critical race theorists... adopt a stance that presumes that racism has contributed to all contemporary manifestations of group advantage and disadvantage.
4. Critical Race Theory insists on recognition of the experiential knowledge of people of color and our communities of origin in analysing law and society.
5. Critical Race Theory is interdisciplinary.
6. Critical Race Theory works toward the end of eliminating racial oppression as part of the broader goal of ending all forms of oppression. (p. 6)

It is through this lens of CRT that I share and analyze the experiences of Antonio, Crystal, Engracia, Jasmine, Mario, and Moriah. Indeed, the issue of race was woven into their transition to CMU, and we have much to learn from these students' voices.

The Role and Subjectivity of the Researcher

Within the CRT framework discussed above, neutrality and objectivity are understood not only as unattainable but also as undesirable entities that lead to the misrepresentation of the experiences of People of Color and detract from the kind of knowledge that becomes possible through relationships (Yosso,

2005). As Yosso explains, CRT "challenges notions of 'neutral' research or 'objective' researchers and exposes deficit-informed research that silences, ignores and distorts epistemologies of People of Color" (2005, p. 73). Thus, in keeping with CRT, relationships are at the core of the study presented here. Over the course of the study, I came to know and care for each of the study participants. Indeed, the comfortable, familiar relationships that developed between each participant and me allowed for rich, in-depth conversations about the students' lives and experiences during their transitions to CMU. In short, it was my goal to understand as best I could, through personal interactions, the lived experiences of my study participants and then to relate those experiences responsibly.

Thus, the attempt to do so "responsibly" is at least two-fold. First, honoring and telling their personal stories does its part to push the conversation on racism forward. As Morfin, Perez, Parker, Lynn, and Arrona explain, "A key aspect of the narrative scholarship in CRT is its focus on how stories of racism are quite personal and appear so for a reason: They attempt to make the reader question whether any person should be subjected to the treatment detailed in the story" (2006, p. 251–2). Secondly, my own positionality and subjectivity must be recognized. As a White female researcher, I do not claim to have intimate, firsthand knowledge of being the target of any type of racism, nor do I claim to understand experientially what it is like to be a Person of Color on a predominantly White campus. This book, though based on the experiences and words of the students in my study, is inevitably my story of what the students experienced. And, although I consistently shared my impressions and writings with the study participants and asked for their feedback, it is, ultimately, my interpretation of their experiences that gets publicly highlighted.

In some ways, this discussion echoes Geertz's (1973) foundational notions of anthropological research. In Geertz's words, "The essential vocation of interpretive anthropology is ... to make available to us answers that others... have given, and thus include them in the consultable record of what man [sic] has said" (p. 30). In representing these students' stories, then, we add them to the "record" of what people have said—a record that has been dominated by experiences of Whites. And both CRT and Geertz call us to go beyond merely adding to this "record." As discussed earlier, CRT requires a redressing of problems vis-à-vis a commitment to social justice. Relatedly, Geertz argues that part of the researcher's responsibility is "...stating, explicitly as we can manage, what the knowledge thus attained demonstrates about the society in which it is found and, beyond that, about social life as such" (1973, p. 27).

It is my hope, then, taking into consideration these inherent issues of positionality, subjectivity, and representation, that my involvement in the discussion will add to a necessarily diverse and multifaceted approach to increasing college access and retention for underrepresented groups as well as combating racism. It is also my hope that my work here sparks deeper examination of the complexity of identity formation as well as of the notions of "inclusion" and "multiculture" and that this work will contribute to a greater understanding across differences, which, in turn, will improve the schooling experiences for underrepresented students.

Organization of the Book

Chapter One introduces the reader to each of the six students through portraiture (Lawrence-Lightfoot & Hoffmann Davis, 1997). The brief portraits are, in essence, my story of who they are, or, perhaps more appropriately, who they *were* as they transitioned to Central Midwestern University.

Chapter Two focuses on the types of support the students have received related to college access and success. Specifically, after discussing the relationship between capital and the types of programs addressed above, I describe the college access/support programs represented in this study. Then, in Chapter Three, I examine the students' experiences with the programs as well as their path gaining access to the programs. I discuss key programmatic components as well as implications for supporting the transition to college for underrepresented students and call into question some common ways of measuring "success" in college.

Chapter Four explores identity formation vis-à-vis race. After discussing the construction of the very notion of race, I focus on Antonio and Mario and the ways in which each student perceived and experienced "race" as he transitioned to CMU and how these perceptions and experiences participated in each student's identity formation.

In Chapter Five, I explicitly address racism. After providing a context for present-day forms of racism and discussing current theories on the same, I pay specific theoretical and practical attention to *racial microaggressions*. Through an analysis of the students' experiences with racism at CMU, I argue for greater understanding and increased use of the term "racial microaggressions" within education generally, and specifically with regard to higher education. I also, however, argue for specific changes in the existing framework of racial microaggressions. Implications for discussions of racism writ large as well as for specific changes on college campuses are discussed.

Chapter Six, with its exclusive focus on Jasmine, a fundamentalist Christian who identifies as Mexican American, addresses the complex relationship between religious fundamentalism and public schooling. Specifically, I apply the notion of familial capital (Yosso, 2005, 2006), which is based in Critical Race Theory, to Jasmine's case. Through an examination of the ways in which her fundamentalist background and her liberal arts college education interact, I discuss implications for the use of familial capital and call for further study of fundamentalism and public education as well as for a nuanced expansion of concept of "multiculturalism."

Chapter Seven focuses on Engracia and the particular and sometimes complicated role that family members can play in one's education. Specifically, in this chapter, I examine the ways in which Engracia's family members—particularly her parents—were influential in the formation of her "school kid identity" (Flores-González, 2002) and, subsequently, how her relationship with her parents became strained as she transitioned to CMU. Finally, Chapter Eight concludes the book and offers suggestions for "getting college ready."

A Glossary of Key Terms Used to Refer to Students

In addition to Students of Color and White students, four other terms are frequently used in this book to refer to students: Latinos, Latino/a(s), Latin@s, and underrepresented students. Below, I define each term as it is used in this book and explain how I use each term to refer to students.

Latino(s)

The term "Latino" is commonly used as a catch-all term for all Latino subgroups, and Mexican-Americans are commonly the largest of these subgroups (Gándara & Contreras, 2009, p. 8). Importantly, the term "Latino" includes people from many different racial backgrounds and thus does not refer to one "race." As Gándara and Contreras (2009) explain, despite the great diversity within the group labelled "Latino," most U.S. Latinos "encounter surprisingly similar educational challenges" (p. 7).

Latino/a(s)

The common use of "Latino/a" instead of "Latino" is meant to include males ("Latinos") *and* females ("Latinas") instead of only males, as reflected in the masculine ending "o."

Latin@

Historically, "Latino" was used to refer to everyone: male, female, and other gender identities. Then "Latino/a" became commonplace, which refers to (and includes) both male and female. Latin@ is the relatively new spelling that is meant to both shorten "Latino/a," and, importantly, be more inclusive in terms of gender identity. In sum, this term challenges the dominance of the masculine "o" ending in Spanish; it recognizes various gender identities instead of the normative binary; and it effectively offers a more concise spelling.

Underrepresented Students

In this book, the term "underrepresented students" includes students from a low SES, Students of Color, and/or first-generation college students.

How I Use These Terms

Because the self-identifications of the students in this study vary, I use the general term "Latin@" as the default term. When referring to a specific student, however, I use whichever term that student uses to self-identify. When quoting research that uses the Latino/a binary, I use "Latino/a."

· 1 ·

STUDENT PORTRAITS

In this chapter, I provide a portrait (Lawrence-Lightfoot & Hoffmann Davis, 1997) of each of the six students in this book. My aim, through using portraiture, is to help each student "come alive" for the reader and become the multifaceted, complex beings they are before moving into the subsequent chapters that focus on specific aspects of their lives. The portraits are meant to be accessible and free of academic language. As Lawrence-Lightfoot (1997) explains, "The attempt is to move beyond the academy's inner circle, to speak in a language that is not coded or exclusive, and to develop texts that will seduce the readers into thinking more deeply about issues that concern them" (p. 10).

Antonio

"So, how would your friends from back home describe you?" I asked Antonio, who was dressed in an oversized white T-shirt, baggy denim shorts, and perfectly clean white sneakers. He fiddled with the large pendant hanging from a thick gold chain around his neck as we wrapped up our first interview in a crowded Collegeville café.

"Funny—like I'm a real funny guy, I guess," he chuckled. "Uh, cool, laid-back. Calm, 'cause, yeah, I'm not good at rushing into things, so I take my time. Stuff like that. And I'm good to hang around with," he finished, adjusting the backwards baseball cap that sat atop his dark, gelled hair.

Over the course of the study, as well as during the years since, the self-description he offered on that June day in Collegeville, just months before starting his college career, represents a handful of characteristics that Antonio considers central to who he is. As I got to know him, I also found that he was cool, laid-back, funny, and good to be around. He always had a welcoming smile, making his dark-brown eyes dance with laughter; indeed, it was rare to see Antonio relate a story that didn't make me laugh at one point or another. His calm demeanor was a near constant in my experience: As if philosophically opposed to rushing, he moved slowly and calmly; and in our conversations, he sat comfortably reclined in his chair, chatting with me easily. He is also a loyal friend who has a close circle of peers he considers central to his life—friends made both at CMU and prior to college.

Of course, there is more to Antonio than his calmness, humor, and friendship. He is also a socially aware, budding activist whose community involvement started before he came to CMU and continues today. He is a sports enthusiast who played high school football and baseball but opted out of baseball his senior year to have more time to "have fun" before moving to Collegeville. He is a confident, thoughtful, social young man.

The son of a Mexican-American father and a White mother from the Midwest, Antonio identifies as "Chicano" or Mexican-American and has grown up in the same urban Lakeside neighborhood his entire life. His father, born in Texas, worked as a migrant worker before moving to Lakeside at 17. "My dad's whole family," he explained, "my dad and all his brothers and sisters and father, they are all migrant workers. They worked the fields in Texas, Oklahoma. They used to pick grapes and all that."

"So how did he come up to Lakeside?" I asked.

"They worked in the fields for a long time, from when they were little until when my dad came to Lakeside to work when he was 17. He left on his own. He came up here because there were a lot of job openings up in the north part of the country back then."

Antonio's father eventually earned a GED and now works at a car parts factory in Lakeside. His mother has a bachelor's degree from the state university in Lakeside and works at a financial planning firm. He explained that although his three older half-siblings, all in their thirties, do not have college degrees, he and his younger brother were always expected to go to college:

> I kinda always knew I would go to college, I guess. Like it was always pushed for me to do it. My parents expected me to 'cause my mom did it. She got her bachelor's degree, and my dad never did—he got his GED—so they always wanted me to get to college for sure. And I was always pushing in that direction since I always did good in school. Plus, they never forced me to get a job, so that helped me realize that I should do schooling instead of getting a job for quick money.

Although Antonio consistently earned good grades, he did not spend much time studying. He explained that he "picks up things quickly" and simply did not need to study much to earn good grades. School, however, was a positive aspect of Antonio's life; he enjoyed school—both academically and socially—and was involved in activities ranging from playing sports to helping organize health fairs designed to educate his peers about issues related to wellness.

Within the Lakeside public school system, students have the option to choose which school to attend, and the vast majority exercise this right. Students attend their neighborhood schools only if they have not chosen a different school. Placement tests are required for acceptance to many of the high schools. Antonio and his parents consciously chose the Lakeside public schools he attended. His parents sent him to a bilingual elementary school, and Antonio, with the encouragement of his parents, decided to apply to Roberts High, Lakeside's premier public college-prep high school, and was accepted. While he nearly attended a different high school because most of his friends were going there, he decided in the end to attend Roberts.

"At first I had thought Herrington," he explained, "because I knew a lot of people that were going there, and I didn't know many that were going to Roberts. But then I changed my mind 'cause I heard Roberts was a good school. It was like a school for the college bound, to help us get there. So then there was only a couple of us from my middle school that went there. There was maybe like six or seven of us. Then like at the end, there may have been like 3 or 4. 'Cause like the other ones dropped out."

"So are you glad you went to Roberts? Were you glad with the choice?" I asked. "Yeah. And I'm glad I was a good student, because it gets you ready for college. I learned a lot, I guess. So I think they prepared me well for college."

Although Antonio had expected to go to college since he was little, participating in the college access program, Pre-College, was a pivotal point in his getting to CMU. As I explain in Chapter 2 Antonio was sent a letter from this program, encouraging him to apply. Upon acceptance to the program in his first year of high school, Antonio received intensive college preparation through summer workshops on CMU's campus, which included courses such as ACT preparation, college writing, and English literature. Thus, Pre-College, a partnership between CMU and various public school systems in the state, provided Antonio with academic preparation for college *and* familiarized him with college life through the required summer stays on campus. What's more, because the same students attended summer workshops year after year, he came to CMU with a built-in group of friends.

Despite the confidence Antonio had in the preparation he received through Pre-College and his college-prep high school, he was somewhat apprehensive about being able to earn good grades at CMU. When I asked him if he was worried about anything in terms of starting college, he explained, "Just grade-wise, I guess. Most likely classes will be tougher because this is one of the higher colleges in the nation, so most likely the classes are going to be rigorous and all that. Just the workload, because I can't study for that long of a period. My priority level too. I don't know. Most of the time, I put fun over school, but I still get my stuff done."

"What are you excited about as far as college goes?"

"I am excited for actual college to start," he said, referring to the fact that he was on campus all summer for the Summer Bridge Semester, and college wouldn't officially start for another two months. "Right now, it's kinda boring because nobody's here. So there's probably gonna be a lot more parties," he finished with a grin.

"Yeah. Excited about the parties?" I asked, jokingly wagging my finger at him. "Uh-hum," he answered mischievously, laughing. "I've heard they're pretty good."

Crystal

By definition, underrepresented students attending prestigious universities are "beating the odds" and "defying statistics." Crystal, however, did this in spades. The oldest of four children, she was raised bilingually in Center City by her mother and grandmother in various struggling neighborhoods and is the first in her family to attend college. Her parents, both from Puerto Rico, divorced when she was six. When Crystal was eight years old, her father was sentenced to 15 years in prison for selling narcotics, and he was all but absent from her life until his release when Crystal was in high school. Crystal's two younger brothers are, in her words, "juvenile delinquents" and heavily involved in gang activity. Her school life has always been distinctly separate from her family members, who she says "are not really into school" and are "kind of crazy."

During our first interview in a bustling Collegeville café on a bright September day, Crystal seemed tired and a bit down. Clad in a sweatshirt, sweatpants, and glasses, Crystal spoke softly but deliberately. A self-described "bookworm," and "serious person," Crystal is someone I rarely saw smile. I did not get to know her nearly as well as the others, however. She did not attend all of the interviews in the study, and we did not spend as much time together as the other participants and I did. Although I was left wishing I could have gotten to know her better, it struck me that throughout the time I did spend with her, her demeanor remained similar to that first day. Indeed, while the others—at least at times—displayed a lightness in our interactions, I did not observe this in Crystal.

Academically, Crystal had been a star since early grade school. Teachers repeatedly took notice of her and gave her access to programs for gifted students at top-notch public schools as well as college-prep programs. After being accepted to Washington High School, a rigorous college-prep magnet school, her mother moved two hours away. Instead of attending a high school closer to her mother's new home, Crystal commuted two hours each way by train to continue attending Washington.

Although Crystal consistently felt successful at school, this success did not come easily. When I asked her about her high school International Baccalaureate program, she said she had "mixed feelings" about it. "You don't meet anybody who's ever gone in that program that doesn't have mixed feelings, because it's really rigorous," she explained. "The classes are really difficult. I did homework for like four or five hours every day, you know? So it's harder than pretty much most [high schools]. I mean, they give you material that college students are reading. So there's a lot of not-sleeping, a lot of tests, and a lot of anger... and frustration. So it can be difficult. And you still have to maintain good grades and it doesn't matter how difficult it is."

Crystal was very clear that the intensity of her high school education and the effort she put forth had prepared her academically for CMU. Cupping her hands around her glass, she asserted, "See, the one thing that doesn't worry me here [at CMU] is schoolwork. Because it couldn't be any harder than what I just finished doing. You know, the heavy textbooks, the reading, the outlining forever. They taught me, like, I'm confident in the notes that I can take, and my reading skills, I think, are pretty good. And my writing—I'm not *the best* and it could improve, but I know that straight off the bat, I'm not going to be struggling to catch up here." In addition to Washington's rigor, Crystal said the ultra-competitive Amigos college-prep program also helped her prepare for CMU.

Despite her academic success, Crystal confided that school "has always been hard" socially and emotionally. "I was the one they picked on a lot in grammar school. I had the glasses and the bad haircut, and I always had a book in my face. I was a bookworm for a really long time. I still love to read. But I was a little dorky back then." Her tone remained solemn when she reflected on the non academic challenges of high school. In contrast to her racially diverse grammar school, Crystal's high school was a place where she felt "different" as a Latina. Although she was no longer "dorky" and did not get picked on in high school, she says there was "a separation because we were the [racial] minorities, and you could count us on one hand. So, you know, it's different. I was different [than the majority]."

Particularly striking to me was Crystal's independence related to the choices she made regarding her schooling as well as her commitment to resist peer pressure. In grade school, when a teacher encouraged her to apply to a well-regarded magnet grade school, she made the decision "on her own" to apply and eventually transfer. In addition, the decision to attend Washington High School "was [hers] completely." While her mom had always been "interested" and "supportive" of Crystal's education, she also showed Crystal "how to be independent, very early." Crystal explained that when it came to decisions regarding her education, her mom's attitude was, "Whatever you wanna do, you just let me know and go do it." Despite her mother's interest, she and other family members could not relate to Crystal's dedication to schooling.

"It's been kinda difficult. It's difficult. They—my family, everybody—don't understand why I would commute two hours to go to school. I tell people, and they're like, 'Why? Why would you do that?'"

"So why do you think you did?" I asked.

"Well, because I was good at it. And the thing with commuting, like when I commuted two hours, it was just because I had started something, and I think it's hard not to finish. I wanted to finish and I didn't want to quit. I had put so much work already into it. I figured, you know, if I didn't finish it, then there would have been no point to start in the first place."

Crystal then spoke of her fierce commitment to "breaking the cycle" by not following the pattern of her family members and friends. "The whole reason I'm here," she asserted, "the whole reason is to stop this cycle that's being perpetuated by my family, and by people around me that I know, which is, you know, getting laid, and doing drugs, or getting married to someone who's gang-banging and doing drugs, and getting pregnant early. I have family members who have done that, and they would tell my mom, 'Oh watch out for her! She will be pregnant by the time she's 16!' and they were all in my face. Because they thought that if anybody is half good-looking at all, or is popular with the guys or whatever, she would end up like that."

A flash of anger glinted in her eyes as she continued sarcastically but evenly, "You know, there is no such thing as a girl really wanting to go to school *that* bad that she would avoid getting pregnant at all costs. 'Cause, you know, it's not that easy. There are so many people who doubt, and it *is* difficult. It has been difficult. There have been times when I'm just like, 'All right, you know what? I don't wanna do this anymore. I wanna sit back and hang out with my friends and do whatever the hell I want.'"

After admitting to this temptation, however, she related her first phone conversation with her CMU roommate, in which she affirmed her commitment to her lifestyle:

> We talked about lifestyles mostly, 'cause I like to have fun, but I don't party. I don't drink. I don't smoke. I'm very reserved on all that. And I'm very, very particular about my friends. Not everyone is going to be my friend. And I think I have a pretty good sense of responsibility and I'm pretty sensible. And I usually have a pretty set schedule. I like school. You know, it gets hard, but I like school. I like to read. I like all the stuff that comes with it.

When I asked Crystal if she could think of specific disadvantages she might have as she enters college, she responded without hesitation. "The only thing I've found so far is, like, the natural advantages that others have had that I haven't, because of where I come from. I don't come from a very [wealthy] family. So just learning how to, you know, do better on research, do better on presentations. And I had to learn the things I should know—things that those I am competing with for grades already know. Just how to make it so I'm in step with them instead of even just a little behind."

Excited that Crystal had, in essence, just offered an astute explanation of cultural capital and how it (or lack thereof) has affected her, I probed, "So how do you think those other people who did have those resources and other advantages, who came from different backgrounds … how did they learn that stuff?"

"Well," she answered,

I think it has a lot to do with family, and just what comes with not having to worry about certain things. Like for us, it's always been work, and you need money [to have these advantages]. Knowing how to do PowerPoint, and how to give presentations and how to speak, and do it well, and where to go. And to have resources, especially monetary ones, to find out what it is you're doing for school.

You know, I've never been one of those to be able to do that because it's just not available to me. And so a lot of it is family, and being taught how to do it. 'Cause a lot of parents do that, you know? If you have the resources, why not give your child the best, you know? The best tutors, the best teachers, you know? So that they learn early how to provide and do things well, and be ahead. It has a lot to do with family and background, the education. The better the education of the parents, I mean, their children are gonna be that much more educated. And so can you imagine how much more they're going to have if you can give them the best of what you had, and you had it really good? You know?

As she finished, I couldn't help but chuckle to myself, recalling my own doctoral-level classes and the requisite scholarly discussions and analyses of cultural/social reproduction theory, which Crystal had just concisely and easily explained over coffee.

By the end of our first interview, I was forming a preliminary understanding of Crystal. *Organized, serious, well-spoken, bookish, fiercely independent, wise beyond her years,* and *solidly dedicated to her education* were emerging as the foundations of this budding understanding. Then, just as I was confidently settling into this image of her, Crystal said something that was impeccably timed to sharply reject my oversimplified profile her. Indeed, my jaw dropped in utter surprise; and, admittedly, as a life-long female athlete, I was delighted: Crystal calmly shared that she was the first girl in the history of her high school to try out for—and play on—the football team.

"I beat out like 40-some guys in the first two days of try outs," she explained casually. I then learned that in the years before high school, Crystal played in a recreational football league at a nearby park and "had a blast." Upon entering high school, she said to herself, "I know I'm crazy, but I'm gonna try anyway." She went on, "I was the first girl to try and actually play with them. And I tried out. And it's so funny 'cause the first day, the coach is trying to, like, scare me off. He's like, 'Do you know what this involves? We're gonna be hitting each other and we're gonna be running around!' And I'm like, 'Yeah, okay, let's go.' And so I did that for two years. And then school got harder, and then I moved too far away, and boys got bigger." After she stopped playing, Crystal worked as the team manager. She also played soccer for three years during high school. Between sports, activities, and working at a bakery, she "was never at home." When she was at home, she says, she was either sleeping or studying.

After taking a brief foray into the lighter topic of sports, Crystal defiantly reiterated her resolve to succeed at CMU, perhaps despite all the forces working against her. "Nothing here will scare me off. You know, I'm not gonna let anything—academically or otherwise—scare me off. I don't scare easy. Some people are, like, scared of school and what that brings. But like I said, it couldn't be any harder than what I've already done." Then, as if giving a nod to the many roadblocks she had faced on her journey to CMU, she stated, "If I had had things handed to me, I wouldn't be here."

Engracia

Engracia pored over the large planner splayed open in front of her, full of color-coded and labeled blocks of time representing the various activities and appointments that filled her schedule. Even though we were well into the evening, her next appointment was closing in on us, so we rushed to find an open window in her schedule to set up our next time to talk. I soon learned that her full-to-the-brim schedule that month was not an anomaly: Engracia had always been extremely busy, mostly due to her deep involvement in school-related activities.

"I went to Lincoln College Prep," she explained proudly, "which is the biggest and most diverse school in [my] state. So that was pretty cool. It was good. I was like the president of the student council, student council representative before that, I was in the Honor Society.... It was so many clubs— orchestra all four years. It was like, I basically just did everything there."

"Wow," I said, feeling tired just imagining the schedule she must have kept. "And why? Why do you think you did everything you could?"

"I've always been like that. I've always liked being involved, since I was young. Like in elementary school I was a cheerleading captain and I was on the basketball team. Also, I was in student council even back then." She also explained that she had a 4.0 grade-point average—no small feat anywhere, let alone at Lincoln, a top-notch high school with a strong reputation—and that she loved school.

"I have only positive memories of school," she said with a shrug and a smile. Adding to her optimistic view of schooling was her acceptance into the highly competitive Amigos college access/preparation program. As I explain in detail in Chapter 2 this program provided her with intensive preparation for college for most of her senior year and the summer before she started at CMU. Significantly, she entered college with the same small group of peers—including Crystal—that participated in the months of preparation with her. In essence, she arrived at CMU with a built-in group of close friends.

I came to know Engracia as an extremely organized young woman who was at once studious, serious, refreshingly direct, *and* bubbly, energetic, and very easy to relate to. She is, perhaps, the only person I know who could be described as "bubbly" without being the least bit flighty or "air-headed." To the contrary, she was always as sharp as a nail, both in her wit and intellect, even after pulling all-nighters to get her coursework done. In our conversations she often checked in with me with a quick, "You get me?" to make sure I was following her rapid-fire speech and train of thought.

The daughter of a Mexican father and Puerto Rican mother, Engracia always wore nicely put-together outfits, subtle make up over her light skin, and her thick brown hair was always neatly styled. Engracia grew up in Center City and made frequent trips to visit relatives in Puerto Rico. Her father works as a waiter, bar tender, and dishwasher, and her mother, formerly a fashion model in Puerto Rico, is a hairstylist and recently bought her own salon. Engracia and her younger brother are bilingual, and, as their parents do not speak much English, she and her family have always spoken Spanish in the home.

Although both her parents have limited formal education—her father completed the third grade in Mexico, and she is fairly certain her mother graduated high school—they have had a deep and overwhelmingly positive influence on her education and schooling, which I elaborate on in Chapter 7. Although they were unable to help her with her homework, Enrgacia's parents were constantly encouraging her to work hard in school and to use education as a way to a better life. They consistently supported her schooling in other ways, such as driving her to school early if she needed tutoring and regularly attending school functions.

Her parents were also protective of her and were strict with her and her brother. Engracia and her brother were not allowed to go out and do much socially, and when they were not at school, they were expected to be in the home, where her parents knew they would be safe. I asked her about the presence of gangs in her neighborhood and school growing up, and she explained that she always resisted any pressure to join a gang and was respected for it. She explained, "Yeah, the boys would try to act like all tough and I'm like, 'Shut up. You got like straight Fs. What can you offer people in like five years?"

"Did you ever say stuff like that to them?"

"No, they knew me. A lot of 'em would ask me out and stuff, but I never was involved with that, so they respected me in a way."

Engracia later told me of the significant role her dad played in protecting her. "I was always known as the girl who had a rabid dad," she laughed. "My dad had like this evil look. I remember one time these gang guys were asking me for my phone number and my dad was, like, staring them down. It was so funny. I was like, 'Ha, tough gang guys!' I loved it."

The irony surrounding gang involvement was not lost on Engracia, as she explained in no uncertain terms. "It's funny," she mused, "Because a lot of the gang kids, you see them at church. They go to church, they're sitting in church, and you're just like, 'You little shit! What are you doing here?' You know? The parents don't know, or don't want to accept it at least. Denial. They're like, 'My kid's not doing anything. He's just sitting outside for five hours.' Yeah, right," she scoffed.

Enrgacia's desire to "give back" to her parents was apparent when she discussed possible majors at CMU. Although she was not sure what she wanted to study, she knew she wanted to make enough money to help her parents financially. Although Engracia has always loved dancing and planned on taking some dance classes and joining various student dance clubs at CMU, she was leery of majoring in dance, both because of the insufficient income she thought she would make and because she feared her parents would not see it as a respectable major. She explained further, "Originally I wanted to study Mandarin and study abroad in China, but you know, I'm not sure because it's such a hard language. I mean I really want to learn it, but maybe I'll do that as a hobby when I'm older, instead of you know, making it my career. But I wanna help my parents."

"Okay," I said, encouraging her to continue.

"Yeah, my dad, all his life, he's always wanted a Rolex. I don't know why. But I was like, 'Okay, I'm gonna get you one,'" she stated, determined.

I came to know Engracia as a motivated, exquisitely organized, and intellectual young woman, who was, importantly, much more than this. Just as with anyone I know well, she defies simple, one-dimensional descriptions. I was fortunate enough to genuinely get to know Engracia, which meant witnessing her endearing, silly side as well. She is the well-prepared student who, ten minutes before a final paper was due in December, sat with me in a Collegeville Subway restaurant feverishly editing her paper. Granted, the paper was well done and ready to turn in before we met; she simply wanted to make it even better. But the frantic, last-minute editing was accompanied by conversation peppered with giggling and frequent obscenities as we raced to beat the clock. She is also the controlled, disciplined person who jumped up and down when I told her I was pregnant with my second child as we walked back to my car after an evening interview. As we got in the car that wintry night, Engracia slipped on the slick sidewalk and was suddenly gone from my sight. I soon heard giggles erupting from the curb, and the graceful, life-long dancer clawed her way in to my car, legs covered with snow, proclaiming, "Oh my God! Seriously, you did *not* just see that!"

Jasmine

[*Author's Note:* By the time my late grandmother was in her mid-sixties, she was a strict adherent to her church's evangelical Christian worldview, which included literal interpretations of the Bible as well as spreading "God's Word" whenever she saw the opportunity. Through my teenaged eyes, her increasingly fervent dedication to the Bible and God had caused her to change almost beyond recognition—and not in a way I liked or understood. As hard as I tried, I could not have a conversation with her that did not quickly turn to the topic of my unsaved status and the dire need for my family and me to turn to Jesus and be saved for eternity. It was as if my grandmother was no longer accessible to me; every time I tried to reach out to her, I was blocked by a concrete wall—thick, impenetrable, and uninviting. What's more, her near constant attempts to proselytize my siblings, parents, and me, was a source of eruptive anger in my childhood home. My father took her "unfounded" and "unproven" religious convictions to be at once fanatical and ridiculous, as well as infuriating and insulting. Any attempt on her part to convert us witnessed by my father sparked an anger to be reckoned with.]

My experiences with my grandmother may help explain why I had a visceral reaction to hearing Jasmine describe, upon minutes of introducing herself, her fundamentalist Christian faith. It was on an idyllic July day when I made the hour-plus drive from Collegeville to Lakeside to meet and interview Jasmine for the first time. I dropped off my then two-year-old son with my parents in the Lakeside suburb I had grown up in and headed into the city. Although I had not lived in the Lakeside area for nearly 15 years, I knew enough to know that the shopping area surrounding the café we had planned to meet at had recently struggled to remain afloat. The neighborhood had become increasingly diverse over the years and is now predominantly African-American and Latin@. As I waited in the café for Jasmine, I noted a welcome departure from Collegeville's relative racial homogeneity: I was the only White person in the café.

During our phone conversation a few weeks earlier, Jasmine had described herself as "a little heavy-set," with brown hair and a *Lady and the Tramp* purse. The latter struck me as curious, since I was fairly certain that this type of accessorizing was not considered "fashionable" or "cool" for a soon-to-be college student, even in a "retro" kind of way. Although I half expected to find out I was mistaken, this matters because I had noticed immediately over the phone that Jasmine sounded younger than her 18 years, and the *Lady and the Tramp* purse punctuated that impression. Her outfit, however, gave her a professional-casual look; indeed, I was surprised by her relatively formal attire. Her floor-length denim skirt was nicely pressed, and her black summery top was neatly accented with white piping. Her thick, wavy brown hair reached down to the small of her back, and part of it was neatly pulled back. Jasmine's olive skin was flawless, without a stitch of make up.

Within minutes of starting our interview that July day, Jasmine referenced her religion and vaguely linked her religion to her choice of dress and lack of make up. When I asked her to elaborate, she replied, "Well, we're Pentecostal Apostolic. We go, like, according to the Bible." I felt myself tensing as a childhood's worth of memories of a grandmother "lost" to her literal interpretations of the Bible rushed back at me. I tried to hide my discomfort as Jasmine easily continued,

> So we believe that, like, you're not supposed to wear men's clothing. So like, for the women, they believe that we wear skirts—they don't push it on you or anything—but my parents just are like, "Let's wear the skirt." You know, it's not that hard to put on a skirt. And a lot of people are like, "Why don't you wear pants?" I'm like, "It's part of my religion and I wouldn't feel comfortable in pants." Since I've been raised in skirts, I wouldn't be comfortable anyway, so, it's kinda grown into me.

As she spoke, I lost my internal battle to push aside memories of my grandmother. As Jasmine talked, I silently assumed I would never be able to have a conversation with her that didn't center on her fundamentalist beliefs, and

I fully expected that in no time she would try to convert me. I expected that religion would dominate our conversations to such an extent that I would learn nothing from Jasmine in terms of what I set out to study—her transition to CMU. On some level, I unofficially decided, in that conversation, that I would not be able write about her much—if at all—in the final analysis.

I was mistaken. Getting to know Jasmine challenged me in deeply personal and professional ways. I was forced to confront my own stereotypes of those who subscribe to fundamentalist religions, I was challenged to enter a world of literature and research that was previously foreign to me, and, for the first time, I had to critically consider the responsibility of public schools and universities to adherents of fundamentalist faiths.

Despite my inner struggle, our conversation continued and Jasmine chatted easily, answering my questions about her family. "Well, my parents got married when they were like 18, I think, and they had me when they were 19. They were just getting out of high school. I have a sister and a brother. My sister is like a year and a half younger than me, and my brother is four years younger than me."

Her mother, from the Midwest, is White and Native American. While she has done some coursework at a local technical college, she does not have a post secondary degree, and works inside the home. Her father was born in Mexico and came to the United States when he was 16 years old. He works in the trades as a floor layer and through apprenticeships and union work has achieved the status of Journeyman.

Though neither parent has a college degree, Jasmine wanted to go to college to "have a better life." Originally, she was set on being a neonatal nurse, because she "loves babies," but explained that she eventually decided she wanted to be a pharmacist. She explained,

> Ever since I was little, I wanted to be a neonatal nurse. Then I found the schooling is like 12 years and I'd have to tell a parent that their kid just died and I was like, "Oh, I couldn't do that." You know, I'd be crying more than the parents. You know, that's a baby you connected with. And for it to die? I'd be just like so devastated. It would be horrible, so I was looking for something else and I came out to want to be a pharmacist, 'cause, you know, you don't have to deal with any naked people. You don't have to deal with saying somebody just died, you know.

We both laughed at her refusal to deal with "naked people," and she continued, laughing, "Yeah, that's my number one thing. My mom is like, 'You can be a doctor or nurse.' I'm like, 'No thank you.'"

As I listened to Jasmine recount her experiences with schooling and share her thoughts on her future career plans, I began to wonder if she understood, even on a basic level, what becoming a pharmacist—and doing the work of one—entailed. She explained that she didn't really like school and was not good at studying. She also mentioned her parents had frequently moved her from school to school and that the urban schools she attended "weren't that great" academically. As she shared her apprehensions about starting college, both in terms of finances and academic preparation, I became increasingly worried about her prospects for graduating from CMU.

"My dad's all about the whole student loan thing. 'Oh God,'" she imitated. "You're gonna be in debt for the rest of your life. What if you don't make it? You'll be in debt, and you won't even have anything to show for it." I'm like, "Dad, I'm going to try my best, okay? Don't make it worse, Dad." As she went on, it was clear that she was unsure about her academic preparation for CMU. "It's kinda hard. Its like, 'Oh my God, I'm going to be in something for almost a decade.' It's hard 'cause like with the proficiency test, the placement testing? I ranged really low on my math. They're like, 'You need to retest so we can put you in a math; otherwise, you can't start your chemistry.' And I'm like, 'But I need my chemistry for pharmacy.'"

At the end of the interview, after agreeing to meet again in Collegeville once the school year had started, I headed back to my parents' house in the suburbs to pick up my son. The vista rapidly changed, run-down streets and boarded storefronts morphing into curving cul-de-sacs and manicured lawns. Before reaching my parents' home, I stopped the car to gather and record my thoughts. I wrote, "I'm worried for her. Is it because she's just more honest about her preparation than some of the others, or does she really have less of a chance?" I concluded my notes that day with, "In some ways I'm expecting her not to make it at CMU. I will be overjoyed and surprised if she does."

Moriah

"I think I want to be in your study," Moriah told me over the phone just two months before starting at CMU, "because I have a lot to say about my schooling. I was *not* prepared for college." My first impression of Moriah, based on that initial phone conversation, was that she was sure of herself and tough, and this made me especially eager to meet her. Indeed, when she confidently strode over to my table at a trendy Lakeside café after a day of work at a nearby bank, my first impression seemed to hold up. She was direct, to the point, and not afraid to ask *me* questions right off the bat. Just after settling in to our table, before I could start recording our first interview, Moriah looked directly into my eyes, elbows firmly planted on the table, and asked, "So, why are you interested in our group?"

Dressed in jeans, sandals, and a green T-shirt that displayed a message in Spanish too faded to fully make out, Moriah was a particularly striking young woman. Her brown skin framed classically indigenous features, and her focus and confidence were accented by an easy laugh.

Moriah was aware of her self-confidence and spoke of it in an effortless, nonchalant way. Toward the end of our first interview, I asked her, "What advantage might you have in terms of succeeding at CMU that others don't?"

"I guess my wisdom—I don't know," she replied. "My mom says I'm conceited, but like, I'm just…" she paused to search for the right word.

"Confident?" I offered.

"Yeah, my confidence, and that I know that I'm gonna be the only one who can do it for myself, so I have to do it. So, I told my mom, no one will love me as much as I love myself. So I can only do it myself. I wanna be successful."

I quickly learned that for years, Moriah, who aspired to be a forensic scientist and eventually work for the FBI, had been relatively independent from her parents, both in terms of finances and schooling. While she spoke highly of her parents and explained she was "close" with them, they were unable to fully support her financially or help her with her academics. In her words, "My dad would always ask me, 'How are you doing in school? Did you do good on your tests and stuff?' And my mom, she was just like, 'You're gonna do what you want. If you don't graduate, that's your decision.' But she's always known that I would stay in school."

Her parents, who have been together for roughly 20 years, are both factory workers and have limited education credentials. Her mother, who was born in Texas and is of Mexican descent, dropped out of school after her eighth-grade year and eventually earned her GED. Moriah is unclear about how much schooling her father had before coming to the U.S. from Mexico at age 20. Largely uninvolved in her schooling, Moriah's parents have been her main source of motivation to earn a college degree and achieve a higher standard of living.

My mom and dad, they struggle because they work in a factory. You know, how much does a factory pay? And they work hard to make ends meet. And I'm like, "I don't wanna work that hard." My mom, she works two jobs, so I see her maybe at night time around eight o'clock, like for an hour, 'cause then I go to bed. So she goes to work—she works overtime at the factory—and then she probably stays there until she has to go to her next job. My dad, he just works one job. He's gotten lazier over the years [she says with a laugh].

"I don't know," she continues, the laughter gone from her eyes, "I just tell myself I don't want to live like that. I don't wanna kill myself. Like my mom, she didn't go to work last Saturday because she was like, 'I'm killing myself and I'm still broke!' And I'm like, 'I don't wanna be like this.' So, I guess that's my motivation."

Growing up, Moriah lived with her parents, her younger brother, her older sister, and eventually her older sister's son and husband. With the addition of her sister's family came added responsibility; Moriah became closely involved in raising her nephew once he arrived. Her older sister, who became pregnant when she was 17 and Moriah was seven, has two bachelor's degrees from local colleges. Moriah also has a brother who is nine years older than her who has a law degree from CMU and lives in another state in the Midwest. Although Moriah received some help and guidance from her older brother, who was clearly successful in his own schooling, he was out of the house by the time Moriah was an adolescent. He did, however, strongly encourage Moriah to attend CMU, insisting that its prestige and reputation would be an advantage for her, and discouraged her from attending the local university in Lakeside.

Moriah made important, weighty decisions regarding her education and schooling on her own, without much input from her family. Perhaps the clearest example of this is the chain of decisions she made regarding which Lakeside public high school to attend. Though she was not told to do so by anyone, she initially decided to apply to Roberts High, Lakeside's premier urban college-prep high school. To her great disappointment, she was wait-listed. She enrolled at her neighborhood high school—a trades-focused high school that aimed at providing students with the necessary skills to start blue-collar jobs directly after high school—but was soon offered a spot at Roberts. She explained, "Maybe a month after school started, Roberts called me and said, 'Oh we have an opening. Do you wanna come?' And I had to give them an answer by Friday, and it was maybe Wednesday."

Explaining her mom's role in her decision to decline Roberts's offer, she said, "My mom was like, 'Hey, that's cool.' My mom's the kind of mom that says if you're comfortable, you do what you want. So, my high school was okay."

"Are you glad with your decision to stay there instead of going to Roberts?"

"I'm glad in the sense that—of what I accomplished, but I don't think my high school prepared me for college."

Moriah was her high school's valedictorian, and although she was proud of her accomplishments there, she did not believe her school was a "great" school, and she had to face peers who only shared her low opinion of her school and who downplayed her accomplishments there. Her cousin, who graduated from Roberts, had a less-than-supportive reaction to her status as valedictorian:

> My cousin was telling me, 'Well, of course you're gonna get a 4.0 'cause that's the easy school,' and stuff like that. It was easy, but I still had a hard time sometimes, and it was challenging for me sometimes, and I worked really hard to stay on top of my grades and stuff. Especially when I started working at my job. I think I earned it. Some people think that it was a cake-walk for me or something. I'm like, 'no, no. I work for my grades.'

Yet, despite her hard work and her accomplishments, she was sure she was not ready academically for CMU. "I took some AP courses, but I still don't think I'm gonna be ready for college." When asked to explain why, she continued, "I think because the teachers focused more on the bad kids. And gave them more attention, yelling at them, stuff like that, when they should have kicked them out," Moriah responded angrily. She continued:

> And they should have paid us more attention 'cause we wanted to learn. And we needed help, you know? Like, I would confront those teachers and they would tell me, "Well the principal will yell at us or get mad at us if we send all these kids out, so we have to deal with them," and blah, blah, blah. And I'm like, "that's not fair 'cause you're taking away from everybody else."

At this point in our conversation, I shared in Moriah's anger at the injustice of her high school education and felt a sense of regret on her behalf that she did not take Roberts High up on its offer to admit her. It was hard for me to see that decision in any other way than a missed opportunity. Despite this, however, I couldn't help having the sense that her confidence, strength, and independence might significantly ease her way through CMU, a university whose size alone makes it daunting to many.

Indeed, although she expressed concern that she would miss her family after leaving for college, she was anxious to get her life started at CMU. Having grown up in the same inner-city Lakeside neighborhood her whole life, Moriah was excited to move to Collegeville and live in a "safe" neighborhood. She explained, "When I went to Collegeville for orientation, we went walking down Main Street at night. And I was like, 'Wow.' You know, it was nice because I actually felt safe walking around at night time. Like if I was walking around in Lakeside at night time, I would be looking over my shoulder. It was just different."

"What else did you notice walking around?" I asked.

"A lot of White people," she laughed. "I mean, I knew that when I applied. It's no big deal to me. As long as, you know, they're not looking at me weird, you know, having racist thoughts. If they're not being racist, then I don't care. I just talk to them. But you know, if someone calls me a 'spic' or something, then I have to fight," she finished, laughing again.

Mario

It's a few weeks into the fall semester, and I am seated in the back of a disorganized array of uncomfortable and impossibly small desks. Donning a baseball cap, jeans, a casual sweater, and what I *think* are trendy shoes, I am trying to "blend in" as students file in for their Spanish 102 class. The instructor is late, and an uncomfortable silence falls over the now full room as we wait for her to arrive. I am stunned to see that it is Mario who saves us from the awkwardness, and I'm captivated as I watch him comfortably and confidently entertain the group of about 35 students. He tells us the horrifying tale of how his house, while he and his father were in it, was recently struck by a car (no one was seriously injured); yet he skillfully spins it to sound funny, hilarious even. When he is done, he says with artful flair, "Anyone else?" and proceeds to facilitate the sharing of others' outlandish stories until the instructor rushes in.

Although I came to expect this kind of confidence and easy humor in Mario as the study progressed, these were not traits I saw in him when we initially met. When we first spoke, during a break in his CMU summer orientation activities, Mario was relatively formal and serious. The CMU student union was abuzz with chatty young men and women and harried CMU staff members charged with orienting soon-to-be college students to their new life. As we talked on a couch in the midst of the activity, I was struck by Mario's intensity and focus. He maintained near-constant eye contact with me and was not for a moment distracted by the chaos around us. I also sensed he wanted me to know that he was a serious student, intelligent, and well prepared for college. His brown hair was cut close to his head, which, combined with his athletic build, clean-shaven face, khaki shorts, sandals, and Abercrombie and Fitch shirt, made for a classically clean-cut appearance.

Mario was born in Texas and for the most part grew up there, and his childhood consisted of uncommonly varied experiences in terms of race and class. For the first five years of his life, he lived with his parents—both of Mexican descent—and sister in a trailer on his grandmother's land in rural South Texas. His father, after serving in the navy for six years after high school, attended a Texas community college and was recruited and given a scholarship by CMU. While his father finished his undergraduate degree at CMU, Mario attended kindergarten through most of second grade in Collegeville. Upon his father's graduation from CMU, Mario and his family moved back to Texas and to the trailer, and his parents divorced. After living with his grandmother while his dad worked in a different part of the state, he moved with his dad and sister once again, and they eventually bought a house in a predominantly White suburb of a large Texan city, where Mario graduated from high school.

Mario also attended two different CMU-based college-access programs. His father's friend, a CMU employee, introduced these programs to Mario and encouraged him to apply. Through the Access to College program (ATC), Mario spent part of the summers after his sophomore and junior years living on CMU's campus and getting a sense of college life. Then, the summer after his senior year in high school, he participated in CMU's Summer Bridge Semester (SBS), which is designed to give underrepresented students an early taste of college coursework and college life. While in SBS, Mario lived in the dorms and took two college-level courses for credit.

The multiple moves Mario endured during his childhood allowed him to experience life in poor, predominately Mexican neighborhoods as well as White, suburban neighborhoods. He sees this as something he is "grateful for" and something that has "opened his eyes to see that you can't be close-minded because people are from different areas."

He further explained, "I know that we moved a lot, and that was one of the things I felt was an advantage, even though technically it wasn't a stable environment that I grew up in. However, you have to disregard the negative aspect of it and look to the positive, and what I see is that because I moved around, I saw different things, and picked up different things as I've gone. And because of this, I've experienced more of the world than, say, a person that grows up in a certain town their whole life."

As I got to know more about Mario's upbringing, it was clear that living for some years in the same lower-income, rural neighborhood in South Texas that his father grew up in had a significant impact on him. After attending part of grade school in this small town, Mario returned there for a semester of high school. When he returned as an adolescent, he saw the town as somewhat of a "trap" that he was glad to escape. In his words,

> I'd say there's about 75 kids in the [high school] senior class, and a lot of those kids are the same kids I went to school with in the 4th grade. So it was nice to go back and see it, but then I also saw how they've been stuck in this little town, and this is how it was for my father, you know. And now I see why he left and had he not left, how different our lives would have been. You know, it would have been repeating the cycle, and that's what it is in that town. It's repeating the cycle: After they graduate high school, or *if* they graduate high school, they go on and they get a job, they get someone pregnant, and they get married. Notice how I said they get someone pregnant, and *then* they get married, because that's unfortunately how it works down there.

Mario went on to explain the "cycle" of having children at a young age and never leaving the small, depressed town:

> It's very sad to say, and I'm sad myself that I have to say it that way, but that's just the way it is—that's the way it happens. It's all because—it's a revolving door because of how they're raised. Their parents did that, their parents' parents did that, and it just is a revolving cycle that unfortunately is going to continue unless you have someone down there to open their eyes and tell them, "Look you have to do something else with your life." You have the valedictorian, the salutatorian, the top ten kids in the graduating high school class, and the furthest they were going? One of them was going to the University of Texas in Austin. That was the valedictorian. The rest of them were going—these are the top kids in school, you know, very smart kids—to community colleges, local colleges, and you just stop and think, like, what a waste, you know? You are the elite of this class; however, because of the revolving door, you're going to stay in that area and you're only going to amount to as much as you can in that area. You're not going to experience the world. You're not going to see different places. You won't even know what you're missing.

"How do you think you came to have a different mind-set than them?" I asked.

"Luckily," Mario started, "I was fed this since I was young because my dad fortunately realized he had to get out of there. So he was in the Navy. And then he got out, and he was doing odd jobs, and then he finally realized, 'Look, I have to better myself and get an education, to provide for a family.' So that's when he started his community college. And then, luckily, he got a scholarship to come up here to CMU."

It is hard to overstate the connection Mario feels to his father, as well as the deep influence his father has had on him. Even I now have an almost larger-than-life image of Mario's father. Like the family portraits young children draw, in which important adults are disproportionately big, my own mental picture of Mario's life has his father looming exceptionally large. Mario's father, his primary caregiver, always expected him to go to college and taught him that an education is the key to success.

"Tell me about you parents' influence on your education," I inquired.

Responding quickly and emphatically, Mario said, "It's all my dad, it's all my dad." He continued,

> Going to college was never a question in my mind, just because of my father. Growing up, that's just something he said, you know, "You need to go, you need to achieve a college education, because if you don't, then look what your options are." He would say, Look, do you wanna be outside doing hard labor? Instead of doing physical labor, you can work hard, but you can be using your mind instead. And that's really what he was always feeding me, like, You're gonna go to college. It was never a question. Never, never, never a question.

By leaving Texas and going to college in the Midwest, Mario was in some ways defying stereotypical ideas about Mexican Americans, which paint a picture of young adults who stay close to home for schooling and careers, and whose community-oriented worldviews overpower the notion individual success. Mario, explaining that he could have gone to any number of local colleges, left Texas because his father "always taught [him] to be an individual" and to "get out and explore." That's not to say that Mario was not raised to love and respect his Mexican heritage. To the contrary, Mario often told me that the level of awareness he has about race and racial identity is because of the many conversations his father had with him about his heritage and about race in the US.

In fact, as I sat with Mario in a Collegeville café for our first official interview, I found myself in the middle of a discussion about how race is "socially constructed," in Mario's words. After I was almost lulled into a familiar space of academic discussions with my peers and students about this very concept, I snapped to attention and asked Mario how he, having just graduated high school, was aware of these ideas. While he struggled to explain how he understood the concept, as I think most of us do, he told me he was learning about it in his summer sociology course at CMU. He added, however, that he "kind of always knew it" because of his dad. When I related this story during an interview with a Latino CMU staff member who attended college with Mario's father, he laughed and exclaimed, "I am sure Mario *does* know all about that! His dad instilled it in him—his dad is the most hard-core Mexican I know!"

Mario's passion for music and its enormous presence in his life can also be traced back to his father, who played in a *Tejano* band during Mario's childhood. Mario explained,

> I just love music because my father played in a traveling band. So growing up with him, I remember going with him [when he'd play]. I remember they had pictures of me when I was little sitting behind his drum set trying to play. I remember going to watch him play a few times, sitting right next to him as he played. And then he's always listening to music. I love all that kind of Tejano music—that's just what I grew up with. I just feel it inside me. And I love all sorts of music, I just love music.

Mario's love of music was to play a significant role in his life at college. He aspired to be a member of CMU's prestigious and nationally renowned marching band, and in late summer he learned he had earned a coveted spot in the organization. This meant, however, grueling physical training and a huge time commitment, including a lot of weekend travel.

The picture of a strong, moral, ever-present father that Mario painted is, in his words, "the opposite" of how he views his mother. His mother, who now has a "good job" driving 18-wheelers for a grocery company in Texas, was largely absent from Mario's life growing up. Because at the time I was the mother of a young son, listening to Mario's account of his mother's place in his life was especially heart wrenching.

> Recently, I guess when I started high school, or 7th grade or 8th grade year, she started coming back around again. Now she tries to buy me and my sister's love, you know. Now that she has the money, she tries. She's, like, trying to make effort. But how do you make up not having a mother? I appreciate that she's trying; however, it's never gonna make up for those years, the young years in my life when I didn't have that mother in my life.

The intensity and thoughtfulness that Mario displayed when talking about almost anything, ranging from sensitive family issues to marching band practice to his courses at CMU, was also apparent when he explained why he feels especially well prepared for CMU. When I asked Mario about disadvantages or obstacles he could face as a student at CMU, he replied,

> Right now, I can't see me having problems here, just because, as I said, I came from a White suburban area for high school, and I included myself, you know, in all the

extra curricular activities as well as the academic side of it. So, hopefully, no. You know, I'm not at a disadvantage in any way. And hopefully I'm as much prepared as I possibly can be.

At the end of our summer conversations, I found myself not only silently rooting for Mario as he was on the cusp of starting his college career but also whole heartedly believing that his confidence was grounded in reality. In the months leading up to the start of the school year, I did not for one moment worry about what his transition to CMU might look like. Indeed, after meeting all the students I've portrayed here, I formed assumptions and expectations about them and their chances of succeeding at CMU. I would soon discover, however, just how complex the notion of "success" can be.

· 2 ·

COLLEGE ACCESS PROGRAMS

Mapping the Terrain

In reality ... going to college begins long before kindergarten; perhaps before conception. The economic situation of parents, their schooling history, the neighborhoods into which children are born and raised; all have powerful effects on children's
aspirations and preparation for schooling before they ever step inside a classroom.
(Gándara & Contreras, 2009, p. 250)

Introduction

Numerous college access and retention programs exist across the U.S. While
there is great variation within the wide range of programs, all share the
foundational goal of mitigating the effects of the uneven access to college
highlighted in the epigraph above. Programs labelled "college access programs" are generally those programs that begin while a student is in middle
or high school, are outside the school's regular curriculum, and are designed
to improve the dismal rates of college enrollment (and, in some cases, retention) among underrepresented students. These "access" programs may or
may not continue once the student is enrolled in college. "College reten-
tion/support programs," on the other hand, start once a student is enrolled

in college. These programs provide various resources to underrepresented students while they are on campus with the hope of increasing retention for these students. Both types of programs may be involved in recruitment efforts as well.

College access programs in particular generally fall into two categories: student-centered and school-centered (Gándara, 2002). Student-centered programs represent the "vast majority" of college access programs, and, as mentioned above, identify specific students from under-represented groups and use various strategies and interventions to prepare them for college (Loza, 2003). The goal of these student-centered programs is to "close any perceived academic gaps in the *individual student*" (Loza, 2003, p. 44, emphasis mine). In contrast, school-centered programs work to "restructure" and "reform" a specific school as a whole, thus equally preparing all students for the rigors of post secondary studies (Loza, 2003, p. 44). Various scholars have argued that the student-centered design of most college access programs is flawed and that more school-centered programs are needed to effectively combat the crisis facing Latin@ and other underrepresented students (Loza, 2003; Gándara, 2002).

Despite the relatively clean categories of "student-centered" and "school-centered" programs, there is little else that is organized and regulated within the world of college access and support, and the reasons for this are multiple. First, although most college access programs begin in high school and end upon high school graduation, there is a growing number of "access" programs that continue into college. Second, there are various college-based "support" or "retention" programs designed to help students succeed (by various means, including combinations of providing academic support and social support) once they arrive on campus; yet some of these programs have begun to support students while they are still in high school. In addition, while most college access programs were traditionally thought to begin in high school, some now begin in middle school or even as early as kindergarten.

Last, sources of funding vary widely across similar categories of programs, resulting in distinct policies across programs that might appear to be very similar. As Gándara and Contreras explain, "...there is no coordinated policy about how to best provide [educational intervention] services for disadvantaged youth" (2009, p. 254). They also argue that this lack of coordination results in a "...rather ad hoc system for providing services [and] means that there has been no overarching thought given to when or how to effectively reach the students" (2009, p. 254).

Further contributing to the lack of clarity surrounding college access and support programs is the relatively low number of studies that have examined the effectiveness of these programs. The few rigorous studies that do exist have produced mixed results; and, curiously, even given these mixed results, program design has not changed (Gándara & Contreras, 2009). Tierney and Hagedorn offer a more specific—and dismal—outlook: "Despite what might be termed 'gallant efforts' by some programs there has not been a dramatic increase in college attendance, retention, and graduation for low income and minority youth" (2002, p. 1).

In this chapter, after discussing the relationship between capital and the types of programs addressed above, I describe the programs represented in this study as well as the process by which the students were accepted into the various programs. I then continue the discussion in Chapter 3 by examining the students' experiences with the programs.

Conceptual Perspectives

College access and retention/support programs aim to provide underrepresented students with, among other resources, the social and cultural capital that middle-class (and, arguably, middle-class White) students have access to, thereby interrupting the cycle of social reproduction (Loza, 2003; Vásquez, 2003). Before examining the ways in which programs attempt to do this, it is necessary to discuss the contributions that Critical Race Theory (CRT) and social/cultural reproduction theory have made to the conceptualization of these strategies.

Critical Race Theory

One of the ways CRT has recently been used to challenge traditional conceptions of Students of Color in U.S. schools is to reexamine our understanding of the ways in which the well-known notions of social and cultural capital (Bourdieu, 1986) have been used in educational research. Social capital (Bourdieu, 1986; Coleman, 1988) can be defined as the relationships that help us attain other forms of capital; and cultural capital is the knowledge that affords access to opportunities for success (Bourdieu, 1986). Various scholars have taken up these notions to help conceptualize student achievement in schools (e.g., Lareau, 2003; Saunders and Serna, 2004; Loza, 2003).

Cultural/Social Reproduction Theory

Cultural/social reproduction theory (Bourdieu, 1977; Bourdieu & Passeron, 1977, 1979) has been used to further conceptualize the lack of equal access to and preparation for higher education within the United States. Multiple studies have shown that U.S. schools operate in ways that are congruent with middle-class values and beliefs and that this way of operating significantly advantages middle class—most often White—students and disadvantages students of lower socioeconomic status and Students of Color (Heath, 1983; Delpit, 1995; Valdés, 1996; Valenzuela, 1999; Laureau, 2003, Conchas, 2001). These studies also show that the result of this inequality is lower academic success for non-White and non–middle-class students. In essence, a cycle of inequality is put into motion whereby middle-class students continue to have access to academic success through the schools' validation of their values and worldviews, and others are denied this access.

Although the use of Bourdieu's constructs within educational research has done much to conceptualize and challenge inequality in our schools, CRT theorist Yosso (2005, 2006) offers a critique of the ways in which these theories have been used within education. Yosso (2005) argues that Bourdieu's theories have ultimately been used to sustain a deficit model of Students of Color in U.S. schools, thereby portraying them as "disadvantaged" and lacking the forms of capital needed to succeed. Yosso uses CRT to expand the traditional view of Bourdieu's theories, which she argues are based on White, middle-class values, to include the forms of wealth that People of Color *do* have. As she explains, "Centering the research lens on the experiences of People of Color… reveals accumulated assets and resources in the histories and lives of Communities of Color" (2005, p. 77).

Specifically, Yosso (2005) draws on the work of sociologists Oliver and Shapiro (1995) to explain how cultural capital is only one form of capital that may prove to be valuable. She uses a model of "community cultural wealth," which she defines as "an array of knowledge, skills, abilities and contacts possessed and utilized by Communities of Color to survive and resist macro and micro-forms of oppression" (2005, p. 77). Community cultural wealth entails at least six forms of capital that Communities of Color have. The six forms are listed below, followed by Yosso's (2005) definitions:

1. *Aspirational Capital* is "the ability to maintain hopes and dreams for the future, even in the face of real and perceived barriers" (p. 77).

2. *Linguistic Capital* "includes the intellectual and social skills attained through communication experiences in more than one language and/ or style" (p. 78).

3. *Familial Capital* "refers to those cultural knowledges nurtured among *familia* (kin)...." It "engages a commitment to community well-being and expands the concept of family to include a more broad understanding of kinship" (p. 79).

4. *Social Capital* can be understood as "networks of people and community resources" historically used by People of Color to attain other forms of capital (p. 80).

5. *Navigational Capital* includes the "skills of maneuvering through social institutions...not created with Communities of Color in mind" (p. 80).

6. *Resistant Capital* "refers to those knowledges and skills fostered through oppositional behavior that challenges inequality" (p. 80).

Yosso's work indeed pushes schools and researchers to recognize the forms of capital that Students of Color *do* possess as assets, thereby reframing the default deficit model used to conceptualize these students. Below, I analyze the students' experiences with various forms of support through the lens of this CRT approach to capital.

Student Support Programs

High schools often lack funding and have to seek outside partners to form college access programs because the limited federal funding for low-income and minority youth school improvement has primarily been aimed at preschool and elementary levels (Gándara & Contreras, 2009). Yet sources of funding for college access and retention/support programs have significant influence on program design and often "drive key characteristics of programs" (p. 271). Gándara and Contreras (2009) have thus grouped high school support programs into five categories based on their sources of funding: private nonprofit programs, higher education-sponsored programs ("K–16 partnerships"), state- or federally funded programs, community-based programs, and K–12 sponsored programs (p. 271). All but K–12 sponsored programs are represented in this study.

In addition to those in Gándara and Contreras's (2009) typology, I add a new category, internal high school support programs, which describes broad variations within the types of support given to the participants at the high school level. The following program descriptions include which students received support, how the programs are funded, and brief explanations of their services and goals. All program names are pseudonymous.

Private, Nonprofit Programs

Amigos. Crystal and Engracia both were a part of Amigos. Although this program self-identifies as a private, nonprofit organization, its "partner" universities contribute approximately one million dollars per cohort of Amigos participants (personal communication, anonymous CMU support staff member). This program is both a college access program and college retention/support program. Serving cohorts of urban students in various cities, Amigos begins in high school and continues on the campuses of participating, or "partner," colleges and universities. Amigos identifies eligible students who then must attend multiple "screening" activities to eventually be selected to participate in the program. Competition is stiff: hundreds of students compete for the ten spots that make up one cohort. Once accepted into Amigos, these cohorts experience eight months of intensive college preparation aimed at:

1. Team building and group support
2. Cross-cultural communication
3. Leadership and becoming an active agent of change on campus
4. Academic excellence (Amigos website)

Amigos participants go to college with their cohort, made up of the students they have been working with intensively for most of their senior year in high school. Once they start college, this cohort meets regularly with the campus support staff member specifically assigned to the group. Amigos participants also have individual meetings with this campus staff member. In addition, all Amigos participants are automatically enrolled in Education for All Students (EFAS) in order to provide them access to tutors and other resources on campus. Finally, all Amigos participants receive a full scholarship for four years as well as a laptop upon starting college.

Higher Education-Sponsored Programs

Access to College (ATC). This program, in which Mario participated, is geared toward preparing underrepresented students for college life at

CMU. Students come to campus for one or more summers during their high school careers. Most participating students qualify for free lunch at their K–12 schools and therefore receive scholarships from the state to cover the cost of the program. The program's website says participants will do the following:

1. Discover if [Central Midwestern University] will be a good match for you and your career goals;
2. Get a head start on your preparation for college;
3. Practice problem-solving skills you will need to succeed academically in college;
4. Work with college instructors on projects that will help develop your writing skills; and
5. Learn how math and science are used to solve real-world problems. (CMU website)

Summer Bridge Semester (SBS) (with additional aid from private grant funding). Antonio and Mario were both a part of this summer bridge program, which is available to any student enrolling at CMU as a first-year student but is designed for underrepresented students. Students take college-level course-work during the summer immediately before starting college and are able to start the school year with up to six college credits earned in the program. The program website explains that SBS aims to help students "adjust to [their] new environment and get a jump start on their college career." The SBS website also states,

> During [SBS] you will learn how to: read critically, write college essays, conduct library research, learn up-to-date computer skills, take notes, prepare for tests, and manage your time efficiently. These skills will help you throughout college. We strive to prepare [SBS] students to join our community of scholars with confidence and leadership skills. (SBS website)

During [SBS] you will also:

1. meet a very diverse group of first-year students
2. attend orientation together with your SBS friends
3. learn about valuable resources and support services on CMU's campus
4. meet with advisors in various areas
5. get familiar with campus buildings
6. enjoy fun social activities

7. enjoy the guidance and friendship of a mentor
8. learn about CMU Student Organizations and how to get involved (SBS website)

State- or Federally-Funded Programs

Academic Student Assistance (ASA). ASA, a state-funded program in which Antonio and Mario participated, offers academic tutoring and advising and is often compared to EFAS. An ASA staff member explained, "[ASA] is an academic support program for Students of Color on campus and disadvantaged students. We work with the student from the time they matriculate until they graduate, which is really unique for most of the support programs on campus." While the frequency of advising meetings varies across the program staff members, if a student is doing "really well," they are required to come in for advising meetings less frequently than a student who is struggling with grades. Staff at both EFAS and ASA monitor student grades as a means to determine their need for advising and support.

      Education for All Students (EFAS). Crystal, Engracia, Jasmine, and Moriah all participated in this federally funded program. EFAS is designed to "provide academic and ancillary support to low-income [college] students, first generation college students, and students with disabilities" (program website). Program staff provide academic advising and tutoring for qualified students. In addition to this support provided during the school year, EFAS offers a summer orientation for its students in lieu of the orientation offered to "mainstream" students who are not a part of EFAS. This orientation includes facilitating discussions with students about the racial and socioeconomic makeup of CMU, with the goal of helping them prepare to be minorities—in one or more ways—on CMU's campus. EFAS serves more than 500 undergraduate students.

Community-Based Programs

Pre-College Program: A Partnership between CMU and K-12 Schools. Antonio participated in this program, which is designed to ease the transitions from middle school to high school and high school to college. Although the Pre-College Program initially focused exclusively on urban Lakeside Students of Color, it has since expanded to include K-12 schools in eight geographic regions within the state. Pre-College initially began working with middle school students and now supports students at the elementary level as well. The program website lists the program goals:

1. Retain pre-college students of color and those from low-income households in school;
2. Help them graduate as motivated, focused young adults who are academically prepared to go to college; and
3. Increase enrollment and graduation rates of students from diverse backgrounds as intregal [sic] to the university's mission. (Pre-College website)

Although formal academic support does not continue once students enroll at CMU, students are encouraged to draw on the social support of their fellow Pre-College participants on campus.

Internal High School Support Programs

I have included this category within the notion of "types of support" because there is considerable variation within the group of high schools that the participants attended and in the ways in which each approached preparing its students for college. All of the participants attended public high schools. Antonio, Crystal, and Engracia attended urban schools specifically geared toward college preparation, and each of these schools required students to apply in order to attend. Jasmine graduated from an urban high school with a large Latin@ population that was not specifically geared toward college preparation. Mario attended a suburban high school with a reputation for having a strong curriculum, and Moriah attended a racially diverse trades-focused school in a poor urban neighborhood that offered no college preparation support.

Social and Cultural Capital as Tools for Gaining Program Access

Student-centered college access programs are often exclusive in their rigid acceptance criteria, such as high standardized test scores and grades (Loza, 2003). This exclusivity results in only the "cream of the crop" among underrepresented youth having access to programs designed to reach struggling students. Loza argues, "the Latino students who exhibit the most need are summarily excluded from participating in the programs, thus leaving them on the margins of the educational system" (2003, p. 43). In fact, it is estimated that no more than five percent of Latin@ students who could benefit from college access programs actually have access to one (Adelman, 2001, cited in Gándara & Contreras, 2009, p. 253). Furthermore, little is known about the educational paths of the students who are lucky enough to obtain access to the programs. That is, at least partly due to poor funding for such research, virtually no programs keep longitudinal data on their students (Gándara & Contreras, 2009).

In this section, through the student voices and experiences, we see that it is not only grades and high test scores that pave the way for participation in programs. Indeed, in addition to a little luck, connections (social capital) and specific knowledge of college life (cultural capital) can play significant roles.

Mario

Mario, as seen above, participated in two summer programs, Access to College (ATC) and Summer Bridge Semester (SBS). ATC brought him to CMU's campus for two summers during high school and SBS for the summer before his first semester at CMU. He also is a part of Academic Student Assistance (ASA), an academic support program for Students of Color and/or "disadvantaged" students. Recall that Mario's father, after serving in the military and attending a community college, received a bachelor's degree from CMU. It was clear to me early on that Mario arrived at Central Midwestern University with significant social capital.

This capital stems directly from his connection with the three Latino men—Jorge, Roberto, and Salvador—who are friends with Mario's father and who currently work at CMU. Specifically, Jorge is an academic advisor at CMU with whom Mario played on a summer baseball team; Roberto is the coordinator of minority programs for the School of Education and was a CMU student with Mario's father; and Salvador is a director of admissions and recruited Mario's dad to CMU years ago. Below, Mario talks about the important ways in which these men have been a part of his transition to CMU:

Julie: So how did you know about ATC?

Mario: So, since Roberto [my dad's friend] works in the School of Education, and he knows about these programs, he's the one who said, 'Hey look, if this program is available, we'll have Mario apply.' So I applied and got accepted and so that's the only reason why I [knew about ATC]—just 'cause of Roberto. 'Cause he showed me these other extra programs that are here.

Julie: And then how did you hear about SBS? Through Roberto, too?

Mario: Through Roberto, too, yes. Well, also last year when I was here, they were saying, 'Okay, after this we'll get you into SBS so you can start just basically coming to school early so you can...get your feet wet, you know, take a couple of classes...'

Not only did Mario's connections to his father's friends give him access to bridge programs, but it also may have eased his way through CMU's application process.

Julie: You just applied [to CMU] on your own, and then?

Mario: Right. I applied on my own. However, I was already in contact with the admissions people.... And then having people that actually work on campus. Okay, well obviously I have...some connections saying, 'Well, okay, at least you can get accepted here.' So...really, I knew I was going to come here when Salvador told me, 'Yeah, we'll get you in the SBS program.' Well, if you get in the SBS program, that means you're starting [regular] classes already. Just 'cause Salvador has such high position...in the university.

While he was participating in SBS the summer before his first year, Mario continued to possess significant social capital. Below he discusses how this social capital allowed him to get into yet another support program.

Julie: And how did you get into ASA?

Mario: The [English professor in SBS]. I went in to go turn in a paper [over the summer] and he asked me if I was in ASA, and I was like, 'No.' He was like, 'All right, we'll go talk to this person and you're gonna be in ASA now.'

Moriah

Although neither parent attended college, Moriah's older sister has two college degrees, and her older brother has a law degree from CMU. As I mentioned in Chapter 1, she was her graduating class' valedictorian but did not feel as though her K-12 education prepared her for college. She is part of the support program, Education for All Students (EFAS).

On the surface, Moriah's connections may appear to be similar to Mario's: She has two direct connections to CMU, both of whom are Latino men. Her brother, who is roughly the same age as Mario's father, attended CMU's law school and still lives in the Midwest. Her brother's friend, who currently works at the CMU law school, has offered his support to her. However, Moriah is only in one support program (EFAS) as compared to Mario's three. And, as we see below, she has significantly less social capital than Mario. Moreover, Moriah's acceptance into the support program was much less personal:

> Julie: So how did you hear about EFAS?
>
> Moriah: Yeah, they sent me a letter with my [CMU] acceptance letter. And I was like, well, I could use the counseling or whatever, if I ever needed it or whatever, so I signed up. And then my brother, he tried to get me into all these programs, too. But a few weeks after I applied and got accepted, he was like, 'Did you look into the EFAS program?' I said, 'Yeah, I'm already a part of it.' 'He said, oh, okay.'

Although Moriah's brother's friend contacted her and offered, "If you need anything, you can call me," the two had no contact during her first semester. Moriah explained, "I haven't talked to [my brother's friend] since [he initially contacted me]. I don't know why. I haven't really thought about talking to him. Though maybe I should."

It appears that not only did Mario have more connections than Moriah, but his were more effective in getting him support. Mario's connections were close family friends with whom he had contact before his fall semester at CMU; Moriah's contact was someone she knew vaguely through her brother. Thus, *familial capital* (Yosso, 2005) weighs in heavily in terms of Mario's connections and their positive impact on his transition to college. In essence, Roberto, Salvador, and Jorge act as Mario's extended family, or *familia*, on campus. Moriah does not have anyone acting in that capacity.

Crystal

Recall that Crystal does not have any family members or anyone within her *familia* who attended college. For most of her childhood, her father was in prison and her brothers were heavily involved in gang activity. While her mother wanted her to get an education, she was not directly involved in decisions related to Crystal's schooling. In her words, she was "marked early" as a very good student, and teachers consistently alerted her to opportunities that would help her get a better education and thus closer to Amigos and college acceptance. She explained:

> I've had teachers who have helped me, who were very good to me, and they were the ones to tell me to apply [to Amigos] and that I can do whatever I wanted, that I was on the right track, you know? Like in high school, I had a history teacher who was very supportive. He helped me with Amigos. And he helped me pick CMU. Because for Amigos you have to get nominated. So I'm in class junior year, and my guidance counsellor brings me out of class, and he's like, 'Okay, tell me what you're involved in.' He's like, 'There's a scholarship that I wanna nominate you for.'

> He could only nominate two people, so the fact that he's nominating me is a big deal. But he explained there was a scholarship for tuition, and it was only for six schools. I hadn't even really considered going to any of them. But I was told they were really good schools. And then he told me that the scholarship was tied to an early decision, so if I got in, I had to go. So I was like, 'Well, wait. I'm just barely starting my third year in high school—I don't want to commit. I was like, 'I don't want to commit to something.' So I told him 'maybe.' And then I was like, 'No, no, don't sign me up!' And then I told my history teacher about all this, and he sat me down, and he's like, 'Crystal, this is a really big deal.' I told him that the guidance counsellor said he would give me the rest of the day to think about it. So my history teacher was really helpful. He was like, 'You can do this. This is more money than you could ever hope for.' He said, 'Just go for it. There's no guarantee that you'll get it anyway. But just go for it.'

In the end, the support and encouragement of her teachers resulted in Crystal "going for it" and agreeing to apply to Amigos and begin the program's rigorous evaluation process. Entering the process, however, meant that were she to be accepted, she was committing to move away from home for college—something, in her words, "that culturally is just not done. You don't leave home for college."

She went on to describe the evaluation process, which involves a series of three meetings of all the applicants. After each "meeting," the group's size is reduced until the final meeting. Crystal recalled:

> Then, we were 25 out of the thousand something students that had started off. So they started cutting down. And then that 3rd meeting, you had to come dressed up. You met faculty from CMU, we met some Admissions Officers and stuff from here. And we had activities and interviews. We got scenarios we had to work through while the evaluators watched us. Then, of the 25, only about ten get chosen. So we're waiting,

we're waiting. You get a phone call. I got a phone call [to tell me I was accepted]. And I cried! That's Amigos. You have to go through a lot, but it's well worth it.

After she explained this process, she reflected on the series of events and teachers who helped pave the way to CMU for her:

And you know, [Amigos] is an inexplicable opportunity. Because I can, you know, trace back and think back on the steps that got me here. I got a letter in grade school to go to a better grade school. To go take a test for a better grade school based on my test scores. Why I was the one to get that? I don't know. I couldn't tell you. But that letter showed up at my doorstep and I went and took the test and went to that better school. And then that led me to more opportunities, to another letter that said, 'Come take a test at this high school, a better high school.'

And I did, and I got into that. 'Cause it was gradual, and then, Amigos, and now I'm here, you know, so really that's what happened. I got letters in the mail about schools that I never heard of, and programs I never heard of, my parents have never heard of. Why? Why weren't the thousands and thousands of other kids getting it? I have no idea.

Crystal's recollection of Amigos' selection process made me at once excited about the innumerable doors that this program had opened for her and disillusioned at the thought of the hundreds of qualified students who did not get the same chance. Crystal seemed to be able to recognize both the significant amount of hard work and sacrifice on her part that contributed to her acceptance at CMU as well as a certain amount of luck involved in the series of events that led to her starting college at CMU. Crystal no doubt had connections, or social capital, that stemmed from the various schools she attended. Her teachers, administrators, and guidance counsellors were the connections that led to significant opportunities for her.

Engracia

Although neither of Engracia's parents attended college, and she had no relatives who attended CMU, as did Mario and Moriah, Engracia arrived at CMU with crucial social and cultural capital, both provided at least in large part by her college prep-oriented high school and the Amigos program. A series of events led to Engracia's acceptance into this ultracompetitive program. A student council president with an exceptional GPA, Engracia had to be nominated by a teacher or community member to be eligible to apply, and she had incredibly stiff competition for entrance into the program, as we see here:

Julie: How did you choose CMU? And did Amigos find you? How did that all happen?

Engracia: I was always involved with student council, so most of the presidents would always go for [Amigos]. But the past two presidents that went for it didn't get it. And I started researching it and originally, I said if I don't get into CMU, I'm gonna go to [a prestigious private university in Center City]. But you know, I don't want my parents to pay all that money, so if I get the scholarship through Amigos, this is the best school. Originally, I wanted Amigos, and I guess it's kind of like tradition … every president of student council and like every president of the senior class gets nominated for it.

Julie: So then you just applied, you got in…

Engracia: Yeah. There were a lot of kids that day. Like the first meeting, you're in a room with like 200 kids. And they make you do these activities where you don't think they're looking at you. Except for that time that someone passes by with a notepad, writing. That's when you're like, 'Oh, boy, they're watching.' And the 2nd one is more comfortable. You get more—you get to show more of yourself as opposed to being in a group of a hundred. And the 3rd is like the first meeting, but there are only 25 people left.

Julie: Okay, wow. That's a lot of people that you had to …

Engracia: Yeah, they say 1,300 people applied, and then like 200 make it to that first meeting.

As I listened to Engracia, my mind drifted to Moriah, who attended a sub par high school which was focused on preparing students to work in the trades rather than go to college and who was in a "support" program at CMU that she did not find helpful. In many ways, Engracia and Moriah, both sharply astute and bright, were opposites in terms of their high school experiences and the resources available to them. My sense was that Engracia's strong high school curriculum and her experience in Amigos complemented each other in terms of preparing her for CMU—the two components were like pieces of a puzzle that fit together perfectly. This sense was confirmed later in the same interview:

Julie: Is there anything that you wish your high school would have done differently to prepare you for college?

Engracia: No, 'cause a lot of the things that the high school might have not done, Amigos did.

Given the strong support Engracia was receiving and how confident she was in her preparation for CMU and her ability to succeed there, I was surprised in a later conversation with Engracia when she told me she was also a part of EFAS. She told me casually, "It turns out, if you are in Amigos, you also have to be in EFAS." I thought of the long waitlist EFAS had and about all the other support at her fingertips through Amigos. While I certainly felt as if Engracia "deserved" Amigos and EFAS and all their benefits, I also couldn't help feeling a sense of injustice on behalf of Moriah, a hard working valedictorian who by all accounts had less privilege than Engracia simply given the disparate quality of high schools they attended.

As I walked to my car after talking with Engracia that day, I recalled Loza's (2003) mandate for fewer student-centered programs and more school-based programs. I wondered what Moriah's experience at CMU thus far would be like if, instead of a handful of students greatly benefiting from expensive programs like Amigos, entire schools and districts were revamped and improved by providing *all* students with the social and cultural capital that Amigos provides, as well as providing rigorous college-prep curricula like the one in Engracia's high school.

Then, as I drove home from campus, my conversations with the study participants thus far settled in my mind and I heard echoes of a meeting I had with a mentor when this study was in its planning stages a year prior. I had originally proposed to study only Amigos students and their transition to CMU, with the intention of learning more about why this program is so widely considered successful. As I explained my idea for the study to this professor, a flicker of anger crossed her normally serene eyes. She stated firmly that she disagreed with the premise of such programs that reach so few and cost so much. She went on to tick off how many changes could be made in the public schools if the amount of money spent on Amigos were available to struggling schools and used to reform them, thereby reaching more students. While there is no doubt much to learn from the successes of the Amigos program, I began to appreciate my mentor's cautionary views on limiting the participants to Amigos scholars.

Jasmine

As mentioned earlier, I was concerned for Jasmine's prospects at CMU even before my first interview with her had ended. She was also concerned. She explained in no uncertain terms that she did not know how to study, read well, or take notes. It was obvious that Jasmine's urban Lakeside high school did not prepare her academically or otherwise for college, and she knew it.

She graduated high school with a 3.6 GPA, although she "never really studied." Her high school education was similar to Moriah's in some key ways: it was not challenging academically, not engaging, and it was a source of insecurity for both young women. Neither woman studied rigorously for high grade-point averages. Both women knew their high school years left much to be desired in terms of academics, and they knew that many of their peers at CMU would arrive much better prepared than they were.

Jasmine arrived at CMU with even less social capital than Moriah, however. She had no family members who had attended CMU and had not participated in any pre-college programs. She did not get accepted to CMU the first time she applied—she revised her application and was accepted on her second try. I asked her how she learned about EFAS, and we see that it was an impersonal letter, as was Moriah's entry into the program; it was not the caring, intimate entrée into support programs that Mario received. I was also struck by how frank the EFAS staff was with Jasmine about her under-preparation for CMU due to the urban Lakeside schools she attended. A portion of our conversation follows:

Julie:	So how did you hear about EFAS?
Jasmine:	They just mailed me a letter and they said, 'Oh, you're gonna be in EFAS,' and, 'Sign up to be in EFAS.' They were like 'You got accepted to Midwestern University EFAS.' And I was like, 'Oh, okay.' 'Cause I guess they don't really expect me to make it [at CMU]. Or, they don't expect me to have an easy time. They said that I'm gonna have a hard time a little bit.
Julie:	Who told you that? Did they say that in the letter?
Jasmine:	I was talking to [EFAS staff] on the phone, and they said that my grades are high and stuff, but in Lakeside, our school is so low. I mean, like the way they teach, it's way lower than a lot of other schools. So they said, 'You're probably going to have a harder time because like here you really have to think about what you're doing.' You have to know how to study. And the school here [in Lakeside], you know, you just have to do your work. You know, it's common sense to do your homework, you know? It's easier to do it, and they said at CMU, you're going to need to study. So it's kind of like they were saying, 'You're gonna be able to do it if you're really set on it, but you know, it's gonna be *way* different than what you're used to.'

Thus, Jasmine, like Moriah, knew before she started CMU that her high GPA in high school was not respected or valued at a place like CMU. EFAS staff saw that Moriah and Jasmine were first-generation college students and minorities and flagged them as students who might need their services. In Jasmine's case, however, they went beyond this initial flagging; they saw the schools Jasmine had attended, possibly in conjunction with other aspects of her application, and went so far as to warn her that she would struggle precisely because of her previous schooling.

Antonio

Like Mario, Antonio came to CMU already having done substantial college preparation outside his college-preparatory high school curriculum. Antonio was sent a letter in his first year of high school asking him if he wanted to be a part of Pre-College, and he applied and got accepted. Although applications to Pre-College were also available in the counselor's office, the letter prompted Antonio to apply. In his words, the letter "talked about getting help with the future, or whatever, through this program, so I applied." The stroke of luck that this letter represented had a beneficial domino effect for Antonio: Pre-College participants automatically attend the Summer Bridge Semester program and are accepted into Academic Student Assistance [ASA] once they enroll at CMU.

Thus, the fact that Pre-College reached out to Antonio had a significant impact on Antonio's academic career: The years after he was accepted into this program were filled with summers on CMU's campus, internships with local organizations, ACT preparation courses, and a summer bridge program that earned him six college credits before the school year began. [Author's Note: The ACT is an exam used in many parts of the U.S. for college entrance. The acronym originally stood for "American College Testing," but the organization is now officially named ACT.] Significantly, after taking the Pre-College ACT prep course, Antonio improved his ACT score by five points. Thus, his admission into Pre-College instantaneously provided him with social and cultural capital that Moriah and Jasmine never had access to.

Thus, we have seen that social capital aids in getting students access to programs whose very mission is to increase social capital for its disadvantaged participants. It seems, then, that the more effective programs are available to the "most advantaged of the disadvantaged"—those who already have some form of social and/or capital at hand. In other words, the Amigos and Pre-College programs are available to a relatively small number of students (ten first-year students for Amigos and 189 students ranging from first year to senior year for Pre-College), whereas EFAS and ASA each serve roughly 500 CMU students. In the following chapter, I continue to examine the programs represented in this study but turn the focus specifically on the students' experiences with each of the programs.

· 3 ·

"TO DROP OUT OR NOT TO DROP OUT?"

Student Experiences after Program Acceptance

In the last chapter, I examined the types of programs represented in this study and the ways in which students gain access (or not) to these programs. In this chapter, I address the ways in which the six students experienced each program. Importantly, my intention is not to evaluate the programs per se. Instead, I focus on the types of support each program offers and how the students experienced that support, and I conclude with a discussion of key programmatic components as well as implications for supporting the transition to college for underrepresented students. Specifically, in what follows, the data and analyses are organized into the following sections: It's Not about the Grades, Personal Connections and Caring Mentors, and Finances. I then offer conclusions about the key program components and implications for rethinking success to close the chapter.

It's Not about the Grades

*Most Students [of Color], including Chicano students, leave campus **not** because of their grades. They leave campus because of…other reasons. People think they drop out because they do lousy in school. That's not the case at all. And I think one of the reasons freshmen [have a hard time] is just the transition, you know? They transition from a neighborhood that is predominantly their own culture to a neighborhood that totally is different from what they*

are used to. That's a huge transition. So they come to this place, they feel isolated, alienated.
They don't see many [people like them]—very few—and they are isolated. There are not
many students like them on a campus like this.

—Assistant Dean, CMU School of Education

Less than a month after starting at CMU, Moriah wrote, "To drop out, or not to drop out: That is the question," on the message board that hung on her dorm-room door. This dismal musing stayed there for most of the fall semester. As we sat at our usual meeting spot, a café not far from campus, the robust confidence Moriah had displayed only three months earlier—even as she asserted she was not academically prepared for CMU—was gone. Hunched over her tea, Moriah explained she was feeling stressed because of all of the work she needed to do in "so little time." Although she said she initially wrote the words as a joke, it was clear to both of us in that moment that this was no joke. I watched the tears well up in her eyes as she said, "Well, I thought I could handle it. I guess I can't. I don't know."

But what did she mean by "it"? What was the "it" that she felt she couldn't handle? Perhaps surprisingly, Moriah's grades were not suffering when she wrote these words, nor did they suffer all semester. In fact, she ended her first semester with a GPA of 3.65. As the epigraph above suggests, Moriah was not considering dropping out because of her grades; indeed, it was a more complex—and grave—situation than that. Moriah was considering leaving competitive, prestigious CMU in part because she was a high school valedictorian who told me in no uncertain terms before the school year started that her inner-city Lakeside high school did not prepare her for college.

In addition to her shaky confidence in her college preparation, however, Moriah considered leaving CMU because she often felt deeply isolated. In her words, she felt "miserable" and "out of place," which I examine more closely in Chapter 4. Indeed, the few weekends she stayed on campus were spent alone. Part of this isolation was because she rarely saw any faces in the crowd that looked like her own—she was not accustomed to being surrounded by virtually all White people. This isolation was also because she had yet to find caring, personal support on campus in the form of an academic staff member who could help guide her through her transition to college.

As she reached for a tissue, I wondered how, on a campus as large as CMU's, a campus that claimed to have abundant resources and support for underrepresented students, Moriah could still be left to feel so alone and without support. I wondered how, in the span of a few months, the strong young woman I had met in a Lakeside café could have been transformed into the down trodden, self-doubting student sitting before me. I recalled meeting her in June, when she was confident even as she spoke of her lacking college preparation: Put simply, she spoke confidently and clearly about her perceived lack of preparation. Yet she had believed she could succeed at CMU, that her strength and confidence would help her do so.

I thought of Antonio, Crystal, Engracia, and Mario—and all the support they had gotten before starting college and continued to get as they transitioned to CMU—and couldn't help but feel a sense of injustice. Why was Moriah languishing, alone, while others were enjoying access to multiple forms of support on campus? Moriah—and for that matter, Jasmine—needed the kinds of support the others in this study received and were still receiving. EFAS, the one "support program" she was technically a part of, felt impersonal and ineffective to Moriah; thus, she rarely used it, and it did not begin to make a dent in her rough transition to CMU.

In many ways, Crystal sits on the opposite end of the spectrum from Moriah in terms of college preparation and support. While Moriah attended mediocre public grade schools and a public high school with a poor reputation, did not feel academically prepared for CMU, and received minimal support on campus, Crystal attended a top-notch magnet grade school and a highly competitive college-prep magnet high school, felt abundantly prepared for CMU, and received robust support before and during her transition to CMU. Here, Crystal explains how significant Amigos has been with regard to her experience at CMU thus far:

> Crystal: I think [my Amigos peers] are just like my family away from home. It's funny because we go to meetings, but we're also going to the meetings to hang out. We help each other out. Like, one of the girls lives upstairs from me and she is having a really hard time of it, and she gets really lonely, and I ask her to come over, or I'll go over there, you know. We're there to help each other. And, if I have a problem in an area that I'm not too good at, I know who to go to. You know, math and science, I know whose strong suit that is.

For Crystal, then, Amigos did indeed provide the "team building" and "group support" included in its program goals listed earlier. In fact, it seems as though the students in Crystal's Amigos cohort—whom she describes as her "family away from home"—formed part of her *familia*, which in turn provided her with *familial capital*. One of the six forms of community cultural wealth listed in the previous chapter, *familial capital* includes "those cultural knowledges nurtured among *familia* (kin) that carry a sense of community history, memory, and cultural intuition" (Yosso 2005, p. 79). Significantly, Yosso uses an expanded notion of family to conceive of *familia* as including "immediate family as well as aunts, uncles, grandparents and friends—living or long passed on…" (2006, p. 46).

Above, we see that Crystal counts on her cohort members for emotional and academic support, as well as provides them support in return. Below, Crystal describes an instance in which she and her *familia* at CMU share a home-cooked meal for her birthday:

Crystal: My birthday is coming up soon, and I'm not gonna be able to go home, so that's kinda hard. 'Cause I have a boyfriend back home. I can't hang out with my guy for my birthday, and it's a big deal. So what I'm going to do is, I'm gonna cook in the kitchen, and [my Amigos cohort and I] are gonna bake stuff. And we're just gonna have dinner. Otherwise, without them, I wouldn't be able to do that. I think something like that would depress me. Not being able to go home is a big deal to me. If I'm having a problem, I know that I can go to my [Amigos cohort] and not have to worry about it. You know, support to help me through it. That's a big deal.

Significantly, then, Crystal explains that not being able to go home for events such as birthdays would "depress her" if it weren't for the support and camaraderie she feels within her Amigos cohort. Thus, we see a vast difference in the type and depth of support Crystal has at CMU when compared to the support Moriah has.

Despite this difference, and perhaps surprisingly, Crystal shares Moriah's disillusionment about CMU's lack of diversity and therefore struggles to fit in with the campus beyond her Amigos cohort. Indeed, Crystal explained that it was difficult that CMU was "so homogeneous." Specifically, she explained that being one of the small number of Latin@s on campus was particularly challenging. In her words, "I'm the only Latin@ on my [dorm] floor, which makes it more uncomfortable. Especially when most people [in my dorm] aren't used to having Latin@s around." When I asked her, at the start of her second semester, how her transition to CMU might have been different without her Amigos peers, she explained that CMU would have been "a lot lonelier" and "a lot more negative." She then asserted, "I mean, it has been hard, period, at this point. But I think it would have been a lot harder if Amigos was not there." Later in the same conversation, when I asked her what she would change at CMU, she immediately answered, "more [racial] diversity." I asked her more about this:

Julie: If you could have more [racial] diversity on campus, what would that change for you?

Crystal: I think it would just make it more comfortable. Which I think makes it easier all around. Like you don't feel as pressured or as alone in working or studying, or just in class. Just to become more integrated in school and enjoy it more socially. So that would be the biggest thing [I would change]. How White it is here did catch me off guard a little bit.

Thus, while Amigos was clearly invaluable for Crystal in her transition to CMU, she still felt racially isolated as a Latin@ on a predominantly White campus. Despite this feeling of isolation, one might still expect Crystal to feel successful at CMU given her impressive K-12 academic preparation, her affinity for and dedication to school, her close-knit *familia* at CMU, and her stellar first-semester grades.

Interestingly, and as we saw with Moriah, Crystal's relationship with and definition of "success" at CMU proves complex in important ways. In January of her first year at CMU, I asked Crystal about her feeling of success thus far. Part of that conversation follows:

Julie: So, do you feel successful here [at CMU]?

Crystal: Academically, yes. I'm really proud of myself in how well I was able to do for the first semester, you know? That makes it all very real to me. So I am feeling academically very, very successful. I took an 'honors option' in history. I've been interested in applying for the Honors Program here.

Later in the conversation, I asked about her answer above:

Julie: You said that academically you definitely feel successful here. So does that mean that there are other areas of success that you're thinking of?

Crystal: Well, I'm doing a lot of personal reassessment, which is a way of putting it. I don't know. It has to do with me not feeling at home here yet, and me needing to at least find something here that will keep me grounded and comfortable, something that lets me feel like this is where I need to be. I know that this is what I need to be doing, but I think being here for such a huge chunk of my time, of my life, I should feel comfortable here. You know, feel comfortable going to class. And

Julie: you know, that I belong on this campus. I've been having a really hard time with that. I separated that kind of success from the academic because it's very different. I know I can do the work, and I know that I'm here for a reason, but just feeling at home here is different. ... I need something that will be grounding for me here.

Julie: And how much does Amigos do that for you?

Crystal: Right now, it does all of that for me. But I'm trying to separate from being so dependent on them because that just keeps me hanging out with the same people all the time. It keeps me connected with just those same people.

Thus, for both Moriah and Crystal—two young women with vastly distinct college preparation and types of support—the biggest challenge to feeling fully successful at CMU is the lack of racial diversity and not feeling "at home," and as if they "belong" on campus. Indeed, Moriah and Crystal's experiences clearly support the CMU administrator's words in the epigraph above, "Although many might assume that Latin@ students struggle at competitive, predominantly White universities because of academic problems, oftentimes this is not the case." Crystal astutely bifurcates her definition of success at CMU, illustrating that one's grade-point average can fall woefully short of representing his or her feelings of success.

Personal Connections and Caring Mentors

It is very difficult for these students to open up [when they come to a support program for help], because the likelihood of the person sitting on the other side of the table is someone like them is very small. But if you have a relationship with them over time, there's a bond, and also they trust that they can confide in you very personal information. I think that [Latin@] students generally feel at ease when they think there is somebody like them on the other side of the table with some authority or power that can make a difference in their life on campus.
—Xavier, Support Program Staff Member

In this section, I contrast the experiences of Mario and Moriah in terms of their connections to caring, personal relationships with campus staff members who were in a position to "make a difference in their lives on campus." The following excerpts show that both Mario and Moriah value close, personal relationships with people in support roles on campus. Both want to be connected with campus employees in support roles who know and care about them. Mario enjoys and acknowledges such relationships, while Moriah notes their absence in her life on campus. Mario explains:

Mario: My dad coming to school here and knowing people here [has] helped
           me tremendously because I have people to go to. Not only as people
           to talk to, but also I can actually meet connections and go from there,
           and that's helped a lot. I mean a tremendous load. I try to see Jorge or
           Roberto like once a week. Just to go in and talk to him.
Julie: Do you kinda just drop in?
Mario: Right. Just drop in and talk. Well, I mean the thing that makes it eas-
           ier was the fact that I had more of a personal relationship with Jorge
           because we played baseball together over the summer. So I mean, we
           have more than just the academic part… we also have like more of a
           friendship, too. So I go in [his office] and he's helped me a lot. He's
           been great for me.

Mario recognizes that he meets "connections" through these family friends, and, as he explains later in the same interview, he plans on using them to navigate the local hospital system and secure an internship in the medical field to bring him closer to his goal of eventually being admitted to medical school. Thus, Mario's personal relationships with these men have provided him with *navigational capital* (Yosso, 2005), making the task of navigating a large university and its affiliated medical institutions a more manageable task.

While Mario benefits from close relationships with several CMU staff members, Moriah longs for support on a personal level. When I asked her how often she has taken advantage of EFAS, the one support program she is in, Moriah explained that she only goes for the required advising sessions because she does not feel "comfortable" on a "personal level" with her EFAS advisor. When I asked her how she would change EFAS to better meet her needs, she stressed the importance of personal connection.

Julie: What would be your dream resource or support program here at CMU?
Moriah: I don't know. I guess like a place in my dorm that had like tutoring and
           writing help. But with someone I was familiar with.

I later asked Moriah about why she is not using EFAS, and her answer again echoes Xavier's words at the beginning of this section:

Julie: So, have you used EFAS? Did you end up using them at all this
           semester?
Moriah: No. I was gonna go to Steve, the writing guy, but like his schedule
           didn't work out with mine. So I didn't go. I don't really feel comfort-
           able going out there.
Julie: Why?

Moriah: I don't know. I just—it's kinda hard for me to ask for help because I
            was always the one who everyone came to for help. So, like I don't
            know. And since I don't know them, I don't feel comfortable with
            them like judging my work, or whatever. So I'd rather not.

This theme of teachers and other school-based personnel *caring* for and *knowing* the students is consistent with Valenzuela's (1999) study of Mexican immigrants and Mexican-American high school students in which she found that while many teachers employed *aesthetic caring* (i.e., caring about instrumental and impersonal notions, such as grades and homework), the students craved *authentic caring* (i.e., caring about students as whole people while nurturing student–teacher relationships to help them succeed in school). Valenzuela claims that the politics of caring at school play a central role in U.S.-Mexican student "failure." She writes that many students of Mexican descent "… prefer a model of schooling premised on respectful, caring relationships" (1999, p. 61), but that too often they do not find these relationships with school-based figures of authority. Gándara and Contreras (2009) concur with Valenzuela and argue that first-generation Latin@ college students "need sensitive counsellors and friends" to provide support (p. 325).

Interestingly, as the study progressed, I began to fill part of the hole that was left wide open for Moriah due to the lack of caring "counsellors and friends" in her life. We often talked about her emotional and financial struggles, I served as her "writing tutor" more than once during her first semester, and I supported her in miscellaneous ways such as giving her a ride to job interviews. Quite fittingly, as I was sitting at my computer working on an earlier draft of this chapter, an email came in from Moriah with the word "Help" in the subject line. She was writing to ask for help with a paper she had written for her Spanish class. I edited the paper just as I would have while working as a college Spanish instructor two years prior, emailed it back to her, and continued working on this chapter. It was simply part of our relationship, and indeed still is.

The rapport between Moriah and me is in some ways the clearest example of how in-depth qualitative research is based on trusting relationships, as I have discussed earlier. Although I certainly did want to "repay her" (to the extent that it is possible) for being in the study and giving me hours upon hours of her time, it was not a give-and-take in the technical sense. Our relationship evolved organically over the months, and supporting her as she transitioned to CMU was a natural part of it.

Finances

It is generally accepted that socioeconomic status is the number one predictor of college admission because of the issues of capital and social reproduction discussed above (see, for example, Deil-Amen & López Turley, 2007; Gándara & Contreras, 2009; Lareau & Conley, 2008). That is, those who already have the financial ability are the ones who make it to college and therefore secure the jobs that allow them to continue to have financial means and social power. As Rueda (2005) concisely asserts, "Ultimately college is about access to resources and political power…" (p. 197).

While financial aid makes college enrollment possible for many who would otherwise not be able to afford tuition, access to financial aid requires capital. In other words, those who are able to secure an effective financial aid package are, by definition, relatively advantaged. Whether through social capital, cultural capital, or both, students with a robust aid package, as well as knowledge of the financial aid system, have had access to knowledge that others did not. Importantly, however, having financial aid does not translate into stress-free finances. Below, I explore the distinct financial realities of the students.

Antonio, Crystal, and Engracia: All Set

As part of the Pre-College Program (Antonio) and Amigos (Crystal and Engracia), Antonio, Crystal, and Engracia received full scholarships to CMU. The Pre-College Program starts awarding money to its participants while they are still in high school, as Antonio explained:

Julie:	Part of the Pre-College program is getting your college paid for, right?
Antonio:	Yeah, but like at the beginning of our junior year [in high school], we get a check for like $300, and then at the end of it, we get $700. We get $1,000 altogether our junior year [in high school] for being in the program. And then with the completion of the SBS program right now, we'll get our scholarship for the free tuition. Like, they'll pay our complete tuition for up to five years of our schooling.
Julie:	How does that feel, to know that you're starting college having everything paid for?
Antonio:	It's pretty good 'cause it's like the most expensive [public university in the state]. It's a lot off of us having to worry about. It is really good.

Like Antonio, Engracia and Crystal enjoy a relatively stress-free outlook when it comes to finances. Engracia explains:

Engracia: I don't even worry about money.
Julie: Good. Why?
Engracia: I have a scholarship. So my parents don't have to pay a single thing.
               I mean, the only money they spent was gas to bring me over here.
               That's all.

Mario: Saved by "A Web of People"

Mario's connections result not only in emotional and social advantages, as we saw above, but in more concrete ones as well. Here, we see that his social capital has a significant positive impact on his finances. Mario explained how his connections paved the way for a significant scholarship:

Mario: Did I tell you about the [scholarship I got]?
Julie: No. I know that we talked about you being worried if your dad was
               going to be able to pay out-of-state tuition.
Mario: Yeah. So our [SBS] professor was pissed off at a lot of the ... people
               in the Pre-College program because he knows that they have a full
               ride and that they're not even putting as much effort into class [or]
               taking it seriously. So he was really mad about that. And he saw that
               I was there, and I was doing my work and I was paying attention in
               class. So he went out and talked to [an administrator] and got her to
               pay my out-of-state portion of my tuition. So now I'm only paying
               in-state [tuition].
Julie: And did you have to apply?
Mario: No, no, no. He did it all by himself.
Julie: So you didn't have to go in and say anything?
Mario: I didn't apply. He took it—because he has such a high credential in
               the university. He was like, 'Look, I need this kid. This kid needs the
               money.' And so [admissions] scrounged around.
Julie: How did he know you needed money?
Mario: I think he heard from my dad's friend, Roberto, who works here at the
               university.... So it was a web of people, and luckily I know the right
               people, I guess, is what it is, and so I got that help.

Until he received this "scholarship," Mario was observably worried about his father being able to pay his out-of-state tuition. He told me more than once that although his dad was paying his tuition for now, he knew that it would not last. He would not be able to stay at CMU, he explained, if he did not find a way to have his tuition reduced. I noticed a significant change in him in him after this reduction in his tuition; he was visibly less stressed.

Moriah: Barely Making Ends Meet

Moriah received three separate scholarships totalling $4,250, two of which were automatically given to her; she did not have to apply. The third, which her guidance counsellor alerted her to, required a brief student profile. Moriah had the sense, which I shared, that if she had had a supportive mentor in high school who was aware of larger scholarships, she very likely would have been able to receive more money for college. Indeed, finances were a near-constant stress for Moriah once she started at CMU. The stress-free financial circumstances of Antonio, Crystal, and Engracia, as well as the greatly reduced stress for Mario, stand in sharp contrast to Moriah's financial reality. Recall that her parents work in a factory, and her mother often works more than one shift to pay the bills.

Unlike Mario, she struggled to pay her in-state tuition; did not receive help from her parents; had no one "looking out" for her financial wellbeing; and she experienced a decline in her financial situation as the semester continued. In fact, Moriah had a hard time convincing a family member to cosign a loan she needed to cover tuition costs. Her financial woes came to a head over winter break, which added to her existing doubts about staying at CMU, as seen in the following excerpt of our conversation:

Julie: So how serious were you thinking, 'Am I going to be able to come back [for spring semester]?'

Moriah: Pretty serious. My sister told me, well, just come back [home] and stay here and go to [a local university]. And then when I talked to my brother, I told him that I was thinking about just staying home. He was like, 'No, you can't do that. You know that CMU is opportunity,' and all the other stuff he was telling me before.

Although she eventually succeeded in getting a cosigner for a loan to cover immediate costs, Moriah is unsure about what the upcoming school year holds and is concerned that she will find herself in the same situation—unable to pay her bills.

Jasmine: It's Not Worth the Money

Jasmine came to CMU with the least social capital of all of the six participants. She did not have any connections whatsoever to CMU and did not participate in any type of college access program before she arrived at CMU. Her only support program at CMU was EFAS, a program that she used "about three times" during her first semester when she was required to meet with her advisor. Although she did apply for some scholarships, she did not do so until later in her senior year of high school, because until that point, as she explained, she "didn't know what scholarships were."

By the end of her first semester, Jasmine was seriously considering leaving CMU and had vague plans to attend a lower-tier state university near her home in Lakeside. While the reasons for her struggles at CMU are many and are further discussed in Chapter 5, we see that finances are part of the picture. Jasmine, who originally had planned on going into pharmacy, reasoned that it may not be "worth it" to stay at CMU since she had realized she was not the "science type" and thus was not going into pharmacy. She explains:

> I came here for prepharmacy. That's what I came here for, to the only pharmacy school in the state. And I miss my family a lot. I'm sorry, but I would rather go home instead of paying $30 at least once a month to go home and have to pay for housing and everything here. I mean, I'm paying [for CMU] on my own.

In the end, Moriah and Jasmine, the two students in the group who did not go to a college-prep high school, received neither extensive outside support to prepare for college nor to succeed once there. They did not arrive at CMU with social networks in place and struggled the most with money shortages. By the end of their first semesters, they were both seriously considering leaving CMU. The other four students possessed significant social capital; indeed, their connections were converted into tangible resources that clearly benefitted them. We are left to wonder, then, what might have been different for Jasmine and Moriah had they been approached by the Pre-College program, as had Antonio, and as a result had received college preparation starting in their middle-school years as well as a full scholarship for the duration of their college careers.

Key Program Components

While the commonly cited necessities for college success among underrepresented youth—strong academic preparation and sufficient financial aid—are crucial, there is more to the picture. Here, I describe two key components of the programs in which the students participated.

Explicit, Early Exposure to College

As high school students, Antonio and Mario had the opportunity to spend more than one summer on CMU's campus through the ATC, SBS, and Pre-College programs. Mario explained this early exposure to college life was "very valuable" and that because of these programs he already "knew what to expect" from college before he started. He also said these programs helped with the "social aspect" of college; he asserted that because of these programs, he learned how to live in dorms and have a roommate and that he was exposed to "all different kinds" of people. This early exposure to college life, through living on campus for three summers prior to starting college at CMU, allowed him to have a smooth start to his college career, which he appreciated:

Mario: I mean, there's gonna be thousands of other kids that are coming in here without this [experience]. Man, that's scary. I can only imagine the feelings they're gonna feel, because I've already felt these feelings.

A few weeks into the school year, Mario again emphasized the importance of feeling prepared for college in terms of knowing how to "do" college life and not necessarily in terms of academic preparation. Here he explains that he felt prepared for CMU and that SBS had a lot to do with that:

Mario: Yeah, I do [feel prepared]. I really do. The SBS really helped because it's like there are anxieties that I probably would be feeling right now that I don't have. So luckily it's just something else I have out of the way.
Julie: So it's not just high school that prepared you for this?
Mario: A lot of it was SBS, just because you're coming to the university in the summer. You're taking real classes. So you already have to deal with all the responsibilities that you're gonna face in college life, and so that's what really helped and that's why I'm extremely glad I did it.

Antonio echoed Mario's thoughts as he explained that the early exposure to college he got through Pre-College and SBS made "a big difference," specifically by giving him a sneak peek of what it was going to be like to have to budget his time and live on his own.

For those who are not fortunate enough to have these experiences before starting college, some college-based programs try to make up for some of what was missed. EFAS, for example, holds its own summer orientation for students who are eligible for the program. While Moriah and Jasmine did not use the tutoring or advising services, nor did they find the program particularly helpful, they did benefit from the program's attempt to expose them to college culture. Both Moriah and Jasmine told me that this orientation was "helpful" to them, explaining that at the very least it alerted them to the fact that they were going to be surrounded by students, most of whom are both White and from much wealthier families than their own. In the end, though, these frank discussions over the course of a four-day orientation that took place a month before the start of classes did not come close to providing the kind of preparation that Antonio and Mario received from their summer residencies on campus.

Caring Mentors and a Built-In Peer Network

As seen here, mentors on campus who care about and know the students can be vital. We saw Moriah yearn for these relationships, and we saw others recognize their importance. Through Amigos, Engracia and Crystal had regular contact with various mentors, one of whom they each met with individually on a weekly basis. They also had an automatic group of peers to lean on—a group they had known for almost a year prior to starting CMU. In Engracia's words, she knew she would "never be alone" because of the Amigos program.

We also saw how Mario benefited from the close relationships with the Latino men on campus who were looking out for him. Additionally, Antonio and Mario came in knowing peers from the ATC, SBS, and Pre-College programs—in fact, they both wanted to "branch out" and meet other people since they had already spent so much time with these students by the time classes started.

Rethinking Success: Beyond Programs and Grades

> Students who arrive at the university with the appropriate A-F requirements, ade-
> quate test scores, and proper grades are not necessarily ready to meet the demands
> of an academic cultural system. Although they may qualify on paper, their ability to
> felicitously maneuver through the system can be seriously hampered by their unfa-
> miliarity and inexperience with the culture of the institution. In other words, they do
> not have adequate social and cultural capital to secure a position within the intellec-
> tual and social realms of an academic community. (Vásquez, 2003, p. 24)

Moriah and I are back at our regular café. She is telling me she is considering
dropping out, but I've drifted off into my own thoughts, feeling angry that
she is left to feel alone and without support. My silent rant is interrupted
when Moriah relates a recent conversation she had with a friend who became
concerned after seeing the words "To drop out or not to drop out: That is the
question" scrawled on Moriah's dorm-room door. She explained:

> So I'm like, 'Oh, I really don't wanna be here. I should just pack my stuff and go
> home.' And then my friend, she's like, 'You know we can't do that. If we go back
> home, there's gonna be nothing for us. We'll be on [welfare]. Do you want us to be on
> [welfare]?' I'm like, 'No.' She's like, 'Okay, then, you gotta stay here.' I don't know.

For Moriah, going back to Lakeside and living off her parents while she
"figured things out" was not an option. Her parents were unable to help her
financially, and the three options as she saw them were to stick it out at
CMU, go on welfare, or work a factory job like her parents, which she refused
to do. She chose to stay at CMU, because, as she explained, "I refuse to flip
burgers for the rest of my life, or work in a factory like [my parents]." She is
miserable at CMU and is on the brink of leaving, yet her high grade-point
average causes her to go unnoticed by EFAS, the support program she is in.
Not one staff member of this "support" program is aware of how much Moriah
is struggling; thus, they do not put forth any effort to help her outside of regular advising meetings, which are designed to help students register for classes.

On the opposite end of the spectrum is Antonio. He is earning mediocre
grades, is happy at CMU, and is very involved in campus activities. He has
found his "niche" on campus, and the thought of leaving has never crossed
his mind. He does not use ASA very much; he does not find it useful. He also
explained that many students he talks to think the program is "unorganized."
Halfway through his first year, he told me he didn't use the program because,
"I don't really need the help."

ASA staff, however, keeps tabs on the grades of the students on their roster, and after seeing Antonio's relatively low grades, they began heavily pursuing him to come in for advising meetings. ASA often puts "holds" on the accounts of those students with "low" grades in order to get the students to come to an advising meeting. The "holds," which prevent students from doing things like registering for classes and checking out library books, are lifted once the students meet with an ASA staff member. Antonio eventually agreed to come in for an advising meeting, the goal of which was to help him study better and budget his time more efficiently. However, as we see below, that meeting never happened:

> Antonio: I know I was supposed to meet with some lady to try to schedule my week out, how much studying I do and all that. But that was supposed to be before my test, but she couldn't make a meeting [during] the times that were available for me—she was busy. So then it was scheduled for another two weeks after, and I was like, 'Forget it, I'm not gonna go.'

As we have seen, programs such as EFAS and ASA use grades as *the* indicator of success: Students on the roster of these programs are not pursued to come in for support if they have high grades. These large federally and state-funded programs have massive numbers of students to serve and only a small handful of staff members to do so. It is common, for example, for an ASA staff member to have 100 students on his or her caseload. So, while it is not surprising that such programs use grades as the sole indicator of success and thus the only gauge of how much support a student needs, it is a flawed system.

Indeed, as Gándara and Contreras (2009) argue, effective and significant school reform could one day make the programs like those in this chapter obsolete. They call for making the following effective aspects of college access and support programs available to all students, thus eliminating the need to rely on exclusive "add-on programs":

> The most important features of ... programs ... include recruiting a critical mass of Latino students; creating supportive peer study and social groups; placing the best teachers in freshman classes; extending program components beyond the freshman year; acknowledging that skill development is cumulative and that some students may require more time to excel; and providing meaningful financial aid. All of these features were present in the most effective college support programs we have seen and need to be replicated widely. (p. 325)

It is significant, then, to note that these scholars do not argue for academic preparation to be the sole or even the most pressing component of college preparation or retention. What's more, Lareau and Weininger (2008) plainly point out that academics and finances are only a portion of the picture of success in college. They assert:

> Thus, above and beyond questions of financial resources and children's 'academic ability,' the stratification system on which higher education is based is one in which individuals have unequal levels of the key cultural resources that facilitate the development of a customized educational career. (p. 121)

Similarly, as Vásquez (2003) argues, college is a "specific cultural system," and attaining success within this system is contingent upon familiarity with its norms (p. 25). Indeed, as seen in this section's epigraph, she argues that a student's K-12 grades may not tell us much about the student's ability to do well in college. For Students of Color, she explains, it is their lack of familiarity and facility with the way college "works"—not grades—that puts them "at risk from the moment they reach its doorstep" (p. 23). The process of acquiring facility with the norms of the collegiate "cultural system" is not something that can happen overnight. Underrepresented students must have early access to the social capital, which in turn can provide them with cultural capital, that White, middle-class students have readily available. In other words, they need early and sustained contact with the university. Unfortunately, however, most college access programs start late in a student's K-12 career and focus almost exclusively on grades and test scores (Vásquez, 2003).

Thus, the all-too-common exclusive focus on grades and test scores before college seriously misses the mark if we are to prepare underrepresented students to succeed in college. Similarly, using only grades as a means of judging students' "success" once in college, as well as measuring the level of guidance they need, is dangerously misguided. These traditional markers of success must be expanded if we are to effectively understand and support the transition to college for underrepresented students. Indeed, the role of capital needs to be recognized. We have seen that social capital is a significant player in how underrepresented students gain access to college access programs, how they gain admission to college, how they fare emotionally once enrolled in college, and even how they manage to pay for college.

In fact, it seems that during the crucial months of transitioning to college, social capital can take precedence over the other forms of capital included in Yosso's (2005) community cultural wealth model. While each student discussed here indeed possessed a combination of each of the forms of capital included in the model—aspirational, linguistic, familial, social, navigational, and resistant—it was social capital that trumped all the rest. For example, social capital certainly both paved the way to college access/support programs and eased the transition to CMU for Antonio, Crystal, Mario, and Engracia. Indeed, the presence of social capital provided significant tangible and emotional advantages for some, and its absence contributed to tangible and emotional hardships, especially for Moriah. Social capital, in the end, helped Antonio, Crystal, Engracia, and Mario pay for college; the lack of it resulted in significant financial stress for Moriah and Jasmine.

Traditional notions of "success" must be reconfigured to include the experiences of underrepresented students, and we must reconsider what it is that a "successful student" brings to his or her schooling. We saw that labeling Moriah a "successful student" paints a dangerously incomplete picture. We need to understand not only why students like Moriah feel unwelcome, alone, and under prepared, but also why they *stay* in college and achieve academic success. Indeed, close, personal relationships and support (social capital) may at times be more accurate predictors of "success" than a high grade-point average. It is this "relational" aspect of college that must be considered as seriously as and in tandem with "academics" if we are to truly understand and improve the educational experiences of all students.

· 4 ·

"RACE SHOULDN'T MATTER, BUT IT DOES"

Racial Selves, Identities, and Belonging

Introduction

This chapter explores the ways in which Antonio and Mario experienced and perceived "race" and belonging as they transitioned to CMU. These perceptions and experiences are inseparable from their identities during this time of transition; and part and parcel of their own identities are the ways in which their peers perceived and responded to them vis-à-vis race. Indeed, the notion of race is woven throughout all the participants' transitions to college. It is, for example, in the fabric that contains their experience of K-12 schooling, access to certain forms of capital, and changing family relationships while becoming college students, all discussed throughout this book. It is inextricably tied to the participants' experiences with as well as the design of the college access and support programs specifically addressed in Chapters 2 and 3. And it is of course omnipresent in the ways in which the students faced racism at CMU, explicitly examined in Chapter 5. While there are certainly other facets to their identities and personal experiences, it was race that repeatedly came to the foreground of my conversations with the students, no doubt in part because of their minority status at a predominantly White university.

Before delving into the students' experiences with race, however, it is necessary to define the very concept of "race." The notion that race is a social construct created to elevate dominant groups and subordinate others, as opposed to an objective category based on biology, is not new. Solórzano, Ceja, and Yosso (2000) explain this notion in plain terms: "...an examination of U.S. history reveals that the 'color line' of race is a socially constructed category, created to differentiate racial groups and to show the superiority or dominance of one race—in particular, Whites—over others" (p. 61). In what follows, we see the subjectivity inherent in a socially constructed category come into play, specifically as Antonio and Mario interact with—and are perceived by—others within the CMU community.

Racial Selves and Racial Ideology

As is to be expected, each of the six students I came to know through this study—who are commonly lumped together as "the same" racially—arrived at CMU with varied backgrounds in terms of race and identity, and each confronted the environment at CMU in his or her own way. Simply put, each had distinct racial selves, or identities. As a result, the degree to which each student engaged in critical thought about race also varied. And, while some students' awareness of and attention to race changed dramatically after enrolling at CMU, for others changes were much less dramatic or even imperceptible. In this section, I review the relevant literature on racial identities and ideology within the context of schooling and school success. I then address these issues in terms of students' voices, stories, and experiences vis-à-vis race and CMU.

Carter (2005) found that low-income African-American and Latin@ students fell into three categories that characterize how they perceived and interacted with their identities, cultural styles, and educational beliefs: "non-compliant believers," "cultural mainstreamers," and "cultural straddlers." Importantly, there is much variation and complexity within each category; however, the following synopses of these categories are helpful. Non-compliant believers "believe in education, but do not always comply with the rules of educational attainment" (p. 12). In other words, their experiences and understandings of themselves as racial and cultural beings cause them to oppose the rules that are commonly accepted as necessary to achieve school success and to be "good" students. While they believe in the value of their own cultural knowledge—knowledge that schools do not commonly honor—they refuse to integrate what Delpit (1995) calls the "culture of power" (Carter,

2005, p. 12). Importantly, the term *noncompliant* does not represent "anti-intellectualism or low achievement" (p. 29). Rather, it is a challenge of dominant cultural practices associated with success. While this group of students "believes" in education, they "slip through the cracks because they comport themselves differently and do not view cultural assimilation as a prerequisite for achievement" (p. 30).

Cultural mainstreamers, on the other hand, *do* subscribe to the dominant culture, or Delpit's (1995) "culture of power," even if it means being rejected by their peers for not embracing their own racial and ethnic behaviors. And, while they articulate that their own racial/ethnic background is "a central part of their identity," they believe that People of Color should be assimilated into the dominant (White) culture. In other words, their approach is to "fit into the system" (Carter, 2005, p. 29). Importantly, while cultural mainstreamers are aware of how their racial heritage differs from that of Whites, they view the behaviors and preferences (e.g., music, clothing, speech) that others associate with middle- and upper-class Whites as normative, or "regular" (p. 13). Some cultural mainstreamers may identify primarily as "human," while others more explicitly embrace their racial/ethnic identity (p. 29).

Finally, cultural straddlers are those who can strategically move between the spheres of the dominant culture and their racial and ethnic communities. They skilfully abide by the school's cultural rules, but they do not do so passively. Carter explains, "Though critical of the schools' cultural exclusivity, cultural straddlers negotiate schooling in a way that enables them not only to hold on to their native cultural styles but also to embrace the dominant cultural codes and resources" (p. 13). Carter found that while both cultural mainstreamers and cultural straddlers do well in school, noncompliant believers struggle.

Importantly, Carter and others (see, for example, Bergin & Cooks, 2002, and Arrellano & Padilla, 1996), challenge much of the work in oppositional culture theory (see, for example, Ogbu 1978, 1987, 1991; Fordham & Ogbu 1986; Ogbu & Matute-Bianchi, 1986), which claims that minority youths, having observed the institutional racism their parents faced with regard to education and job opportunities, develop oppositional identities. According to this theory, they decide that school success is incompatible with their identities as People of Color and perceive school and academic success as the domain of Whites. Thus, they view doing well in school as "acting White," and they resist this behavior. Carter's findings, in addition to those of the others named above, stand in direct opposition to this theory. She found that Students of Color do *not* in fact resist doing well in school and do not see educational success as the domain of Whites. Rather, she found that students who resisted "acting White" were instead resisting adhering to what is considered culturally "normative or 'natural'" in the U.S.: "the generic American, white, middle-class patters of speech and mannerisms, dress and physical appearance, and tastes in music and art forms" (Carter, 2005, p. 53). For African-Americans in Carter's study, resistance to "acting White" was about "maintaining cultural identity, not about embracing or rejecting the dominant standards of achievement" (p. 53).

Just as attitudes about schooling and engagement with schooling are part of one's identity formation, so is phenotype. In her counter story, Yosso (2006) discusses the issue of phenotype—one's physical characteristics—and the ways in which it interacts with and affects racial identities for Chicanas. A character in her counterstory, Michelle, is a light-skinned, green-eyed Mexican American. Michelle, who is often mistaken as White, says that she receives privileges as a result of being light skinned (Hunter, 2002). However, along with the advantages she enjoys, she endures many racist comments made in her presence; the perpetrators consider her to be White and thus a "safe" person to include in their racist conversations.

Judgments based on skin tone are not only made by Whites; internalized racism has brought these judgments within the Latin@ community. Yosso (2006) explains, "With negative images of Chicanas/os in the media and textbooks that stereotype or ignore Chicanas/os altogether, it's no wonder that Chicana/o students tend to internalize ideas that dark skin is not attractive, speaking Spanish is not 'normal,' and that anything Mexican is inferior" (p. 108). Thus, argues Yosso, it is not uncommon for Chicanas/os to judge each other in terms of their "degree" of *Mexican-ness*, based on skin color, lifestyle, language, and background. Terms like "coconut"—meaning "brown on the outside, White on the inside"—are sometimes assigned to those thought to be "less Mexican" (p. 108).

As this body of literature suggests, racial identities and ideologies are complex and individual; yet there are observable patterns that can be traced across groups. While these patterns and the above findings are helpful in deepening our understanding, I am leery of labeling the participants in my study, thus assigning them to a fixed category vis-à-vis their racial identities. They are complex, evolving individuals who each have unique backgrounds and stories. Carter's three categories discussed above are the result of a much larger study: Her findings are based on surveys and interviews with 68 students as well as surveys of the students' parents. The long, frequent, in-depth discussions I was able to have with my participants afford a different type of insight. Thus, while I was not able to see patterns across a larger group, as did Carter, I had access to more complex stories of fewer students. The lived experiences of Antonio and Mario, as well as the others, contribute to their having characteristics of more than one category and highlight the shades of grey between the categories.

Student Experiences

Below, I explore the intersections of identity and perceptions of race through focusing on the voices and experiences of Antonio and Mario. I do also, however, bring in the voices of Engracia, Jasmine, and Moriah. Their experiences are organized into the following sub sections: "Very Mexican" in Collegeville: Antonio; Liminal Spaces: Mario; Phenotype and Belonging; Counterspaces and Campus Involvement; and The Case for More Diversity.

"Very Mexican" in Collegeville: Antonio

Antonio's T-shirt caught my eye as we grabbed a table in the crowded restaurant. It was modeled after the uniforms of the delivery company, *UPS*, and the caption on the front read, "What Can Brown Do for You?" It was a shirt from one of the many Latino-focused campus groups he was active in, Group for Latino Men. At this point it was months into the study, and Antonio and I often comfortably talked about racial issues, both writ large and in terms of CMU's campus. These conversations were, as were almost all my conversations with Antonio, laid back and low key. In my experience, "laid back" was his M.O.

When it came to specifically explaining how he identifies himself racially and talking about his heritage, however, Antonio spoke with passion and intensity. It was clear at the outset that Antonio has a clear racial identity; being Chicano is central to his self-perception, and he is proud of his racial and ethnic heritage. Antonio's father was born to Mexican immigrant parents in Texas and was a migrant worker until he moved to the Midwest, where he met Antonio's mother, who is White. Months ago during our first interview, Antonio told me that he identifies as either "Chicano" or "Mexican American," and that he thinks he "looks very Mexican." On CMU's predominantly White campus, his appearance and dress—gelled, black hair and goatee, a thick chain necklace with a large pendant, baggy pants and T-shirts—easily label him as "other," and specifically as Mexican American. Although his mother is White, he identifies as Chicano. Antonio explains, "I look really Hispanic and stuff like that," and that because of this, he "stands out" and "gets stared at" at CMU and in Collegeville.

Thus, Antonio's phenotype and style of dress clearly marked him as "Hispanic." As we continue to see below, in a discussion of Mario's racial identity, phenotype is significant. Although Antonio's phenotype alone caused Whites at CMU to "look at him weird" and treat him differently—a form of racism, closely examined in Chapter 4—it also made it "easy" for him to "fit in" with Hispanics on campus, and his choice of dress made it easier yet. In other words, people around him did not question his racial identity, neither Hispanics nor Whites. He was not considered "half White" in some circles and "half Mexican" in other circles. He cleanly fit into one category, and his phenotype helped him do so as far as others—both Whites and other Hispanics—were concerned.

Antonio's clear self-identification as Chicano/Hispanic/Mexican American remained constant throughout the ten months I spent time with him, and he did not struggle with his "Whiteness." He enjoyed a positive and close relationship with his mother and her extended family, *and* he never felt "less Mexican" because of having a White mother and a father of Mexican descent. The saliency of Antonio's racial identity is apparent in the following conversation when I asked him how he would describe himself to a professor:

Julie:	So how would you describe yourself to a professor? Let's say you're emailing a professor and you wanted to get into his or her class.
Antonio:	I'd have to say I'm Mexican-American, whatever. Tell 'em what my status is—like how I am. Tell 'em, like, my skills, that I'm a hard worker, dedicated, stuff like that. Introduce myself, maybe give like, my background, what schools I graduated from and all that.
Julie:	And so you would include your—your ethnic background, or your racial background?
Antonio:	Yeah, I'm normally do. I'm used to doing that.

I then asked him how he would describe himself to a future roommate whom he had not met yet:

Antonio:	I'd say my race probably 'cause I'm proud of my race, so I'm not afraid of saying it. So I'd say that. And then tell him things I like to do, I guess, like hobbies and stuff.

Later in the conversation, I followed up on his assertion of being "proud":

Julie:	So you said that you're proud of your race?
Antonio:	Yeah.
Julie:	How do you think that happened? How do you think that you're proud of it, and [that] you would say it as you're describing yourself to somebody?
Antonio:	I don't know. I always grew up with it. Like I was never raised to like ignore it or something, like to try to pretend I'm not it. I was always raised with it.

Thus, the first thing Antonio would say by way of introducing himself to both a professor and a future roommate is to identify himself racially. Describing his work ethic and hobbies would come after his racial identity. He went on to explain that he liked the fact that he was raised to be aware of and proud of his "race," which he acknowledges is a large, diverse, group:

Antonio:	I've always liked [how I was raised in terms of my race]. I like my race, too, like how it is, all that.
Julie:	What do you like about it?
Antonio:	Like how we're so diverse. Like how big we are too. Like, we're everywhere. We're all kinds and stuff. And like we don't have a specific quality in order to be Hispanic.

Here, Antonio is "making room" in the category of "Hispanic" for all types of Hispanics. Although he does not explicitly say it, he is tacitly making room for those who, like him, might be categorized as "bi racial," or "multi racial," and identify as Hispanic.

I often "checked in" with him throughout the study to see if being on a predominantly White campus had any effect on his racial identification. His answers were very similar, and the following excerpt is representative of those check-ins:

Julie:	Has there been any change in how you see yourself since you've been here?
Antonio:	Not really. Like racially-wise, no. I'm not trying to like act like I'm White or nothing. I don't try to… adapt to that culture or something. I'm staying how I am, I'm not really changing much.

Although I did bring up the notion of "acting White," Antonio asserts that he is not "acting White," and that he has not changed as a result of living on CMU's predominantly White campus. We see that to him, "acting White" means "adapting" to White "culture," which is in line with Carter's findings. He does not include school success in his definition, nor does he at any time in the study bring up "acting White" in conjunction with his academics.

Antonio, then, had a clear Chicano identity that stayed constant through-out the study, as did his pride in his racial and ethnic background. His moth-er's being White did not seem to complicate or confuse his self-perception, nor did his lack of fluency in Spanish. Although he grew up hearing Spanish, and can understand it well, he is not a fluent speaker. He took Spanish in high school, including an AP/IB Spanish course, and took Spanish 102 during his first semester at CMU. When I asked him if he at all felt "weird" taking Spanish at CMU *and* being Mexican, he simply responded, "No, I'm not weird about it," and went on to tell me what they were currently studying in class. Although he decided not to continue with Spanish at CMU after his first semester because he didn't like the grammar-focused way it was taught, he is confident he will become more fluent in Spanish through contact with friends and family. At roughly the same time he made this decision, he decided to minor in Chicano studies.

Thus, we see that issues that may complicate or confuse one's racial identity—namely being labeled "bi racial" and not speaking fluent Spanish—did no such thing in Antonio's case. In fact, I imagine he would say these aspects of who he is only add to and enrich his "Hispanic-ness," an umbrella term, in his view, under which all kinds of Hispanics fit and are welcome. We also see that he does not fit solely into one of Carter's categories, yet he most closely aligns with the characteristics of the "cultural straddlers" cate-gory. While he is able to move between the dominant culture and his own, he most often stays within his own culture. He actively resists "acting White," and, as we will see later, is an involved student. Antonio's clean, simple way of talking about his "very Mexican" identity and appearance stands in sharp contrast to Mario's thoughts on his racial self and his experience with race, as we see below.

Liminal Spaces: Mario

A few weeks into their first semester, after they learned I was formerly a Spanish teacher, Mario and Antonio asked me if I would be willing to help them with some of the grammar-specific topics being addressed in their Spanish 102 course. The two young men, who were friends and had met through

Summer Bridge Semester, walked through my office door—about ten minutes late—for our weekly Spanish "tutoring" session. Antonio entered with a comfortable smile on his face, Mario with a furrowed brow. Antonio laughed casually, "Sorry we're late—it's in our blood." Mario, clearly upset at the joke's showcasing the stereotype of Mexicans' propensity for being late, firmly said, "Dude, *don't* say that!" Shaking his head while looking down, Mario repeated this repudiation of Antonio's joke. Antonio, still chuckling, assured Mario that he was just joking. Mario never laughed or smiled, and we got right to work.

This snapshot of the two young men is symbolic of some of the differences between them. As mentioned above, although the two students are friends and have a fair amount in common, Mario's identity and experience vis-à-vis race at CMU can be contrasted with that of Antonio. Like Antonio, Mario's father is from Texas and is of Mexican descent. Also like Antonio, Mario is not fluent in Spanish; the two actually enrolled in the same Spanish 102 course. Mario and Antonio both decided to minor in Chicano studies at CMU. However, unlike Antonio, both of Mario's parents are of Mexican descent, and Mario has light skin and a phenotype that is often mistaken for White. Also unlike Antonio, Mario struggles to explain his racial identity, he decidedly does not talk about race as a central part of his identity, and he has trouble "fitting in" racially.

Mario's parents divorced when he was a young child, and he has lived with his father since the divorce. Both his parents speak Spanish. He describes the difficulty he has when trying to identify himself racially to others:

Mario: My mom's parents were born in Texas; my dad's parents were born in Texas, their parents were born in Texas. So it's kinda like, what do you say? 'I'm American? I'm a Texan of Hispanic descent?'

According to Mario, his light skin, manner of speaking, and choice of clothes—his summer attire usually consisted of form-fitting T-shirts, cargo shorts, and a short, beaded necklace—often cause others to assume he is White. He explains this below as he reflects on his distant relationship with his maternal grandfather and becoming "Americanized":

Mario: I was never close with my grandfather on [my mother's] side because he only spoke Spanish, and growing up, we understood [Spanish] to an extent, but we weren't very fluent, and we didn't speak it. So, he had a bias towards us and … he was upset with [my mom] because we only spoke English, and we didn't speak Spanish. He wanted us to be more, you know, traditional, and not be, I guess, technically, Americanized.

But, however, because we have always lived with my father and that side of the family, that's how we were raised. We were raised to see both sides of the culture. It's like, we're in a White society, so you have to adapt to that. However, don't ever forget your culture, you know, where you come from. And so that's how I am right now. I mean, I choose to dress how I want to dress; I choose to speak how I want to speak. However, a lot of times I get considered as being White.

In Mario's above words, we hear echoes of Carter's "cultural mainstream" category, in which people, as Mario puts it, "adapt " to "White society" and "don't ever forget [their] culture," or in Carter's words, "integrate with" the dominant culture without forgetting who they are (Carter, 2005, p. 13).

After years of living in predominantly Hispanic neighborhoods, many of which were also low-income neighborhoods, Mario moved to "White suburbia" with his father and sister before his first year in high school. He spent most of his four years of high school attending a large, predominantly White suburban school. Unlike Antonio, who was accustomed to being surrounded by Hispanics in Lakeside, Mario grew accustomed to being surrounded by Whites during his high school years in suburban Texas. Also unlike Antonio, he says he consciously does not bring up his race in conversation. We see his thoughts on these issues as my conversation with him continues, a conversation in which we hear echoes of Carter's notion of "cultural mainstreamers"'":

Mario: And [being considered White] has a lot to do with [partly] being raised in White suburbia. However, a lot of people there forget that I am Hispanic. I am [of] Mexican descent. They don't know. Because I don't bring it up. I mean, there's no reason to bring it up. I don't see why race has to play a huge part of who a person is.

However, it's something I never forget. You know, it's always there. Then, when I go home, or [hear] music that my father listens to, I understand that, and I love it because that's what I grew up with. However, other people from the outside don't know that about me because I don't bring it up, because I see no reason to bring it up. I'm not gonna be—I'm not a person who's going to be just throwing it, waving it in front of people, saying 'Look, look at me. Look what I am.' Why? In fact, it seems to me that defeats the purpose. You know, I'm a *person*. I'm not of a certain group that I have to show ... who I am. That's just the way I think, you know?

Julie:	Yeah. So how does it make you feel when you are considered White?
Mario:	It's upsetting, because I'm like, 'Okay, I'm White in your eyes; however, you don't know me because you don't know where I come from. You're automatically assuming this about me; however, I'm not White.' A lot of times, I actually get that I'm half White, half Mexican because I'm so light complected [sic]. And that's just 'cause that's my mom's side of the family. They're all Hispanic-Mexicans. They're just light-complected [sic]. And I for some reason got the light complexion. My sister, she's more dark-complected [sic] like my dad. So that's just how it turned out. So I always get considered as being half White, half Mexican.
	And I always tell 'em, 'No, I'm full,' so it's always shocking to people. And like growing up in White suburbia, a lot of people didn't actually know I was Mexican until they saw my last name. And I was like, 'Yes, I am, but … it has nothing to do with anything. I just—that's who I am. I'm a *person*. Why does race have to be involved, is how I see it.
Julie:	And is there one group that thinks you're either White, or half white, more than another? Is it usually Whites who think that, or is it usually Mexican Americans?
Mario:	It's both, it's both. It's really hypocritical and it's really funny because, like, I've been coming to the programs up here on [CMU's] campus for like the last two years, and they are mainly minority programs. So [the Students of Color in the programs] think I'm White. Yet when I'm … with all my other friends in White suburbia, they know I'm Mexican. You know, so no matter where I go it's like I never fit in. And I'm just like, 'Why does it matter? You know, I'm a person.'

Akin to Carter's notion of "cultural mainstreamers" identifying as "human," Mario yearns to identify and be accepted as "a person" (Carter, 2005, p. 29). He does not believe race should be central to discussion, and he is aware that he chooses to dress and speak in a way that may cause people to assume he is White. In some ways, the assumption on the part of many Hispanics that Mario is White, combined with his feeling that he does not "fit in" with Hispanics, points to Carter's claim that cultural mainstreamers risk rejection by their Latino peers for "refusing to embrace their own racial and ethnic speech codes and musical, interactional, and social styles" (p. 13).

However, Mario's situation is more complicated than that. He happened to be born with Anglo-like features and skin tone, as opposed to his sister, who has a much more stereotypically "Hispanic" phenotype and skin tone. He is judged by others as not being Hispanic, or at least being, in Mario's words, "more White than…Mexican," to which he asserts, with a touch of anger in his voice, "No, I'm full." He perceives that others think he hovers in a space *between* "White" and "Hispanic." And although his racial background is "something [he] never forget[s]," he feels as if he does not fully "fit in" with Hispanics *or* Whites.

Interestingly, in our first three interviews, Mario asserted repeatedly that race doesn't and shouldn't matter; but, at the end of our third inter-view, he began to think differently about this issue in relation to his iden-tity and how others perceive him. Interestingly, he did not continue to assert that race "doesn't matter" in our subsequent conversations. After a lengthy monologue in which Mario seemed to be "thinking out loud" about this issue—and at times contradicting himself as he worked through the nuances of his racial ideology vis-à-vis his identity—I pushed him to clarify his thoughts:

> Mario: Then it's like, 'Wait—just because I don't say anything, you know, or bring up anything in my culture doesn't mean I am [White].... I'm Mexican, and I talk about my culture when I'm with my culture because you can. Because they get it, they understand. ... Just because [I] don't talk about it doesn't mean I don't really think about it.'
>
> Julie: Well, you were saying that maybe that means that race doesn't matter, but in a way, somebody could also say that it means that race *does* mat-ter—because they're automatically assuming that you are what they want to assume you are, you know? They assume you are White, and you're not.
>
> Mario: Right. Right, yeah. That's what I was kinda struggling with. When I was explaining it, I was like, wait, [race] shouldn't matter, but it *does*.

We see, then, just how complex identities can be. We see the importance of phenotype in Antonio and Mario's self-perceptions as well as how others see them. Antonio, who might be labeled "bi racial" because he has one White and one Mexican parent, comfortably and proudly identifies as Chicano. He does not struggle with the imposition of others' perceptions of his "Whiteness," or where he should "belong" racially; his phenotype and choice of dress guard against these impositions. Mario, who is not "bi racial," is forced to confront others' assumptions that he is White based on his phenotype, choice of dress, and perhaps his manner of speaking. He feels that he is not fully accepted by Whites or Hispanics: He is "too White" for Hispanics and just different enough to stand out among his White peers. Both young men are aware of their appearance vis-à-vis living in Collegeville: Antonio is conscious of standing out and Mario blends in. Similarly, Antonio is decidedly not going to "adapt to [White] culture," while Mario believes one *should* "adapt" to "White society."

We have seen that the construct of "race" has distinct roles in each young man's life and self-perception. Phenotype, parental lineage, background, and the perceptions of others interact in unique ways to help form the young men's different relationship with race, their own identities, and a sense of belonging at CMU.

Phenotype and Belonging

Just as variations in phenotype are linked to one's self-perception and others' conceptions of one's racial identity, as I argue above, so may phenotype help shape one's experiences with and perceptions of belonging. Antonio explained above that he "gets looks" on campus, which he attributes to the fact that he looks "very Mexican" in a predominantly White community. Mario, on the other hand, has a phenotype that many mistake for White, and this confounds his understanding of his own racial identity. Unlike Antonio, Mario *doesn't* get "looks" from the Whites in Collegeville, which, as we will see below, is something Mario is very much aware of—and, perhaps unexpectedly, is not necessarily a positive aspect of Mario's experience at CMU.

Although this chapter focuses on Antonio and Mario, I also bring in the voices of Engracia, Jasmine, and Moriah here to illustrate my point that phenotype plays a part in shaping one's interaction with Whites at CMU as well as one's experience with belonging at CMU. Moriah, who has brown skin and classically indigenous features, felt very out of place at CMU and attributed most of this to the fact that she is not White, and nearly everyone else is. As we see in detail in Chapter Three, she often felt that people stared at her as if she should not be at CMU, as if she didn't "belong."

While Moriah was aware of—and uncomfortable with—the lack of diversity immediately upon arriving at CMU, it took Jasmine a couple months to reflect on how it affected her. Jasmine often told me that people don't realize she is not "full" Mexican and that she is also White. And as Engracia, who knew Jasmine through a class they took together at CMU, explained, "Jasmine is always like, 'People always see me as a Mexican. They never consider the fact that I'm also White.'"

In contrast, Engracia—whose mother is Puerto Rican and father is Mexican—has light skin and does not look indigenous. In an interview with Engracia, she recounted discussions she had had with friends about "getting stared at" by Whites in Collegeville:

> Engracia: I haven't dealt with [getting stared at] much. Maybe I just haven't focused on it. Because my friends are like, 'Oh, they're staring at me.' I'm like, 'Well, why are you looking at people? Why are you looking to see if they're looking? I mean, they're probably looking at you because you're looking at them.' That's how I see it. You know, when I'm walking and I smile at someone and they don't smile back, that pisses me off. But I don't care. Whatever.

A moment later, however, Engracia acknowledged that perhaps her appearance is part of the reason that she hadn't dealt with the unwelcoming looks that so many of her friends, who are also People of Color, claimed to have experienced. Significantly, I did not ask her specifically about her skin tone or phenotype; she brought up the topic of her appearance on her own, as part of the same conversation excerpted above. She continued,

> Engracia: My friends say that I look White. I'm not sure. Personally, I don't think it. But at times when people are talking about racism and stuff, I'm like, 'Hmm, maybe that's why I've never dealt with it.' But I don't really think I look White. But at times that's why I think I haven't really dealt with that because I don't look that much like [a Latin@].

Interestingly, the issue of appearances and getting looked at on campus came up organically—with no prompting from me—in our group interview in April when I asked the students what surprised them about CMU. It was clear that each of the students had thought about physical appearances in conjunction with how they—and others—were treated on campus.

> Julie: Do you have anything [you want to add about anything that surprised you], Antonio?
> Antonio: When I walk around, I'm like, 'Damn,' seeing all the people pass me by, sometimes people staring. The surprise is sometimes walking on the street, some people staring. That was more of a surprise than anything.
> Engracia: They stare? Like what do they stare about?

Moriah: They just look at you like they're trying to cut through you with their eyes. It's like really annoying. It doesn't bother me as much as it did in the beginning.

Here we see that Antonio and Moriah have similar experiences regarding being the recipients of these "looks," and Engracia is curious about them. Soon Mario joins in, and we see below that for him, in some ways, *not* getting these looks makes him feel left out and represents the ways in which Whites misjudge him. Engracia then echoes his thoughts, and we see that they agree that the result of *not* getting unwelcoming stares is complex and emotional. The conversation continued:

Mario: I mean, the stares and stuff like that, that's one thing that I've never experienced personally, because I know I don't look Mexican. And I take offense to why they don't assume I'm Mexican. Yet I'm 100% Mexican. I just don't look it. Like I have no 'half-White' in me. Like this kid over here, you know [gesturing to Antonio, who is sitting next to him], he looks more Mexican than I am, and he's actually half, and I'm not. I'm full. And like that's one thing that always like irked me. It's just like they always assume, 'Oh boy, you know where I'm coming from, you're White.' And I'm like, 'No, I'm not.' I mean, no way am I White. I have no connection, I have no blood, no White blood in me whatsoever. I don't know. I mean, in a way I can say, 'Well, I can't say I've experienced those [looks],' but at the same time, it's a sad situation.

Engracia: It's like you're aware of it and you kinda belong to it, but you don't feel like you're going through it.

Mario: Yeah, that's it! That's exactly what it is because in a way you almost feel like you *should* be going through it because ... [*Mario is cut off by Engracia*]

Engracia: Because all your friends are going through it.

Mario: Exactly! Like why should you be excluded from it? And then when you are, you're kinda like, well, I don't know. It's a weird circumstance, a weird situation to be in. And like I get along with, I hang around with a lot of White friends. And 'cause a lot of these Whites, these people I hang out with, they don't see me as Mexican. And I'm like, well, I'm not gonna like show any of my like Mexican heritage around you because you're not going to understand it.

Engracia: No, and I don't feel like I should be expected to walk around with my Puerto Rican flag and my Mexican flag to tell people.

Mario: Right, right, and then they tell you, 'Oh, well, you're more White anyway.' And I'm like, '*Excuse me?* Just because I don't act a certain way in front of you that you consider as Mexican or Hispanic or whatever

Engracia:

> you wanna call it, doesn't mean a damn thing. In a way, they're not even including me in my culture that I'm a part of. They don't give me the benefit of the doubt. And it just kinda doesn't make sense. It's sad because ... [*Mario is cut off by Engracia*]

Engracia: You know what I do sometimes? I'll just start talking Spanish sometimes. Just so that people know. 'Cuz a lot of people think I'm mixed— like I'm White, with Italian or Serbian or something.

Thus, we see that there can be a sense of exclusion that occurs when, because of a misjudgment made by Whites, Students of Color are *not* subjected to getting stared at and being made to feel excluded. Whites often assume that Mario and Engracia are "one of them," and as we can see, this assumption causes frustration, sadness, and confusion—perhaps especially for Mario. Once again, we see that Mario feels that others do not allow him to be a part of a group that should uncomplicatedly be "his" group. Recall Yosso's (2006) argument, discussed earlier in this chapter, that lighter-skinned Latin@s who are judged to be White often witness racist comments, endure the guilt of receiving some of the privileges reserved for Whites, and face the frustration of witnessing darker-skinned peers be subjected to racism.

It seems, then, that Yosso's point(s) should be expanded upon. We also see here, through the voices of Mario and Engracia, that *not* being subjected to "stares" and exclusionary looks on campus represents a certain kind of power that Whites hold. In essence, Whites are deciding to which racial/ethnic group Mario and Engracia belong (or don't belong) and are treating them accordingly. Engracia has the ability to use Spanish to claim her identity; but Mario, who understands Spanish but does not speak it fluently, does not have this in his arsenal. Thus, White power and privilege, phenotype, and even language can interact in multiple ways to affect the ways in which students like Mario and Engracia experience race, belonging, and the ways in which they understand their own identities.

Counterspaces and Campus Involvement

Much of Mario's social life revolved around his membership in CMU's marching band, a highly regarded and time-consuming organization. As we chatted about his social life at CMU, Mario explained that he had made a conscious decision not to surround himself exclusively with Latin@s. He explained this decision to me:

Mario: Even though I enjoy that a lot of the Latinos stay together, in a way to me that's like isolating themselves. And like they only kinda hang out with themselves and do their own thing. I'm just kinda like, 'Alright, there's more people here besides, you know, this little group.'

                In a way [socializing with only Latinos] is good, 'cause like you can come back to your culture, but then at the end, you're kinda like, 'Alright, that's not all I want. I don't want to experience everything I've already experienced.' You know, this is supposed to be a new experience.

Julie: Yeah, you have to find that balance?

Mario: Right, exactly. And I've been trying, thinking, you know? I'm going though that right now, trying to find a way to do that.

Julie: And most of the people you hang out with in your dorm are White?

Mario: Yeah, oh yeah.

The theme of being, in Mario's words, "in a rut" socially came up more than once toward the end of the study. Mario wanted to "branch out" and experience new people. It is clear that he did not immerse himself in the Latin@ community at CMU; what is unclear is how much of this decision was based on—even if unconsciously—Mario's feeling of not being fully accepted by the Latin@ community. In any case, we see that he longs to have new experiences and not just experience "everything [he's] already experienced." He intimates that he is "used to" Latin@s and says clearly throughout the study that he is "used to" being around White people. Thus, he is hoping to find ways to connect socially with people other than the groups of people he is "used to," namely Latin@s and Whites. Being in the marching band—which is almost exclusively White—makes this "branching out" harder because of its gruelling practice and performance schedule. In sum, just as Mario struggled to find his "place" racially on campus throughout the study, he also struggled to find a social niche that is *not* tied to these two racial worlds, worlds he feels he is floating between.

Antonio, on the other hand, became very involved with the Latin@ community at CMU. He was an active member of four campus groups that are student run and Latin@ focused, and he began to take on leadership roles in some of these groups. Although most of these groups are open to non-Latin@s, they commonly attract exclusively Latin@ members. The activities associated with these groups range from volunteering in the area schools to discussing current social issues such as immigrant rights to traveling to national meetings to, as Antonio says, "throw[ing] good parties."

It was clear to me that Antonio had found a sense of community through these groups and that he enjoyed "giving back" to the Collegeville-area Latin@s through the volunteer efforts of these campus groups. One of the groups provides Latin@ mentors for elementary school children, and Antonio participated regularly in this effort. He explained, "...nowadays a lot of kids don't wanna speak Spanish to their friends, and all that, and [we] do that with them." In his words, these groups give him "a way to meet new people." He also explained that being a part of them is "definitely positive, because you meet other people who have a lot of like similarities ... and that's good to have."

Antonio has found what are often called "counterspaces" (Yosso, 2006) or safe spaces (Hurd, 2004), which allow marginalized students to come together, feel welcome, and, specifically, combat racism. As Gibson, Gándara, and Koyama (2004) write, "...when appropriate and welcoming spaces are not created for marginalized students, they will create alternative spaces of belonging ..." (p. 12). In addition to finding a space to "belong," these student-led organizations also "...have historically played a large role in community building and in helping Chicanas/os survive both socially and academically" (Yosso, p. 123); and, as we see in Antonio's case, they provide an opportunity for students to "give back" (Muñoz, 1986; Yosso, 2006). I was also struck with the amount of time Antonio dedicated to these groups. As a student in Yosso's counterstory explains, "Even on weekends, Chicana/o students work and socialize in these counterspaces, reinforcing that history of building community and 'giving back'" (p. 123).

Mario and Antonio's social lives look very different, then. Although the two young men are friends and do cross paths socially, Mario spends much of his time with the marching band and longs to connect with "new people." Antonio, on the other hand, has immersed himself in the Latin@ community at CMU, mostly through various Latin@-based student organizations. The differences here between the two young men's experiences are significant yet subtle: Both Mario and Antonio consistently reported being happy at CMU and having a "good" social life. However, the counterspaces Antonio took part in helped give him a sense of belonging and purpose; and, while Mario was happy at CMU and had many friends, he did not have, and was seeking, a "niche" into which he felt he belonged and was welcome.

The Case for More Diversity

As we have seen, the students' sense of belonging at CMU is directly connected to how they believe they are perceived by the predominantly White community at CMU. In addition, for Engracia and Mario, other Latin@s may (mis)judge them and thus influence their sense of belonging. For all of the students in the study, however, it is Whiteness that is the "norm" to which each is being compared. Throughout the course of the study, the students frequently asserted that there is a dire need for more racial diversity at CMU and that increased diversity would help significantly with their tenuous sense of belonging.

In my last individual interview with Antonio, we returned to the notion of what Antonio referred to as the "ignorant" White students at CMU. These students, he had earlier explained, were the students responsible for racism, ignorant comments, and contributing to CMU's unwelcoming atmosphere for Students of Color. I asked Antonio what he thought could be done to educate them and therefore improve race relations and the overall climate at CMU. A portion of this conversation follows:

Julie: So … we've talked about, you know, how it's such a White campus. We've talked about that, and about dealing with some of the ignorance and insensitivity of some of the White students on campus. So what do you think it would take to educate them, or to change them, to make it better?

Antonio: I don't know if it's possible, but probably more diversity on the campus. Like I think that's the best thing. Like to be surrounded with it and actually experience it. Instead of just seeing the stereotypes like from TV or movies, whatever. Like that's probably like the best way.

Julie: Yeah?

Antonio: The classes [that address race] don't really do much. Like when you learn about it in like sociology class, like okay. It doesn't help too much. Like especially the one I took in the summer [with the Pre-College program]. It was just weird. 'Cause it was kinda like directed towards White people. We were like just like, 'Yeah, we know this. We've lived through it.'

Julie: And were there any White people in your class?

Antonio: Oh, no, no, no. That was the Pre-College program, so, none!

It is significant that after Antonio asserts that "more diversity" at CMU is the "best thing" in terms of educating the White students and improving the climate, he then discusses one of the efforts at CMU to do just that. While he acknowledges that there are courses at CMU geared toward educating students about race and race relations in the U.S., he argues that the courses are "geared toward White people", and were not helpful for his Pre-College cohort. He also told me he fears that "not enough" White students enroll in such courses.

Mario, who is "comfortable with White people" and is "used to being around White people," also makes the case for more diversity at CMU. His involvement in CMU's marching band, discussed in detail in Chapter Five, causes him to be surrounded by White people even more than he might otherwise be. I also asked Mario, in my last individual interview with him, to share his thoughts on what could be done to work against what he had experienced as the ignorance and intolerance of some of the White students on CMU's campus. Part of our conversation follows.

Julie: One thing we talked about is dealing with the ignorance and intolerance of some of the White students on campus. So what would you do to maybe make things better?

Mario: I suppose you need to be exposed to it to really understand.

Julie: Exposed to what?

Mario: To more people in the culture. Because a lot of White people here don't have any contact [with People of Color] whatsoever. Automatically, [they're] assuming stereotypes because that's all [they] know. And the only way to solve it is to actually have them interact with more people.

Julie: You think that can be done in a college setting?

Mario: It would be really hard here because there's not enough people here for them to interact with. And that's why this stereotype just stays here in this campus because you don't see [Students of Color] as much. So if there's not enough [Students of Color] here for [Whites] to interact with, again, we [Latin@s] are all just thrown together and we're just one in this large group. And because of that, they can kind of overlook you and say, 'Yeah, okay, I understand.' I mean, the only way for that to even change here, you would have to have more Latino people at this university....

I mean, that's the problem with this university. I mean, tenfold. I mean, granted, it's one of the top universities in the nation; however, that's one of the problems is the fact that there aren't many minorities here. I know that they're trying to get more, and they're trying to recruit as many as possible, but the fact that if you don't have—I mean, this school isn't really advertised to minorities.

And, how are you gonna get more if it's not being advertised? And a lot of minorities tell me, they're like, 'Why would I want to go there to a school that I'm not even going to feel comfortable at if I can just go to this different school here where I'll feel more at home?'

Like Antonio, Mario asserts that higher numbers of Students of Color, and Latin@ students specifically, are needed to educate the majority of students at CMU and thus improve the atmosphere at CMU. In fact, Mario asserts that increased diversity is "the only way" to achieve these goals. We also see that the lack of diversity, in Mario's experience, clearly causes Students of Color to not "feel comfortable" and not "feel at home."

As well, and finally, although CMU has a well funded and well advertised "diversity plan," Mario gives voice to an oft-heard complaint: CMU's advertising to and recruitment of Students of Color is lacking. As our conversation continues, we see Mario's struggle with others' perception of his "in-between" racial status come to the surface. Even in an imagined diverse CMU, Mario is not sure he would fully "fit in":

Julie: So, let's just say a miracle happened and within a year, diversity is way, more here. How would it change how you personally feel on this campus?

Mario: I think you would feel a little more at ease just because you have more people to connect with. You would just feel more at ease because there's—you would likely have more celebrations and parties and stuff that are more leaning towards your culture. And you know, that's nice to have when you're a thousand miles away from home, you know?
That's how I would see the change, you know, for me personally. Because I mean, who knows? I mean, granted, I might not be [accepted] in that group, but who knows? Maybe I'll find that same situation I was telling you before: 'Oh, no, he's too White for us,' you know? Who knows? I could get that because I always got it before, you know?

As this chapter shows, then, Mario's experience with race, identity, and "fitting in" is anything but clean and simple. Indeed, these issues are complex and emotional for Mario, and he has considered them deeply and critically. While he asserts that more racial diversity at CMU is necessary, he concedes that it may not change what he perceives as his liminal status on campus. Indeed, he fears rejection from his imagined Latin@ peers at CMU were it to become more diverse.

Conclusions

Through their own words, we have seen the ways in which two young men who are often lumped into the same racial category and are even friends differ in terms of racial identities, racial ideology, and their sense of belonging on campus. We have also seen just how individual and complex identities can be and how significant one's phenotype and the assumptions of others can be in one's identity formation and self-concept. We have also seen how phenotype, biology, and self-identification interact in sometimes unexpected ways to form one's identity vis-à-vis race.

Indeed, Antonio and Mario have very different relationships with the notion of race and their own racial identities. Antonio's is easy and relatively uncomplicated and is a source of pride for him; Mario's is bumpy and intricate and at times a source of confusion for him. Importantly, this is *not* to say that Mario is any less proud of his racial and ethnic heritage than is Antonio; in fact, through getting to know Mario, I learned he is clearly proud of his heritage and background. It is as if, however, he does not feel *allowed* to be who he is: a Texan, a light-skinned Mexican-American who grew up in Hispanic neighborhoods as well as a White suburb, who dresses the way in which he wants and speaks the way in which he feels most comfortable. Many people see his skin, his phenotype, his clothes, and hear his manner of speaking and assume he is White. Others know he is Mexican but wonder if he is perhaps not *fully* Mexican, or "not quite Mexican enough."

Antonio is, based on his parental lineage, Mexican and White but identifies as Mexican/Chicano/Hispanic. He "looks Mexican" and is always assumed to be so by others. He is not constantly challenged to defend and explain his race and identity because they are uncomplicatedly his. Antonio most closely fits with Carter's (2005) category of "cultural straddler," which allows him to move strategically between the dominant culture at CMU and his own, thereby benefitting from the resources available through the dominant culture. He explicitly refuses to "act White" or change in any way his racial identity now that he is at a predominantly White university. Aiding in these efforts are Antonio's various memberships in "counterspaces" (Yosso, 2006), or safe spaces on campus made up of Latin@ students.

Mario, conversely, most closely fits with Carter's (2005) notion of "cultural mainstreamers," who believe students must adapt to the dominant White culture while still maintaining their own cultures. He enjoys membership in a mainstream, highly respected campus organization, but he longs to connect with "new" people [meaning people who are not Latin@ or White]. He struggles to find a niche in which he completely and wholly "fits," including, and perhaps especially, in terms of race.

Much of the attention at universities in terms of diversity is focused on the obviously marginalized students: There are explicit efforts to support underrepresented minority groups, as well as low-income and first-generation college students. A student like Mario, however, might literally be overlooked in efforts to ensure all students are included and have a place on campus. Mario does not visually stand out as "other." In fact, by many accounts, he fits in seamlessly at CMU; he looks like his White peers, he enjoys college life, and he is a member of the well-respected marching band. But he in fact is struggling to find a niche that accepts him fully as a racial being. The eloquent words of Gloria Anzaldúa (1987) help clarify this paradox as well as the need to expand our vision of diversity. She writes:

> I am visible—see this Indian face—yet I am invisible. I both blind them with this beak nose and I am their blind spot. But I exist, we exist. They'd like to think I've melted into the pot, but I haven't. We haven't. (p. 86)

While many Latin@s can relate to her words, Latin@s like Mario—and possibly Engracia—may not. Mario is "invisible" for different reasons. His racial identity, uniquely his own, is invisible to many; thus, he is assumed to belong to the normative category of "White." His appearance blends him in at CMU, and does *not* "blind."

The students' experiences discussed here point to the need to rethink approaches to multiculturalism, especially on predominantly White campuses. Indeed, CMU would do well to heed Carter's (2005) call for schools to "move beyond" what she calls "symbolic multiculturalism," consisting of ethnic celebrations and well-timed recognition of prominent historical People of Color (p. 14). We must create a true multiculture, one in which *all* students—regardless of phenotype, "biology," and presumed "category"—are welcome and allowed to claim their own identities. To be sure, all students at CMU need to have, in Carter's words, "interactions with people who are multiculturally adaptive and fluent" in order to begin to come together as peers, celebrate differences, and combat racial stereotypes (p. 14).

Before we can hope for such interactions and understanding across difference, however, campuses like CMU are in need of significantly more

Students and Faculty of Color, as both Antonio and Mario clearly tell us above. Only then will we be able to pave the way for all students to be able to claim their own identities as well as set the stage for a campus community that is willing to engage explicitly and critically with the reality of race in the U.S. Only then will *all* students have the chance to belong and find their place.

· 5 ·

RACISM, COLLEGE, AND THE POWER OF WORDS

Racial Microaggressions Reconsidered

[*Author's Note*: Parts of this chapter were originally published as: Minikel-Lacocque, J. (2013). Racism, college, and the power of words: Racial microaggressions reconsidered. *American Educational Research Journal*, 50(3), 432–465.]

> *They [White students on campus] look at me like*
> *I shouldn't be here, like I don't belong here.*
> *Like, 'You need to go back where you came from,*
> *'cause you don't need to be here.'*
>
> —Moriah

Recall from Chapter 1 that Moriah started her first semester at CMU with abundant confidence in her ability to succeed in college. Although she was aware that the sub par neighborhood high school she attended did not provide her with ideal college preparation, she believed she could make up for that disadvantage. As we saw in Chapters 2 and 3, however, her confidence was swiftly dashed and she frequently considered dropping out of college. Her struggles, however, were not rooted in academics; she consistently maintained a 3.65 grade-point average. Although she experienced significant financial stress, the principal cause for her discontentment was the feeling that she did not belong. Predominantly White CMU was not a welcoming place for her—she constantly felt she was treated as an outsider. Indeed,

Moriah rarely saw any faces in the crowd that resembled her own, she often was stared at by White students as she walked through campus, and she witnessed various forms of racism on campus. Not surprisingly, she soon began to feel "miserable" and left campus nearly every weekend to visit the larger, more diverse city in which she grew up.

Unfortunately, Moriah's experience of feeling isolated and "out of place"—as well as of being the target of racism—can be common among Students of Color at predominantly White institutions (PWIs) (Feagin, Vera, & Imani, 1996; Strange & Banning, 2001; Patton, 2006; Everett-Haynes & Deil-Amen, 2009; Yosso, Smith, Ceja, & Solórzano, 2009;). And, as examined in Chapter 3 too often our collective focus is on measurable outcomes such as grade-point averages, the rates of college acceptance, and graduation rates and what those trends can tell us about underrepresented college students. While these numbers are certainly important, they do not tell us enough about the students' *experiences* in college.

Many times, the college experience for underrepresented students is reduced to "success" or "failure" based on grades and graduation rates alone. If a student graduates, there is a collective pat on the back, and the student's college experience is moved to the "success" column on a spreadsheet. But if that student was unhappy during her entire college career, if she left campus every chance she got, and if she couldn't wait to simply finish her degree, deeming her college experience a straightforward success is missing much of the story. There are important lessons to be learned from the lived experiences of underrepresented students at PWIs. Indeed, much can be learned from the resilience of underrepresented students who face isolation and racism; and embedded within their stories are crucial lessons about how institutions need to change to meet the needs of all students.

In this chapter, I examine the racialized experiences of Antonio, Crystal, Engracia, Jasmine, Mario, and Moriah. Through the lens of Critical Race Theory (CRT), I analyze the students' experiences with racism, and I argue for specific ways in which college campuses must address and combat racism. Specifically, I use current frameworks of *racial microaggressions* (Sue, 2010; Sue et al., 2007b) to explore racism through the voices and experiences of the students themselves. I argue for greater understanding and increased use of the term "racial microaggressions" within education generally, and specifically with regard to the transition to college for underrepresented students, as a way to decrease racism on campuses. I also, however, draw on the field of critical applied linguistics to contend that the term "microaggression" is at times misused within academia, and that this misuse has potentially negative consequences. Finally, I argue for an expansion of the existing framework of racial microaggressions to include the recognition and naming of a "contested microaggression."

College Campuses and Racial Microaggressions

Although we know that encountering racialized and other discriminatory experiences can have a deep impact on the ways in which underrepresented students perceive—and interact with—their college environment (Minikel-Lacocque, 2013; Camille, Fischer, Mooney, & Massey, 2009; Yosso, et al., 2009; Yosso, 2006; Strange & Banning, 2001; Solórzano, Ceja, & Yosso, 2000; Hurtado, Milem, Clayton-Pedersen, & Allen, 1999; Feagin, Vera, & Imani, 1996), research that closely examines the perspectives of Latin@ students who begin their college careers at selective, four-year institutions is particularly rare (see, for example, Yosso, Smith, Ceja, & Solórzano, 2009; Yosso, 2006; MInikel-Lacocque, 2015; Minikel-Lacocque, 2013).

Today, racism is most often expressed in covert ways; indeed, overt racism is "usually not socially condoned," and instances of overt racist acts in the public discourse are "rare" (Solórzano et al., 2000, p. 61). Racism, many argue, is more commonly expressed through *racial microaggressions* (Pierce, 1974; Sue, 2010; Sue et al., 2007b). More than three decades ago, psychiatrist Chester Pierce introduced this concept, insisting that it is the insidious, hard-to-identify, subtle racist injuries that we must pay attention to if we are to understand and combat racism (Pierce, 1974). While overt, violent expressions of racism by consciously racist individuals still exist and cause irreparable harm, this subtle, common form of modern-day racism most often comes from well-meaning individuals (Sue et al., 2007b; Sue, 2010; Dovidio & Gaertner, 2000; Solórzano et al., 2000).

Although there are various working definitions available, relatively little is known about microaggressions; indeed, they are seldom researched. Studies that explicitly examine racial microaggressions in educational contexts are particularly rare, though the few that do exist address microaggressions on college campuses (Minikel-Lacocque, 2013; Solórzano et al., 2000; Yosso et al., 2009; Yosso, 2006). Yet throughout the years, scholars have argued that these subtle forms of racism have a deep and lasting impact on race relations as well as on the health and confidence of the targets of such racism (Pierce, Carew, Pierce-Gonzalez, & Willis, 1978; Pierce, 1995). Thus, while microaggressions are thought to have a significant impact on individuals as well as on race relations writ large, they are difficult to study empirically, and theories surrounding them are in a relatively nascent state.

A Taxonomy of Racial Microaggressions

Most of the current literature on microaggressions comes out of the field of psychology, and the majority of it is published by D. W. Sue (see for example, Sue, 2010; Sue & Capodilupo, 2008; Sue, Capodilupo, Nadal, & Torino, 2008; Sue, Nadal, et al., 2008; Sue, Bucceri, Lin, Nadal, & Torino, 2007; Sue et al., 2007;). Providing significantly more detail than the original notion of racial microaggressions, Sue (Sue et al., 2007b, Sue & Capodilupo, 2008) developed a taxonomy of racial microaggressions, represented in Figure 5.1.

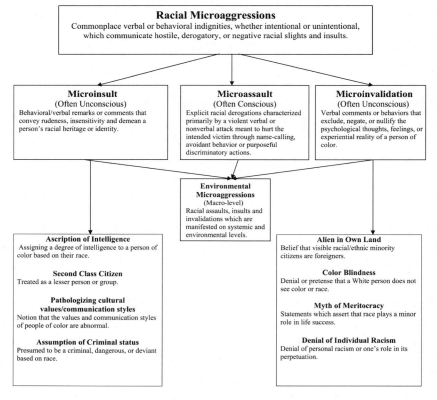

Figure 5.1. Categories of and relationships among racial microaggressions.
Source: Sue, D.W., Capodilupo, C.M., Torino, G.C., Bucceri, J.M., Holder, A.M.B., Nadal, K.L., & Esquín, M. (2007b). Racial microaggressions in everyday life: Implications for clinical practice. *American Psychologist, 62*(4), p. 278. Reprinted with permission.

Thus, as Figure 5.1 shows, these researchers have broadened the original notion of racial microaggressions to include both unintentional and intentional insults in the form of verbal, behavioral, or environmental "indignities." Further, the taxonomy also calls for racial microaggressions to be divided into the categories of *microinsults*, *microassaults*, and *microinvalidations*.

Below, within the context of Latin@ students' experiences at CMU, I bring together Critical Race Theory and the concept of racial microaggressions. I argue that Sue's framework of microaggressions has much to offer the field of education with regard to understanding and combating racism. I also, however, challenge certain aspects of Sue's taxonomy and argue for specific changes and additions to be made. Indeed, the union of CRT and notions of racial microaggressions represents a symbiotic relationship. That is, the notion of recognizing and naming the offense of covert racism is in line with the tenets of CRT; at the same time, CRT necessitates a critique of some of the ways in which microaggressions have been theorized.

Critical Race Theory and This Chapter

With specific regard to higher education, Morfin, Perez, Parker, Lynn, and Arrona (2006) point out that, taken as a whole, CRT research in higher education has highlighted the microaggressions and racial harassment that Faculty of Color often face as well as hostile racial climates and racial profiling that Students of Color encounter at PWIs (see, for example, Taylor, 2000; Solórzano & Yosso, 2000; Solórzano, 1998; Villalpando & Delgado Bernal, 2002; Patton, 2006; Teranishi, Behringer, Grey, & Parker, 2009). Additionally, they underscore the function of CRT to challenge "the experience of White European Americans as the normative standard" (Morfin, Perez, Parker, Lynn, & Arrona, 2006, p. 251).

Similarly, Teranishi, Behringer, Grey, and Parker (2009) challenge the exclusive use of "normative framing" to examine equity issues within education. Dominant paradigms, they explain, are often used to identify the ways in which distinct racial groups are "unevenly distributed across a particular outcome (for example, participation or graduation)" at the exclusion of a deeper probing of inequality (p. 59). CRT, on the other hand, highlights the "needs of marginalized populations, which are often overlooked, as opposed to the agenda served by normative frameworks" (p. 59).

For my purposes here, then, normative frameworks conceive of the needs of Latin@s in higher education within the same paradigm that the needs of White, middle-class college students are understood. Thus, Latin@ college students are viewed from a deficit perspective. To combat this deficit orientation, the experiences of underrepresented college students must be brought to the foreground of academe. Specifically, CRT calls us to highlight these experiences by "providing thick descriptions of students' stories related to campus environments and college experiences" (Teranishi et al., 2009, p. 59). Through focusing on students' perspectives and insights into their own educational lives, I emphasize their voices as "expert" sources of knowledge. As Ladson-Billings and Tate (1995) explain, "a theme of 'naming one's own reality' or 'voice' is entrenched in the work of critical race theorists" (p. 56–57).

In addition to calling on us to name racism and honor the perspectives of those who are injured by racism, CRT pushes us away from perceiving Students of Color as victims. Indeed, CRT requires us to recognize the resilience of Students of Color (O'Connor, 1997) as well as various other assets and forms of capital they bring with them to their college careers (Yosso, 2005, 2006; Yosso et al., 2009). Indeed, while much of the literature on racism refers to targets of racism as "victims," this work does not. In fact, the practice of referring to "victims" of racism is counter to CRT, as it eclipses the agency of those who are targeted by racism and places a label on those who do not self-identify as "victims."

Finally, it is insufficient to name and recognize racism and other forms of oppression; CRT also mandates a focus on redressing problems with the aim of working toward social justice. Scholars must "translate theory into practice" in pushing for change through and beyond their roles and work within academe (Ladson-Billings & Donnor, 2005, p. 292). My work here is an attempt at doing just that: Through applying theory to lived experience, I will highlight some of the ways in which the "practice" at PWIs can be altered to bring about change.

Racism at CMU

In this section, I analyze the data on the students' experiences as they transitioned to college. The analysis is divided into the following six subsections: Getting Stared at and Feeling Isolated; Ignored at the Bus Stop and Angry Bus Drivers; Stereotyping; Insensitivity and Ignorance; Online Hatred at CMU and Intentionality: Not So Micro; The Nickname Story: A Contested Microaggression.

Getting Stared at and Feeling Isolated

Moriah experienced isolation at CMU on a daily basis. She often felt stared at and singled out as different from her fellow students, and the lack of racial diversity caused her to feel alone. Recall that toward the end of her first semester at CMU, Moriah parodied Hamlet's famous words by posting "To drop out or not to drop out, that is the question," on her dorm-room door. Significantly, it was not academics that caused her to feel this way; rather, Moriah repeatedly explained that she felt "miserable" at CMU because of her experience within the overwhelmingly White student population.

Antonio related similar experiences but was less outwardly bothered by them. In my first interview with him, he explained that he is treated differently in Collegeville than he is in his hometown, which is much more diverse:

> Antonio: …Here, we're on a campus where most of the White people are, I guess. But in [my hometown], I live on the south side. And so that's mostly Spanish or like my own race, and… I don't know. There's discrimination there [in my hometown]. Of course there is everywhere…. But I could tell people look at me when I walk in stores [in Collegeville], like they look at me weird 'cause I got like my goatee and all that. Like I look really Hispanic and stuff like that. I'm not being treated *really* bad, but I'm treated different than [I] normally [am].

Staring at someone on the street—in both of the ways described above—because he or she appears to be "other" certainly fits under the original definition of racial microaggressions; indeed, unwelcoming or untrusting stares can be considered "automatic" and "unconscious" acts of racial discrimination. In Moriah's case, the stares she received fall into the category of "microinsult" (Sue et al., 2007b; Sue & Capodilupo, 2008); specifically, they have the potential to communicate Sue's microaggressive theme, *you do not belong* (Sue, 2010, p. 77). While this is also true for the types of stares Antonio describes, the stares he gets while walking into stores in Collegeville may also carry with them, in Sue's (2010) words, *assumption of criminal status*; that is, the store owners may presume—whether consciously or unconsciously—that as a Person of Color, Antonio is "dangerous, potentially a criminal, likely to break the law, or [potentially] antisocial" (p. 36).

In addition to the unwelcoming stares, the lack of diversity on CMU's campus had an effect on all the students in the study. For example, after weeks of staying in her dorm room and feeling isolated, Moriah decided to attend a multicultural alumni event in the hopes of connecting with another Latina. Unfortunately, the experience only exacerbated her feelings of isolation, as we see in her words here: "I was TRYING to integrate myself—but there were no other Latinos there—not one. So I wasn't even represented. I really wanted to leave, so I left. I wish I wouldn't have gone."

Thus, Antonio and Moriah experienced feelings of isolation, and they perceived a lack of being welcomed by the CMU and Collegeville communities. Significantly, the ways in which Antonio and Moriah experienced microaggressions are not often visible to campus personnel who are charged with supporting students during their college careers. These instances are unlikely to come up at a meeting with an advisor or other support staff, meetings which are often focused on grades and course schedules, yet they have the power to affect students' experiences in college. Put differently, these microaggressions—as well as those discussed below—can affect the students' quality of life and how they feel about being in college.

Ignored at the Bus Stop and Angry Bus Drivers

Antonio had been coming to CMU's campus during the summers with a college access program, Pre-College, since his sophomore year in high school. In our first interview, when I asked him about his perception of Collegeville, racism came up almost immediately:

Julie:	What were your first impressions of Collegeville?
Antonio:	That it was big, I guess.... I've seen discrimination, especially on the city bus.... There was a couple of times when there would be like a group waiting at the bus stop, and we'd see the bus, and it would just keep going by and it wouldn't stop. And [it] wouldn't be filled up either. It would just pass by.
Julie:	Was it supposed to stop at that stop?
Antonio:	Yeah, and they kept going. So we complained and all that, so they don't really do it anymore.

Antonio went on to explain that in a separate incident, he and his friends had recently taken the bus to the mall and happened to be on the bus when the high-school-aged Pre-College program students were taking a group field trip to the mall. There was some commotion caused by the group's inexperience with using their bus cards. He explained:

Antonio: They weren't trying to be annoying or anything.... The bus driver just got angry right away. He just got pissed and he was just like, 'Go, go, go!' Like he was yelling at 'em, sorta. You could tell he was really angry and all that, getting all angry over nothing really, 'cause [the students] didn't do nothing. There was just a big group coming on the bus, and he was real angry, real quick.

Julie: What do you think the reason behind that was?

Antonio: Well, because we're all minorities, like in the [Pre-College] program.

Julie: Discrimination?

Antonio: Yeah, most likely. Because I don't think he'd get mad if it was just like a group of White kids, 'cause he'd think like that would be all good. He expected us to be all rowdy and stuff. ... He was all angered and peeved and stuff.

In both of the incidents Antonio relates above, we see instances of a *microinsult*. Specifically, the [White] bus driver not stopping to pick up Antonio and his Pre-College peers (even though they were waiting at a regular bus stop) potentially reflects Sue's (2010) microaggressive theme of *second-class citizen*, through which certain groups are treated as "lesser" (p. 28). This microinsult also possibly carries an *assumption of criminal status* and may echo findings of studies that claim that "Blacks" hailing a cab in Manhattan are 25% less likely to be picked up than Whites (Sue, 2010). The second microinsult, when the [White] bus driver seems to become disproportionately angry with the young Pre-College participants for not having their bus passes ready, also has the power to communicate the derogatory themes named by Sue such as *assumption of criminal status* and *second-class citizen*.

Stereotyping

During their first semester at CMU, Antonio and Moriah both related instances of experiencing racial stereotyping, an offense that is in accordance with Pierce's (1974) definition of microaggressions, as well as Sue's (2010) and Sue and colleagues' (2007b) notion of microinsult. In the first example, as Antonio was explaining that he feels like he "sticks out more" in Collegeville as compared to in his diverse hometown, he recalled comments made by a Resident Assistant during a dorm meeting:

Antonio: I stick out more .... Like I was at my friend's [dorm] floor meeting, and they were talking about Halloween, and [the Resident Assistant] was saying that you can't have racial costumes. So [the R.A.] was like, 'No drunk Mexicans or anything.' She was just putting things out there like as examples. I'm not originally from the floor, and they don't have any Hispanics up there. So I was just starting to laugh, 'cause me and two other friends ... we just started laughing.

Later, when I explicitly asked Antonio if he had experienced racism during his first few months at CMU, he first said "not really," and then told me the following story:

> Antonio: Well, not really... I'm known as being Mexican and stuff. Like, there's one guy on my floor, he was drunk, he was like, 'Hey, Antonio, c'mere. This girl doesn't believe anybody is more hairy than me.' He's like, 'You're Mexican, you're hairy.' I'm like, 'Well, that has nothing to do with it.' I'm like, 'What?' I just laughed at him 'cause he was drunk. I was like, 'Who cares?'

Antonio's lack of outward anger about these comments made by Whites begs the question, If the "subject" of the stereotype claims to be only mildly bothered (or not bothered at all), can one conclude an offense such as a microaggression occurred? Antonio is the expert when it comes to his own reactions and experiences. I argue that we must in fact go beyond this question; indeed, key questions here are, What is being said by and through the comments? What is being "accomplished"? Or, in Geertz's words, "The thing to ask [about a specific behavior] is not what their ontological status is." Rather, he explains, "[t]he thing to ask is what their import is: what it is...that, in their occurrence and through their agency, is getting said" (1973, p. 10).

It is clear that the perpetrators are using stereotypes of Mexicans, and that they are "othering" Mexicans generally and Antonio specifically. While his reactions in both of these instances ostensibly fit with his laid-back personality and easy laugh, it may be more complex than that. He brought up these offenses when we were discussing his identity in the context of CMU more broadly; it was clearly something he remembered and wanted to discuss. Further, I expect that Antonio has endured countless racial offenses made by Whites and that every one of these, whether or not they registered on a conscious level for Antonio, have significantly contributed to his ideas about and relationships with Whites on and off campus.

For example, as we were discussing Antonio's social life, he explained that he only hangs out with "a couple people from my [dorm] floor, but not too many." Although his circle of friends does include some White students, he explained that the White students on his floor "stick to themselves," "hang out in their groups" and are "clique-y," and that they are "not [his] type." When I pushed him to explain what he meant by "not his type," he elaborated:

> Antonio: I don't know. Like kinda typical White people, sort of. ... What I mean, like, a lot of them are dumb, kinda like. They do stupid things. ... Some of them are cocky. I don't like that kind of people. It's just the drinking they do, too. And they can't handle their stuff [referring to alcohol]. They'd always be, like, out of it, like after they had like two beers. And I'm like, 'GOD!'

Thus, it is possible that these microaggressions may register for Antonio on a deeper level and are in part responsible for his ideas of what a "typical White guy" is: someone who is stupid and gets drunk too often. Here we see Pierce's claim ring true that the "cumulative weight" of racial microaggressions causes significant strain in racial relations writ large, this time for Latin@–White relations (Pierce et al., 1978, p. 66). Put simply, a lifetime of seemingly harmless racial microaggressions has contributed to Antonio's negative perception of what "White guys" are like. Viewed this way, we can see very real possibilities in terms of the significance, or Geertz's "import," of these offenses.

In a final example of stereotyping, we turn to Moriah once again. She and her boyfriend, who, in her words, is Puerto Rican and "looks black," were offended while at a local pizza restaurant. Moriah recounts her experience of what happened when a White woman, who Moriah guessed to be in her thirties, approached them:

> Moriah: She said to [my boyfriend], 'Excuse me, excuse me.' She's like, 'Can you run fast?' I was like, 'Just 'cause you're Black doesn't mean you can run fast!' [My boyfriend] was like, 'I *can* run fast, but I wasn't gonna give her the satisfaction of going into that stereotype.' I was like, 'These people are so ignorant!' I was *so* mad!

Indeed, Moriah explained that while walking home that evening, she was "shaking" because she was so angry and that the experience made her feel like yelling in the middle of the street.

In these examples, we witness various ways students can be faced with stereotyping, as well as the distinct reactions on the part of Antonio and Moriah. In each of these instances, however, it is possible that the perpetrators did not consciously mean any harm; indeed, they are probably still unaware of the offense they caused. Another example of this "subconscious" type of racism, as experienced by Jasmine, is discussed below.

Insensitivity and Ignorance

In December of her first year at CMU, Jasmine attended a Christmas party organized by her Bible study group on campus. Jasmine had not found many activities in which she felt she belonged at CMU, and her Bible study group was the exception. She had been looking forward to the Christmas party for weeks; but, unfortunately, a comment made by a White member of the group deeply offended Jasmine and caused her to end her affiliation with the group. She explained:

> Jasmine: I was having a good time and then we went around in a circle and shared our Christmas traditions. This girl was talking about how her family went in the back of a truck down to Florida for one Christmas, and she was with all her cousins in the back of a truck, stuck back there with presents and stuff. And then she's like, 'I don't know why people would wanna come from Mexico in a truck to begin with because it was *so gross!*'
> And right away, I was gonna shout, 'That was uncalled for!' But I was so angry and caught in the moment. And there were people actually *laughing* at this. That was a blatant racist comment, you know? That was not right. She shouldn't have said that. Why does she find it okay to say it? It was just like a smack in your face, that there's racism out there, you know? I was having a good time and then she just ruined it. In two seconds, she just ruined it.

Again, we see a White person make a comment in passing, and by all accounts in a seemingly light hearted manner, that deeply offended one of the study participants. What's more, the person who made the comment was completely unaware of its potential to hurt and offend. It is quite probable that the offender in this case never did become cognizant of the effect her words had on Jasmine that evening. The insensitivity toward (and lack of knowledge about) the immigrant experience revealed by this student's comment is something to be addressed in the effort to combat racism and other forms of oppression. It is important to note, however, that regardless of the reasons behind the comment, Jasmine found them hurtful.

The stories related thus far fall in line with Pierce's original conception of racial microaggressions; although they can cause strong reactions in the target, they can be seen by witnesses as "subtle," and most often the perpetrator is unaware of his or her actions. They also map nicely onto Sue's taxonomy of racial microaggressions, which provides language with which to understand, classify, and discuss the sometimes amorphous nature of these types of offenses. The incidents I describe below, however, point to certain areas of Sue's taxonomy that call for additions and alterations.

Online Hatred at CMU and Intentionality: Not So "Micro"

> As far as I'm concerned, I say let minorities get into college, but only after all the academically qualified applicants get in first. Then when the minority students who are not prepared for college-level coursework flunk out of school they'll have no one to blame but themselves. You want a chance for a better life? Earn it!
>
> —Anonymous post to Central Midwestern University's website

During the spring semester of the participants' first year, debates flourished on CMU's campus regarding the university's "holistic" admissions policies, which take into account the racial background of an applicant. In classes and special forums alike, the campus community discussed, in essence, affirmative action and its place in CMU's admissions process. During this time, Engracia sent me a link to an op-ed article in CMU's online student newspaper in which the [White] student author argued that this "holistic" policy is racist because it does nothing to help prepare academically under prepared minorities for the challenges they will face at CMU. He argued that instead of utilizing such a policy, CMU should focus on improving urban public schools so that minorities *are* prepared for college.

While Engracia disagreed with the author's stance, it represented one side of the debate. Further, she was not overly bothered by what she considered to be an uninformed point of view. The long list of posted reactions to the article, however, was deeply upsetting. I include two of them below:

1. [T]he public schools are doing just fine. You're wrong to assume that public schools are good substitutes for good parents. Ultimately, this isn't a choice that the rich white suburbs are going to have to make for the poor black inner city. This is a choice that the inner city is going to have to make to abandon their current culture, sell-out, and join the rest of educated America. This choice starts at home.
2. Yeah, suburban kids are coddled by rich suburban parents and teachers until they are ready to be handed off to White Bread University. The

inner city parent, not giving a damn, stares at the wall all day, ignorant to the world around them. They say, "child, I don't give a damn what you do. Education and learning are fine, but so is drug dealing and making babies. I wish I had gold teeth... what was I saying?" C'mon, everyone gets what they earn. Being born on the wrong or right side of the tracks does not PREDETERMINE your life. If you PERSONALLY give a damn ... you will find PERSONAL success. The ultimate blame lies with you.

In these comments, we see what is commonly referred to as "the myth of meritocracy" expressed in distinct ways. In short, the myth of meritocracy represents the belief that we all, regardless of race, gender, or socioeconomic background, are afforded the same chances for success: If we want to achieve success, we must simply "earn it." Specifically, if you are a Student of Color who is failing or even struggling in college, you are just not working hard enough. This belief in the singular power of hard work, coupled with the lack of acknowledgment of various inequalities such as the poor schooling opportunities in inner-city and low-income neighborhoods, is certainly communicated through the above online posts. For example, the comments, "This is a choice that the inner city is going to have to make" and "This choice starts at home" are infused with this assumption that the will to succeed alone will result in success. These portions of the above online comments certainly fit with the original notion of racial microaggressions: racist comments made by someone who is most likely not aware of their racist nature and who may very well defend the (perceived non racist) merit of these comments. In excerpt two we also see the myth of meritocracy expressed, albeit in an overt way. Comments such as "C'mon, everyone gets what they earn" and "The ultimate blame lies with you," beg a deeper consideration of what should be classified as a "microaggression" and what is in fact outside of this category.

Further, portions of these online posts indeed go beyond what could be conceived of as "unconscious" and represent what many would consider to be intentional expressions of hatred. Perhaps the clearest examples of this intentional hatred are contained in excerpt number two, in which the post's author claims that "inner city" parents do not "give a damn" and value "drug dealing and making babies" as much as they value education. These are not the subtle, often unconscious, frequently made comments that inspired Chester Pierce to coin the term *racial microaggressions*. They are intentional, conscious, and less common when compared to microaggressions as originally conceived.

The openly racist comments posted anonymously combine traditionally covert and overt modes of expressing racism. These types of comments, often reserved for private settings in the past, are in a very public forum; indeed, here we are privy to a specific variety of "private conversations" that can contain racial microaggressions (Solórzano et al., 2000, p. 61). Through the Internet, one can utter, from beneath the protective veil of anonymity, things s/he would be ashamed to say in person to a public audience. Indeed, the Internet has provided a unique opportunity to witness racist behavior that would otherwise be incredibly difficult or impossible to capture. To be sure, while the racism contained in these posts would still be present and palpable, without the Internet, we would not have access to these verbatim expressions of racism.

The participants' reactions to the openly racist comments posted online were immediate and significant. Although the individual interviewing phase of the study was over by the time Engracia alerted me of the article, the group interview provided insights into the participants' reactions. Engracia and Crystal, the two participants who had read the article, initiated a discussion about it when we met as a group:

Crystal:	...I mean, people are twisted. And the thing is that—yeah, I was just a *little* upset (*with a sarcastic tone*)—
Engracia:	I cried a little. Not cried like *tears*, but like one little tear fell down with that one comment ... the comments were the worst. It was like, 'Minority parents just stare at the wall all day ignorant of the whole world and tell their kids, you can get pregnant, no you can go to school, or you can get pregnant and sell drugs—that's much better. I can't wait to buy a gold tooth.' I was like—
Crystal:	It was a really bad article. I don't know if you guys read it— (*The rest of the students shake their heads "no."*) It was this guy who went off on affirmative action and how it shouldn't be part of admissions.... And so here, on top of that, it was an opinion column so nobody had a name, and then under it they had comments. People were allowed to comment [anonymously]. And like you will hear the most ignorant comments. And I went *off* during our [college access group] meeting after I read the article. I was *so* pissed.
Engracia:	'Just [admit them] and let them fall on their faces when they get here.' I was like, 'I probably have a higher degree of [education than you do].'
Crystal:	That's what I'm saying. It's like, look at the minority students on this campus and ... you can you really tell that a good chunk of them are involved, are doing things. And I just gotta say, ask the people in our [classes] who has the biggest GPA and then we'll talk. And then we'll talk.

Engracia: I mean, the *comments*—

Crystal: It will make you realize how ignorant like the majority of people are.

Engracia: That was like the one time that [the racism on campus] really bothered me. ... That was like the first time that I was like, 'Holy shit! There are people [here] that don't like me.' So that's why it was a big thing for me.

Thus, it is clear that the overt racism contained in the online comments caused no confusion in terms of the participants' reactions; Engracia and Crystal were deeply hurt and never questioned the intentions of the perpetrators. There was no grey area to these offenses. Indeed, it is the openly racist nature of these comments, as well as the students' reactions to them, that brings me to question the prefix "micro" being associated with this type of racism.

Sue includes the notion of a *microassault* in his taxonomy, and his definition of this type of microaggression certainly does fit the type of hatred present in these online posts: Recall that he defines microassaults, which are often conscious acts, as "Explicit racial derogations characterized primarily by a violent verbal, nonverbal, or environmental attack[s] meant to hurt the intended victim through name-calling, avoidant behavior, or purposeful discriminatory actions" (Sue, 2010, p. 29). Sue explains that of the three types of racial microaggressions, microassaults are the most similar to "old-fashioned" racism. He also posits that due to the modern-day condemnation of overt racism, microassaults are most likely to be expressed under certain conditions, such as some degree of anonymity.

Thus, it is not the definition of *microassault* that I challenge; rather, I question placing this type of racism under the umbrella term of *microaggressions*, and I argue that doing so can be misleading. It is possible, I contend, that using the prefix "micro," which means "small," to identify this type of racism could be confusing at best and harmful at worst. Teaching targets and perpetrators alike that offenses such as writing the online comments included in this section, displaying Nazi swastikas and Klan regalia, and using racial epithets are *micro*assaults, a breed of *micro*aggressions, has the power to mislead both groups.

While it is not my intention to create a hierarchy of pain caused by racist offenses, the language we use is powerful and anything but neutral. More specifically, a critical view of language claims that language is always political—as it is inseparable from the social status of the interlocutors—and that it reflects and reproduces social relations and their embedded power structures (Bourdieu, 1991; Pennycook, 2001). Drawing on the work of Foucault (1980) and Lemke (1995), Hawkins explains, "Embedded [in language] are ideologies, beliefs, and values, which are carried out and reproduced through the unfolding social interactions" (Hawkins, 2005, p. 27). Put simply, words carry significant power. They have the potential to help maintain various inequalities—whether it be inequalities within a given conversation or inequalities on a societal level.

It follows, then, that using the prefix "micro" to describe the above online posts as well as other blatant, intentional racist acts may very well carry with it a message that Sue's work is precisely trying to avoid. Given the history of racism in the U.S., as well as the established pattern of racism's injuries being denied and diminished by those with more power historically (read: Whites), attaching "micro" to certain racist aggressions has the ability to maintain power dynamics with respect to racism. In other words, the use of this term may invalidate the anger and hurt caused by such acts as well as empower the perpetrators to believe their actions and words are somehow less egregious than those racist acts not classified as "micro." Indeed, commonplace, unconscious microaggressive racist acts should not be lumped together with overt, intentional forms of racism that have no place in any category dubbed "micro." Thus, I argue for this breed of racism to be called "racialized aggressions" rather than *micro*aggressions.

While the current discussion may be accused of being "nit-picky" or of mincing words, I contend that increased clarity surrounding the terms we use to understand and discuss racism is necessary. It is with the hope that educational settings generally and college campuses specifically develop facility with the notion of racialized microaggressions that I argue for greater clarity of the terms we use. Indeed, the scholarly work discussed here, once incorporated into universities' approach to combating racism (as well as that of practitioners outside the university such as teachers and therapists, among others) has great potential to affect change on campuses across the country. Without the increased clarity I am arguing for, however, this potential is significantly diminished.

The Nickname Story: A Contested Microaggression

Thus far, I have argued both for a change in the current language we use to talk about overt, intentional racism specifically and for greater clarity surrounding the definitions we use to understand and discuss racism generally.

In this section, I return to the original notion of racial microaggressions (subtle, hard-to-name, everyday unconscious acts), and again argue for a change in—or, more precisely, an addition to—the language surrounding microaggressions. Here I consider what happens when the target of a microaggression contests the perceived racist act; specifically, I contend that when a microaggression is contested, it spills over into a new category of experience that must be recognized and named as such.

Scholarly conversations on racial microaggressions have historically focused on the act itself and not on what happens after the act is committed. The small amount of research on the aftermath of a microaggression includes reactions shared among same-race peers (Solórzano et al., 2000; Yosso, 2006), as well as various documentations of microaggressions that are addressed by the target and often end in physical assaults of him/her (Feagin, Vera, & Imani, 1996,). There is also literature that theorizes about the psychology behind reacting or not reacting to microaggressions (Sue et al., 2007b), and, finally, work that explores group reactions to microaggressions (Yosso et al., 2009).

Taken as a whole, however, the existing work in this area is minimal. Indeed, the paucity of research on—and language for—the aftermath of a microaggression represents a gap in this relatively new area of inquiry. This gap was particularly salient for me as I sat across the table from Mario and listened to his story of contesting a microaggression during his first few weeks on CMU's campus. As we spoke, it became clear that the *aftermath* of the original microaggressive act, as opposed to the initial microaggression itself, carried most of the weight for Mario.

Mario had earned a spot in CMU's prestigious marching band, an organization that is highly respected both campus-wide and nationally. For years, it had been one of Mario's goals to become a member; thus, he was extremely excited to be a part of this group, which entailed adhering to a rigorous training and travel schedule. Due, in part, to the time-consuming and close-knit nature of the band, its members were Mario's immediate community at CMU; most of his time outside of class was spent with them. The band's make up reflected the racial demographics of the larger campus: The band was overwhelmingly White, and Mario was one of two Latinos in the group.

In October of his first year, Mario explained that one of the marching band's many time-honored traditions is the "nickname tradition." Upperclassmen in the band, and sometimes alumni, assign nicknames to each first-year student in the band. Thereafter, all band members from that point on are expected to address their younger peers by their assigned nicknames and never their actual names—no exceptions. These nicknames are not meant to be nice; indeed, Mario explained that according to the tradition, the more upset the recipient by the nickname, the better. The scenario was reminiscent of the lore surrounding fraternity and sorority hazing; underclassmen must submit if they want a coveted spot in the group.

In this case, however, Mario was given a nickname that he felt was racist, and he protested the name on the spot. His protests were denied. The involved upperclassmen and alumni refused to admit that it could possibly be racist and even offered an explanation as to how and why it was not racist. As seen below, Mario struggled with how to integrate the offense and seemed tentatively convinced that he should not be offended.

Mario:	Like when I got my nickname for the band, I thought it was racially motivated because my nickname is *Burro*. [*Author Note: Burro*, meaning 'small horse' or 'donkey' in Spanish, is commonly used as a derogatory term, most closely translated as 'ass' or 'idiot.'] And I was like, 'Whoa!' Well, this came up because apparently last year there was a senior whose [last] name was Thoroughbred. And I reminded them a lot of him because he was also a football player [like I was] … so, they were like, 'Wow, y'all are so alike!' So they always would call me … 'Mini Thoroughbred.'
	So when the upperclassmen and an alumni [sic] came to one of the parties, the guy decided that my name would be *Burro* because *Burro* is like a small horse, and Thoroughbred is a horse. I thought it was like [a Mexican horse or donkey, in a negative way, 'cause I'm Mexican], and I was like, 'Whoa!' [sounding angry] … I thought it was racially motivated. And [they said,] 'It didn't have anything to do with race, like it shouldn't. It's just a nickname, you know.' So I was like, 'Uh, okaaaay' [sounding hesitant].
Julie:	What did you do? Did you say [anything]?
Mario:	Yeah. They were like, 'No, it has nothing to do with race.' They were like, 'It really doesn't.' I was like, 'Whoa [*sounding angry*]! Does this have to do with race?' He was like, 'No, no, no, no, no it doesn't. Don't think it does, you know, 'cause it really doesn't.' And then so, okay, it made sense what it was. I was okay [with it], 'cause they would always call me 'Little Thoroughbred' and stuff, so the fact that they went from his name and they gave me *Burro*, like the little horse, it was meaningful.
	I went home and googled it. Someone told me, 'Just go google "*burro*" and see what comes up, so you can figure out what it kinda meant. And everything that came up were horses and donkeys. I was like,

'Okay.' So, I'm okay, I was like, 'All right.' At first, I was like, 'Change
it,' just because I didn't like it, but if you don't like it, that's why it
stays. Like every year, they pick like one freshman to be part of the 'fat
family'…. Fat, *Porky* and then *Fatso*, and then *Chubby*….

As Mario described his initial reaction to his nickname, it was clear to me
he had been angry and that he initially felt confident in protesting *Burro* as
his nickname. After his initial reaction, however, things got less clear for
Mario; he indeed struggled with how to perceive this and how to make sense
of it.

In the upperclassmen's refusal to value Mario's complaints that the name
was racist *to him*, which is what should matter, we see Davis's (1989) words
about microaggressions ring painfully true: The nickname assignment and the
refusal to heed Mario's protest were indeed "stunning, automatic acts of disregard" (p. 1576). Mario's convictions that his nickname was steeped in racism
ignored, he was left to face his bandmates' "… unconscious attitudes of white
superiority" (Davis, 1989, p. 1576). It seemed as if the band members did
not truly hear Mario, a phenomenon we also see reflected in Davis's work on
microaggressions in the legal system. Like the court of which Davis writes, it is
as if the group of band members was "capable of this microaggression because
cognitive habit, history, and culture left it unable to hear the range of relevant
voices and grapple with what reasonably might be said in the voice of discrimination's victims" (p. 1576). In sum, the band members, in positions of power,
denied Mario the right to define his own reality; by negating his protests and
claiming his reaction was invalid, they defined his reality *for* him. And, as Sue
(2010) points out, "…the power to impose reality upon marginalized groups
represents the ultimate form of oppression" (p. 37).

As Feagin, Vera, and Imani (1996) explain, these attitudes of White
superiority can flourish in certain settings called "home territories." In their
words, "home territories" are those spaces in which "the occupants have a
broad freedom to act, which is coupled with a sense of control over the area"
(p. 58). CMU's marching band can certainly be considered a "home territory"
for the White upperclassmen and alumni responsible for Mario's nickname
and the refusal to change it. The marching band is made up of almost exclusively White students and is nested within a predominantly White campus.
The band is very well respected both at CMU and nationally, and a spot in
the band is coveted by many. The band has many time-honored traditions,

including the assigning of nicknames. The White upperclassmen and alumni were clearly at home and in control; they had the power, and they knew it. Echoing Davis's comments cited above, they had years of history to fall back on: Unpleasant nicknames have always been given to first-year students, and the more disliked the name, the better.

Roughly a month later, Mario shared some of his additional thoughts:

> Mario: ... It was like, out of all the names there could have been, you know? A *trillion words*, you know? And I was just like, it had to be *that* close to being racial, you know? And that's why it still gets me, and it's still there. I mean, so, no matter what explanation they give me, there's still to me gonna be that little 'thing' there. In a way that's part of like the White privilege and a lot of these other things you learn in sociology.... That's the whole thing of White privilege. It's an invisible privilege that they don't realize they have, but it's there. And it's apparent to everyone else that it's there. And that's what's happening. I don't know. It's tough, but yeah, it exists, and it's there.

In this story, we see a racial microaggression expand and spill over into a new and different category, that of a *contested microaggression*, which I define as the process by which the target of a microaggression names and contests the perceived racist act. Given the very nature of microaggressions, it is most likely that these protests will be met with denial on the part of the perpetrator; however, more research is needed on this process. As Mario's story illustrates, a racial microaggression can be recognized as such by the target, can be named and protested, and the perpetrators may refuse to take responsibility.

Significantly, Mario's story is not named in the literature. Mario considers his band mates to be his community at CMU, and he looks up to the upperclassmen in the band. As a first-year student, along with his first-year peers, he is very much aware of the subordinate role he occupies in the band and all its traditions. Like many other campus organizations such as sports teams and fraternities, first-year students need to work their way up through the ranks and earn the right to be leaders in the group—and in this case, to someday be doling out nicknames instead of receiving them. In other words, Mario's story differs from the typical microaggression in the literature in that it occurs within a space in which he "belongs" (albeit partially, as evidenced by this story). He does not experience a microaggression while walking on the street or in the elevator, perpetrated by strangers whom he may or may not see again.

He faces a microaggression within a group of people he likes and cares for. It is a group he happily participates in by choice; indeed, the perpetrators are in some ways his role models.

Conclusions

Colleges and universities seem to function as incubators for the soon-to-be (or wannabe) guardians of the status quo (Ladson-Billings & Donnor, 2005, p. 295– 296). I have argued here that racial microaggressions should be conceived as they originally were: as derogatory acts that are most often unconscious on the part of the perpetrator; as commonplace occurrences; and as offenses that have alternative, non racially motivated explanations that often cause the targets to feel conflicted and invalidated. I have drawn on the field of critical applied linguistics to argue that adding intentional, overtly racist offenses to the category of "microaggressions" has a deleterious effect in the effort to combat racism for two reasons. First, it has the potential to diminish the harmful nature of the act as well as diminish the target's reaction to the aggression. Second, expanding the original notion of microaggression to include "microassaults" takes away from an essential message that the concept of microaggressions has the power to communicate to a wide audience; the insidious, slippery, sometimes hard-to-name nature of microaggressions is *precisely* where their power lies to cause damage. It is the "cumulative burden" of these commonplace acts that can have drastic effects for the target (Pierce, 1995). Furthermore, the fact that it is difficult for perpetrators to recognize them as potentially racist offenses contributes to their commonplace nature. Thus, I have argued here for these overt, intentional racist acts to be called "racialized aggressions."

Our understanding and use of the term "microaggression" is not complete, however, without more fully considering and naming what happens after an offense has occurred. As Sue (2010) points out, if microaggressions are recognized as problematic, then reactions such as anger are "understandable and normative" (p. 58). However, if a microaggression is not recognized as such and is considered acceptable, then any reaction to the act can be seen as "pathological" (p. 58). Indeed, a lack of awareness of the offense on the part of the perpetrator places the target in a difficult position. In Sue's words, "they are damned if they don't (take action) and damned if they do (take action)" (p. 58).

Given this catch-22-type dilemma, those instances when the target *does* contest a microaggression need to be recognized and named as such. Within the notion of microaggressions, itself a relatively new area of study, research is needed on *contested microaggressions*. Understanding the experience from both the targets' and the perpetrators' points of view would significantly add to our understanding of the various processes at work surrounding a racially microaggressive act, thus helping in the effort to curb racism. This understanding, however, is not enough. Explicit attention must be paid to affecting change with regard to the college experience for underrepresented students.

Specifically, prior research offers four characteristics that are commonly thought to be necessary for nurturing a positive campus racial climate:

1. the inclusion of students, faculty, and administrators of color;
2. a curriculum that reflects the historical and contemporary experiences of people of color;
3. programs to support the recruitment, retention and graduation of students of color; and
4. a college/university mission that reinforces the institution's commitment to pluralism. (Solórzano et al., 2000, p. 62)

Missing from this list, notably, is the explicit mention of racism and available support systems to deal with racism. Thus, I argue for a fifth element to be added to the list, which should read, *programs designed to explicitly address racism*. In my many conversations with the students and the campus support staff in the study presented here and in my frequent visits to first-year courses, I learned that constructive, explicit discussions of racism are rare at CMU, as are outlets that successfully support targets of racism. Until this has changed, we will continue to be "guardians of the status quo," as highlighted in the epigraph above.

As we have seen, Moriah struggled to a significant degree to stay at CMU. She did, in fact, remain enrolled, and she consistently earned As and Bs. On that basis alone, many would argue that CMU served her well and that her experience as a college student was a success. That is, however, a dangerous assumption. Moriah and the rest of the study participants all faced various instances of racism, and these experiences deeply affected how they felt as students at CMU. Is it enough that students get passing grades and possibly graduate? Put simply, no. It is not enough. We must look beyond the normative frameworks for success (Morfin, Perez, Parker, Lynn, & Arrona, 2006; Teranishi et al., 2009) and examine the college experience for under-represented students. As CRT calls us to do, we must "break new ground" and "reconstruct" in our efforts to redress inequality (Ladson-Billings & Donnor, 2005, p. 291).

Thus, I propose the creation of a program on our campuses that directly addresses racism. Specifically, this program would have as its central goals (1) raising awareness and understanding of racism among majority students, (2) offering a common language with which to talk about racism, and (3) providing a support system to empower students to contest racial microaggressions when they do occur. In essence, I am arguing for an infrastructure to be built on college campuses as common practice. The infrastructure would include regular, visible classes and forums on race and racism, some required, some optional. Also included would be required, in-depth trainings for faculty and staff members to increase their sensitivity to and awareness of racism and its far-reaching effects. These trainings would enable them to successfully facili-tate conversations in the classroom, whether these conversations be planned by the instructor or initiated by students. Additionally, new-student orienta-tions would consistently include open, direct conversations about racism on college campuses.

Importantly, this infrastructure needs to be focused not only on blatant, overt racist acts but also on the seemingly "innocuous" microaggressions as well. The notion of "subtle" racism must be named in classes, support groups, and social settings so this insidious form of racism can become part of our common conception of racism. Incorporating this common, often overlooked form of racism into the language we use is essential in the effort to under-stand and combat racism; specifically, White students, faculty, and staff must become well versed in these concepts.

We must take caution, however, when incorporating the notion of micro-aggressions into the battle against racism. Increased clarity surrounding the language of microaggressions is necessary if we are to commit to "open and honest discussions of race" in classrooms with the hopes of increasing "harmo-nious race relations" (Sue et al., 2009, p. 188). Indeed, having these conver-sations with students means opening up the scholarly conversation on racial microaggressions to a much larger and more diverse (racially and otherwise) audience than is present within academia. In making these scholarly, some-what private conversations about racism accessible to a public audience, the terms we use must be clear and consistent.

This research, as well as the campus program proposed here, has the potential to go a long way toward Geertz's call to sort out "the structures of signification" and determine "their social ground and import" (1973, p. 9). This represents, however, only a part of what must be done. As Ladson-Billings and Donnor assert, "[b]ut even with the strides made by...new studies, they still represent a very small crack in the solid, almost frozen traditions of the university" (2005, p. 295). This book is intended to be a part of the effort to add to those cracks, an effort that must continue until the foundation crumbles, thus paving the way for necessary reconstruction.

· 6 ·

"YOU SEE THE WHOLE TREE, NOT JUST THE STUMP"

Religious Fundamentalism, Capital, and Public Schooling

[*Author's Note:* Portions of this chapter were originally accepted for publication in *Curriculum Inquiry* (Minikel-Lacocque 2015. "You See the Whole Tree, Not Just the Stump": Religious Fundamentalism, Capital, and Public Schooling. *Curriculum Inquiry* Copyright © 2015. The Ontario Institute for Studies in Education of the University of Toronto, Wiley.]

> *You start connecting [things]. It's like you see the whole tree, not just the stump. Here at CMU, education-wise, it's really hard. They really want you to think in a different way. It's like, 'Make your own idea about it. I don't want you to think what I'm telling you., It's so hard because I'm so used to being told what I need to think.* —Jasmine

A recent report by the Association of American Colleges and Universities (AAC&U) details its current vision for higher education in the U.S., titled, "Liberal Education and America's Promise," or "LEAP." In this context, "liberal" is not a reference to political leanings; rather, it refers to the type of education described and promoted in the 2011 AAC&U report discussed here.

Taking into consideration the changing landscape of the global economy as well as input from employers, the AAC&U describes its "New Framework for Excellence" as,

… education that intentionally fosters, across multiple fields of study, wide-ranging knowledge if science, cultures, and society; high-level intellectual and practical skills; an active commitment to personal and social responsibility; and the demonstrated ability to apply learning to complex problems and challenges. (AAC&U, 2011, p. 9)

At the heart of this education is "engagement with big questions, both contemporary and enduring" (AAC&U, 2011, p. 2). The report also outlines specific "Essential Learning Outcomes," which all students should begin working toward during their K-12 schooling and continue throughout their years in higher education. Importantly, these learning outcomes include "inquiry and analysis," as well as "critical and creative thinking" (p. 7). The report decidedly calls for a move "away from the ivory tower of the academy," a shift which calls for applicable, practical skills as well as sophisticated intellectual skills (p. 3). Having described a new vision of learning for the nation, the organization's president claims, "So-conceived, liberal education is a necessity, not a luxury" (p. 3).

Similarly, philosophers of education Brighouse and McAvoy (2009) contend that the university's current focus of delivering information is dangerously narrow and argue that the university should guide its students to think critically and ethically. They contend that the university should be used, in part, to "encourage students to puzzle about how they ought to live in the world" (p. 174). In other words, if the university is to produce "educated people," it must also pay attention to students' moral development. Indeed, they define "educated people" as those who know how to "think ethically, practice good self-care, reflect before they act, and critically think about the messages they receive in the modern world" (p. 171).

Given the changing demographics of the United States, however, we must ask ourselves: What happens when a student's family values are in conflict with this vision for education writ large and higher education specifically? Is it a simple case of a cultural mismatch? Does the educational institution bear any responsibility to the student who may be struggling as a result of this conflict?

In this chapter, I examine one such case by focusing exclusively on the transition to CMU for Jasmine, a fundamentalist Christian who identifies as Mexican American. Specifically, I apply the notion of familial capital, one of the forms of capital in Yosso's (2005) community cultural wealth model, which is based in Critical Race Theory (CRT). Recall from Chapter 2 that CRT has been used to reexamine the ways in which the notions of social capital and cultural capital are applied to Students of Color; what's more, Yosso's model challenges the deficit view of Students of Color and highlights the various forms of capital that Students of Color do possess. *Familial capital* in particular is defined as "those cultural knowledges nurtured among *familia* (kin) that carry a sense of community history, memory, and cultural intuition" (Yosso, 2005, p. 79). Further, using an expanded notion of family, Yosso conceives of *familia* as including "immediate family as well as aunts, uncles, grandparents and friends—living or long passed on…" (2006, p. 46).

This chapter, then, is an analysis of the ways in which the influences of family and religion interact with identity formation and the college experience for Jasmine. Through an examination of the ways in which her familial capital and her U.S. public education interact, I suggest ways in which we must rethink the idea of familial capital as well as expand the concept of "multiculturalism" to include the category of religion. Importantly, this examination of Jasmine's experiences is not prescriptive in nature; rather, the purpose here is to raise questions, encourage discussion, and push theory forward through an examination of the lived experience of a young, Latina, fundamentalist Christian college student.

U.S. Latin@s and Demographic Shifts

As a group, U.S. Latin@s have been getting a significant amount of attention regarding two recent trends: population growth and religious affiliation. Indeed, even the popular media have reported on these trends (The Associated Press, 2013; Dias, 2013; Geis, 2006). In one example, a newspaper article opens, "Welcome to the new off-white America," and goes on to explain that non-Hispanic whites "will lose their majority around the year 2043" (The Associated Press, 2013). In another example, the cover of TIME *Magazine* displays two (brown) hands positioned in prayer, over which reads in large letters, "The Latino Reformation: Inside the new Hispanic churches transforming religion in America" (Dias, 2013). The article then details the dramatic shift, elsewhere called a "mass migration" (Geis, 2006) of U.S. Latin@s away from Catholicism and into fundamentalist protestant religions. A third trend, however, that has not been discussed as much outside academia is the low rate of educational achievement among Latin@s, documented earlier in this book.

Given these trends, it is very likely that stories like Jasmine's will become much more common. Jasmine's case is uniquely rich in its ability to showcase the ways in which family, religion, and public, liberal education interact. At precisely the time of the AAC&U's effort to redefine liberal higher education in the U.S., Jasmine's case forces a laser-like focus on the necessary questions surrounding the purpose of higher education as well as the institution's responsibility to its students as it attempts to carry out its purpose.

U.S. Latin@ Families and Schooling

Various studies have addressed the role of family in the schooling of Latin@s (Stanton-Salazar, 2001; Gibson et al., 2004; Gándara & Contreras, 2009; Gándara, 1995; Antrop-González, et al., 2005; Yosso 2006; Auerbach, 2002; Flores-González, 2002), but none has focused specifically on the family's role in the *transition* to college for Latin@ students. Much of the research in this area examines college preparation, most of which is focused on the preparation of disadvantaged students (Deil-Amen & López Turley, 2007). Additionally, when it comes to understanding the effect of family on the transition to college, past studies (most of which are quantitative) have centered on the family's socioeconomic status (SES) and its influence on college success, which has been found to have a significant effect (Deil-Amen & Turley, 2007).

Lareau and Weininger (2008) add race to the equation and state, "… studies have established that college access, enrollment, and graduation are linked to various dimensions of stratification, including social class and race" (p. 118). The reasons behind this association are unclear, however. Lareau and Weininger argue that middle-class students enjoy and benefit from cultural capital in the form of their parents' knowledge of the college application process and the college experience generally. Conversely, working-class and poor students' parents often do not have this knowledge; thus, these students rely on school personnel to help them with the process of getting into college. In essence, college students find themselves on an uneven playing field as a result of variation in cultural capital.

There is a distinct lack of literature based on qualitative studies that specifically examine the role of family in Latin@ students' transitions to college and that bring to light the more nuanced personal stories, experiences, and viewpoints of the students themselves. However, a diverse body of literature from various academic disciplines, when brought together, offers insight. The relevant literature speaks to the issues of persistence in college, identity formation in relation to schooling, and religion and schooling.

Perhaps the most well-known theory on college persistence comes from Tinto (1993), in which he argues that a lack of congruence between a student and the college context will impede progress and lead to eventual withdrawal. In order to successfully transition to college, Tinto asserts that students must pass through the following stages: (1) separation from communities of the past, (2) transition between high school and college, and (3) incorporation into the society of college. While separation from home communities can present stress for all students, Tinto claims that for students from disadvantaged backgrounds and for those from families who have not gone to college themselves, this separation is often more painful. Additionally, his theory stresses the importance of social relationships and involvement in university-based groups and posits that the more "central" one's membership is to mainstream campus life, the more likely the student will persist in college.

Tinto's tangential consideration of Students of Color, however, has drawn much criticism (see, for example, Stanton-Salazar, 2001; Cabrera, Amaury, Terenzini, Pascarella, & Hegedorn, 1999; Tierney, 1992, 1999; Nora, 1987; Nora & Rendon, 1990; Yosso, 2006). CRT theorist Tara Yosso (2006) offers an alternative framework that she argues more accurately reflects the transition for Chican@ college students. Specifically, instead of Tinto's phases of separation, transition, and incorporation, Yosso argues that many underrepresented students move through the phases of culture shock, community building, and critical navigation. She highlights students' use of families as support to ease the culture shock of college; separating from them, she argues, would take away sources of strength. Next, Chican@ students start to build new supportive communities—"counterspaces"—on campus in order to combat the effects of a "hostile campus racial climate" (p. 122). Finally, instead of simply incorporating themselves *into* the college culture, students are able to critically navigate *among* the multiple worlds of family, home communities, and college without forfeiting their identities and cultures.

With regard to identity formation in school contexts, Flores-González (2002) argues that schools either foster or hinder the development of a "school kid" identity and that one's "school kid" or "street kid" identity ultimately has an impact on school success and graduation. Specifically, her work points to the importance of congruence of students' multiple worlds; that is, when students' worlds (such as school, sports, community activities, and family) are similar, their "school kid" identity can be expressed across these worlds in non conflicting ways, thus supporting persistence. In contrast, those who leave school often experience "role strain" caused by the "irreconcilable con-flicts" among their conflicting student world identities (p. 23).

Fundamentalism, Schooling, and Identities

While there are many variations within the category of fundamentalism, a com-mon thread among them is the strict, literal interpretation of scripture. Before focusing on Jasmine's specific religious affiliation, it is important to address how some religious scholars conceive of fundamentalism writ large. Almond, Sivan, and Appleby (1995a) place fundamentalism "in a category by itself" and consider it to be "neither a 'new religious movement'… nor simply a 'traditional,' 'conservative,' or 'orthodox' expression of ancient…religious faith and practice" (p. 402). Rather, they conceive of fundamentalism as a movement formed in opposition to the influences of the modern world. In their words, fundamen-talism refers to "specific religious phenomena that have emerged in the twen-tieth century…in the wake of the success of modernization and secularization" (p. 403). What's more, these scholars contend that fundamentalism is "reactive to and defensive toward" modernization and secularization, and, further, that fundamentalists believe that the loss of members to the secular world leads to "the erosion and displacement of true religion" (p. 405). Fundamentalism, they explain, is a "militant effort to counteract this trend" (p. 405).

Sivan (1995) uses cultural theory to explain that fundamentalism is an "enclave culture" and that the enclave in general is a response to a group's problem with its boundary. The group (in this case a group sharing religious convictions) is losing members to the tempting "central community," which enjoys "prestige, cultural hegemony, and access to … resources" (p. 17). In response to this threat, it wields moral persuasion in an effort to "seal a porous boundary" (p. 17). Sivan explains, "Devoid of coercive powers over its mem-bers, it cannot punish them; lacking sufficient resources, it cannot reward them. The only control to be deployed in order to shore up the boundary is moral persuasion" (p. 17).

One way the enclave enacts moral persuasion, bequeaths moral rewards, and shapes its authority is to construct a "wall of virtue," which places the "oppressive and morally defiled" mainstream society in "sharp contrast to the virtuous insiders" (p. 18). Significantly, staying within the "walls of virtue," and apart from the outside means one's soul will be saved. Indeed, the outside is seen as "polluted, contagious, [and] dangerous" (p. 19).

Jasmine, a fundamentalist Christian, specifically identifies her religion as Pentecostal Apostolic. Pentecostalism is a branch of conservative Christianity, which is a larger category most commonly associated with literal interpretations of the Bible. Well-known Pentecostal preachers Jim Bakker, Benny Hinn, Jimmy Swaggart, and Pat Robertson helped increase the visibility of Pentecostalism and even became so popular in the late 1990s that they are now part of U.S. pop-culture. Commonly referred to as the fastest-growing branch of Christianity, Pentecostalism's defining features are *glossolalia*—also known as *speaking in tongues*—and lively, emotional church services.

Within Pentecostalism there are many denominations, including Pentecostal Apostolic, also referred to as Apostolic Pentecostal. Sometimes called Oneness Pentecostalism or Jesus Only Pentecostalism, Apostolic Pentecostalism is defined by its belief in the "Oneness of God." In the early 1900s, this group "abandoned the traditional expression of belief in the Trinity [Father, Son, Holy Spirit], and accept[ed] the oneness of God" (http://www.religioustolerance.org/chr_pent.htm).

Historically, U.S. Latin@s have overwhelmingly been Catholic; however, that trend has started to shift dramatically as more and more Latin@as leave Catholicism for fundamentalist religions such as Pentecostalism. The *Washington Post* (Geis, April 30, 2006) called this shift a "mass migration of Latinos to charismatic Christian movements" and reported that 30 years ago, an estimated 90% of Latin@s in the U.S. were Catholics. Today, that number is 70%, a figure that holds steady only because of high birth rates and the arrival of new immigrants. The article explains that "Most other Latino Americans—9.5 million of them—are Protestant, usually Pentecostal or another evangelical denomination" (p. A03).

Yet, despite this spectacular trend, popular notions of multiculturalism have not typically included religion. Indeed, Schweber and Irwin (2003) argue that multicultural scholarly debates have centered around inequities and differences related to race, gender, class, sexual orientation, and disability, and that too few scholars have examined religious identities or minority religions as significant aspects of multicultural education. Schweber and Irwin assert that multiculturality must be expanded to include religion "as a category" and that the very concept of a multiculture calls for scholars to closely examine the ways in which religious communities (including fundamentalist ones) teach, as well as investigate the various effects of that teaching. In academic circles, it is increasingly more common to include religion and fundamentalism in notions of multiculturalism. (See, for example, Boudreau, 2009; Stonebanks & Stonebanks, 2009; and Sensoy, 2009.)

Schweber and Irwin point out that there has been little exploration of the self-concepts and identities of fundamentalist students in the academic literature. Just as the literature discussed above treats of the notion of identity as complex and layered, Schweber and Irwin remind us of the comparable complexity of the self-concepts of fundamentalists and caution against assuming simplicity. They write:

> In much of the educational research to date, fundamentalist students' conceptions of self and other have been neglected … except as targets at which to aim critiques of religious extremism more broadly…. Despite authors' concessions that categories of race, gender, and sexual identity shift and change, fundamentalist Christians are typically conceived of, or at least written about, as an unvariegated, monolithic block. While it is tempting to hang on to fixed categories, especially perhaps when considering fundamentalist religions, religious identities are as unstable and complex as categories based on race, gender, and sexual identity. (2003, p. 1697)

In his provocative article, Berliner (1997) writes of two nearly incompatible worlds, fundamentalism and democracy. In the world of fundamentalism, there is no room for critical thinking, negotiation, or intellectual shades of grey. Rather, a black-and-white and right-or-wrong philosophy prevails. In the world of democracy, on the other hand, the ideals of negotiation, tolerance of difference, and compromise reign. My concern and focus here, however, are very different than those of Berliner. Berliner is concerned with the ways in which the "religious right," consisting of fundamentalist Christians, seeks to change and even abolish the nation's public school system in order to fulfill their religious agenda for schooling.

While Berliner's (1997) work is important, my focus here is not about the ways in which fundamentalists are working to change our schools; rather, my concern is about how fundamentalist students fare *in* our public schools. Specifically, I am concerned that fundamentalist students like Jasmine often struggle in our public universities, and I argue that the stark differences between the worlds from which these students come and the collegiate settings they enter may be at the root of their struggles. Berliner writes succinctly of this difference: "The problem is that [the fundamentalist Christian Right's] world allows no politics, no negotiation, and their views are often irreconcilable with those held by most of the educational community" (p. 412). Interestingly, this statement holds true for both Berliner's cause *and* mine: Berliner means that these characteristics are a problem when it comes to educators trying to work *with* fundamentalists on issues surrounding our public schools, and I claim these characteristics of fundamentalism are a problem for students like Jasmine as they try to succeed in the world of public schooling.

In Jasmine's Words: The Data

Jasmine, whose mother identifies as White and Native American and works inside the home, and whose father was born in Mexico and is a floorlayer, has had a complicated relationship with schooling for years. Growing up in Lakeside, a diverse city about an hour from Collegeville, Jasmine was frequently moved from school to school due to her parents' dissatisfaction with the public schools to which their family had access. Jasmine did not consider herself academically successful and was not involved in many school-based activities.

After initially applying to CMU, she was wait-listed. Upon eventually getting accepted, staff from CMU's branch of the federally funded support program, *Education for All Students* (EFAS), contacted Jasmine and explained, in her words, that she "barely got in." They also explained that due to her relatively weak academic record, she would be required to take part in EFAS, which is specifically aimed at helping underrepresented students through tutoring and advising sessions.

Within minutes of starting our first interview, Jasmine referenced her religion and vaguely linked her religion to her choice of dress and lack of make up. When I asked her to elaborate, she replied, "Well, we're Pentecostal Apostolic. We go, like, according to the Bible. We believe that you're not supposed to wear men's clothing. So, we believe that women [should] wear skirts...." Jasmine communicated in many ways that she feels a very strong connection not only to her religion but also to her church. On multiple occasions she told me of her tight-knit church community and her fondness for it. I asked her once to explain further, and she smiled, "I just love my church, 'cause we're like a big family." In the next section, I analyze the data on Jasmine's experiences as she transitioned to CMU. The analysis is divided into the following subsections: Jasmine and Fundamentalism, Before CMU: A Wary Relationship with School, Facing Ambiguity, and, Intersections. I then finish the chapter by offering concluding thoughts and implications.

Jasmine and Fundamentalism

It is important to first take a closer look at some aspects of Jasmine's religious belief system and practice. Like the fundamentalist students and teachers in Schweber and Irwin's (2003) study, Jasmine and her family have a faith that encourages them to "submit fully to God, a God whom they view as omnipotent, omniscient, loving and good, and a God whom they view as fully directing their lives" (p. 1698). Evidence of this driving belief can be seen in my conversation with her in which she explains how she understands her path to CMU. During that conversation, Jasmine was clearly energized by the idea of God helping her by providing her with "blessings." Her face lit up and she spoke with an intensity and excitement I did not often see in our interviews. An excerpt of this conversation follows:

Jasmine:	It's a miracle being here anyway. People think I was really weird, just applying to one college, and one of the hardest colleges to go to.
Julie:	You didn't apply to anywhere else?
Jasmine:	No, this is the only college I applied to. And then I got a tape recorder from you, and then I met a lot of people here. I didn't think I would fit in, but I have a lot of people that I know. There's a bunch of stuff that doesn't happen to normal people.
Julie:	So why do you think those good things have happened to you?
Jasmine:	I think they're all blessings, really. I kind of think college is like a testimony.
Julie:	A testimony? What do you mean?
Jasmine:	At church we have these things, when good things happen to you, it's like God blessing you, testimony of what has happened to you and what God has given you. I think college is my testimony because I'm the first person in my whole family to come to college, I got accepted to the college I wanted to go to, the only college that I [applied to]. And I found a church two days after I came here…. And then I needed a tape recorder, and you gave me a tape recorder. And it was like, whoa! God's just providing for everything here.

Here, we see that Jasmine, in many ways, "turned her life over to God" and trusted that God would provide for her and would help her do what was right. Instead of referring to her grades or test scores as reasons she got into a selective university, she cites her "testimony" from God. In Christianity, the term "testimony" can be used to refer to one's story of becoming a Christian or to the ways in which God blesses him/her or to the ways in which one lives in accordance with his/her beliefs. Here, Jasmine uses the term to refer to how she believes God has blessed her (i.e., acceptance into CMU). Thus, Jasmine's religious convictions and the central role of her church community formed a foundational aspect of her identity and worldview. Below, I explore how a worldview centered on Christian Fundamentalism interacts with public schooling for Jasmine.

Before CMU: A Wary Relationship with School

Given Jasmine's fundamentalist lifestyle and belief system, including a literal interpretation of the Bible, it is to be expected that ideological differences arose between Jasmine's beliefs and her public school education. Although Jasmine attended a religious school during early elementary school, her family was unable to afford to keep her there and thus relied on the public school system for the rest of Jasmine's K-12 career.

Due to the vast ideological differences between her parents' views and those of her public school teachers, Jasmine changed schools repeatedly. In total, Jasmine attended roughly 12 schools before enrolling at CMU. A key issue that contributed to the multiple school changes was that of evolution being taught in Jasmine's science classes. Jasmine related several stories about her experience in public school science classes, and in these stories she made clear that she and her parents believe that teaching evolution is wrong. Her views are echoed in Apple's (2006) work examining the religious right and its effects on educational policies. Apple explains that for the vast majority of fundamentalists, teaching evolution in schools would not only "undermine Christian morality, but … the very act of drawing a line from apes to humans would invalidate their belief that human beings were created in the image of God" (p. 129). In a more dramatic explanation of fundamentalists' stance on evolution vs. creationism, the leader of the creationist group Answers in Genesis explains,

> Students in public schools are being taught that evolution is a fact, that they're just products of survival of the fittest. There's not meaning in life if we're just animals in a struggle for survival. It creates a sense of purposelessness and hopelessness…. (Belluck, 1999, p. A13, quoted in Apple, 2006, p. 127)

The weight of this issue is reflected in Jasmine's words as she explains what it was like to be a fundamentalist Christian in public school science classes:

Jasmine: It was hard 'cause I have a Christian background, so the whole the-
                ology with science was horrible. I'm like, 'That's not right, that's not
                true,' you know?

Julie: You mean, not true, what they were teaching in science class?

Jasmine: Yeah, the whole billions and billions of years. And, you know, a little
                kid [is] taught one thing, they're gonna stick to that, you know?

Julie: So did you run into the same issues at [one of the high schools you
                attended] with science education?

Jasmine: Yeah. I started to understand that you're gonna have to deal with that,
                you know? You're going to have to deal with the different science
                issues, so just listen to them, learn what you gotta learn, but you don't
                have to believe it. You just have to put up with that because evolution
                is what's taught today, so you're just going to have to separate what
                you believe in and what's taught.

Julie: So it wasn't too bad for you at [the subsequent high school you
                attended] in that respect?

Jasmine: Well, it was a little hard. My science teacher is a major evolutionist.
                I think it's like his religion. He said one day when we were watching
                a movie that Christianity was as stupid a religion as this religion they
                had in the movie. In the movie they have a religion that they believe
                that the world began with a sneeze. And he said that Christianity was
                as stupid a religion as that. And I was like, 'You know what? You don't
                need to be saying that. We put up with what you believe. You should
                put up with what we believe.' So I was like, 'That's kind of rude, you
                know.' He seriously believes we were monkeys. And I'm like, 'I don't
                mind yours; don't try to put down mine like that.' I understand evolu-
                tion and stuff, but I also know what I believe.

As I listened to Jasmine relate this story, I saw a distinct shift in her. When
she spoke of the impending start of college, for example, she appeared nearly
despondent; when the topic changed to her religious beliefs, however, Jasmine
straightened up and asserted herself. I was impressed by her courage to defend
her beliefs, and I quickly learned that although she may lack confidence in her
academic skills, she possesses great confidence in other arenas.

Changing schools so often did indeed take its toll on Jasmine. Through
Jasmine's stories on this topic, it was clear to me that she experienced isolation and discomfort in school at various times. She also mentioned more than
once that changing schools so frequently made her academic life more challenging than it might have been otherwise; teachers expected her to know
material that was not covered at her previous school, and she often felt like
she was trying to catch up to her peers because of the lack of continuity.
Looking back on her first semester at CMU, Jasmine cited the fact that she

"changed so many schools" as part of the reason for her feeling academically unprepared for college.

Indeed, only minutes into our first interview, it became clear that Jasmine did not feel prepared for CMU and was extremely nervous about being able to succeed there. She told me, "It's still hitting me that I'm going to college. I'm like, 'What am I getting myself into?' All these years of learning, [and I] don't like school to begin with. I don't know." Jasmine then explained she did not feel prepared for CMU by her K-12 schooling and that although she tried activities such as student council and math club in high school, her involvement was inconsistent. In her words, she "wasn't really involved in school." She attributed this inconsistency in part to her school being far away from her home and to her lack of transportation for after-school activities. She said, "I couldn't keep up with [school clubs] because my school is far…so it was hard to get home. My parents were not really big on picking [me] up…." In addition to her lack of involvement in school, it was also immediately clear that she did not have a positive academic self-image. She candidly stated in our first interview, "I'm horrible at studying, taking notes, and writing" and that she was "worried most about studying [at CMU]. I'm not much of a studying type." As I got to know Jasmine better, I learned more about her—and her parents'—complicated relationships with school.

Put simply, Jasmine's parents' relationships to her schooling were complicated at best, untrusting at worst. These relationships affected Jasmine in various ways. Concretely, Jasmine experienced a significant lack of continuity academically, which made school difficult for her. Socially, Jasmine's frequent moves made it difficult to have close relationships with peers and teachers. On an ideological level, not only were her beliefs challenged and devalued by some of her schools, but Jasmine also received clear messages from her parents that school was not a place they trusted. Instead, school was a place from which to be protected. Indeed, her parents' relationships with public schooling are emblematic of the enclave culture discussed above, whereby the insiders (Jasmine's family and church community) "fight" the "dangerous" outside (in this case, the public schools) in order to save souls (Sivan, 1995, p. 19).

Although Jasmine's parents encouraged her to get an education and go to college, this encouragement was cautious. In Jasmine's words, "My parents are like, 'You can go to college if you want, but you're going to have to pay your way through,' and I was like, 'Okay, I'll try.'" Although Jasmine and her parents figured out a way to pay for her college expenses, the additional bills put a financial strain on her and on her family. Her father's conditional support of her going to college stemmed from his concerns over Jasmine's accruing debt and her commitment to staying in college. Regarding the latter, Jasmine explained that she and her dad had an "unwritten contract" about her staying in school. Her father told her, "I want you to promise me that you're going to do this. I don't want you to start something and not finish it. I want you to get something out of it." Jasmine confided that she felt like her father's comments sometimes added pressure, which "made it worse" for her in terms of believing she could stay in college and succeed.

Facing Ambiguity

All new college students hope to feel a sense of belonging on campus, whether it is akin to Tinto's (1993) second stage of transition or Yosso's (2006) community building. The ultimate goal of these phases is, in Yosso's words, to be able to "critically navigate" between the worlds of home and college, no matter the background of the student. To be sure, achieving that goal is easier for students from White middle-class backgrounds who experience little dissonance between their worlds. Jasmine found herself unable to travel through either of these stages. As she began to find herself struggling to fit in at CMU, she drew on her ties to her family and their religious beliefs to help her sort out her difficulties at CMU.

Although Jasmine said she felt like she fit in at CMU more than she had expected to, she repeatedly told me she felt lonely, which was very difficult for her. Although she knew people she considered friends, she explained that she and her friends "really don't hang out." Just as Jasmine's ideological and religious viewpoints distanced her somewhat from her K-12 schools, at CMU, Jasmine again found herself faced with the chasm between the beliefs she was raised with and those of her new surroundings. What's more, Jasmine was repeatedly called on to explain and defend her religious convictions. This, as we see below, caused Jasmine to feel alienated and confused as she tried to navigate a new world filled with ambiguity and not with the black-and-white certainty to which she was accustomed.

Marriage Equality

As we sat down for an interview one month after Jasmine started her first semester at CMU, I sensed that she was overwhelmed. In this first month,

Jasmine faced a jarring clash of worldviews that proved to be monumental in her brief college career. Local elections were to be held within weeks, and the most publicized issue on the ballot was the legality of gay marriage. CMU's campus and the surrounding town of Collegeville—both politically liberal—were abuzz with talk of this hotly debated issue, and Jasmine found herself virtually surrounded by people who supported gay marriage. What's more, she was repeatedly asked to explain her stance on issues such as this. Jasmine's struggle was palpable as she spoke to me:

> Julie: Have you run into any conflicts [related to your religion] as far as being here at CMU?
>
> Jasmine: Well, a friend asked me how I stood on the gay [marriage] issue 'cause she really wanted to know about the whole Christian thing. It's a confusing subject because I wasn't raised being taught these things. I think they should have rights, but I don't agree that it's okay to marry the same gender. It's like I stand on both sides of the line. If I ask my Dad, I know he's gonna just be like, 'No, it's wrong.' And I need *more* than just that. I need it explained to me. I need to know what I can say to support my religion, you know? It's a big thing, because a lot of people wanna ask that question, 'Where does your religion stand?' And I felt so bad 'cause I didn't have the answer to it. I just need to *know* it.

Here, we see that Jasmine was being pushed to think critically about these issues on her own, in the absence of her parents or church community. As she straddled the black-and-white world of her upbringing and the collegiate world filled with shades of grey, her confusion was palpable. She wanted to check with her father to make sure she was saying the "right" thing when asked to explain her religion's stance on the issue *and* she wanted more than to be told gay marriage was wrong; she wanted it explained to her. Indeed, when she ventured into the world of democratic thinking, she felt lost and wanted to return to what Peshkin (1987) calls "a polarized world where things are either this or that, not this *and* that" (p. 9, quoted in Berliner, 1997). In essence, she straddled these two modes of thought without the ability to "critically navigate" them (Yosso, 2006).

Debatable Faith?

During the transitional months at CMU, Jasmine faced many similar incidents in which her college surroundings clashed with her faith. It was, however, when her faith and coursework came into direct conflict with one another that I began to see more clearly how her academics may be affected by the lack of congruence between her two worlds. In her freshman English course, Jasmine's first writing assignment was to write a paper on a "debatable topic." For Jasmine, this paper represented much more than an assignment:

> My paper for English was about why I'm a Christian. It was supposed to be a debatable paper, and I said that Christianity just makes sense. And [the instructor] was like, 'Okay, some people are just gonna shoot you down right there. You need to make this paper logical. You can't be basing it on faith.'
>
> Christianity *is* based on faith, so it's kinda hard to be like logical. I said they found Noah's Ark, and he's like, 'Really?' He's like, 'Okay, people are not gonna believe this. They will totally think you're wrong and just put the paper down.' He really helped me a lot because I was like, 'Oh my goodness.' I didn't really understand how to debate it…. I think I have the main idea what I'm gonna do now [for my next draft], but it's gonna be difficult doing it.

Jasmine and her instructor, in essence, were speaking different languages. They each had very different understandings of the task at hand, and the disconnect was striking. The assignment, to write about a debatable topic, implicitly required Jasmine to recruit skills of argumentation and critical thinking to convince her critically thinking audience of her point. It was not clear that Jasmine, situated within her world of black-and-white truths, understood the implicit need to recruit these skills. Berliner (1997) argues, in fact, that these skills are underdeveloped or nonexistent in students with religious affiliations similar to Jasmine's. For this assignment, she stated what she regarded as the Truth and was surprised when it was met with disapproval. Explaining her faith in a "logical" manner was not something Jasmine had ever had to do. That, coupled with the academic aspect of learning how to improve her writing skills, caused Jasmine significant stress.

Hypnotists and Hairdos

Roughly a month later, as Jasmine explained the ways in which her religious beliefs were being challenged at CMU, she related the aftermath of going to a campus function that featured a hypnotist:

> I was talking to [my dad] about it. He was like, 'We don't believe in hypnotists.' I'm like, 'Really? I didn't know that.' I got [upset] …. I had bought CDs from the hypnotist [but after I talked to my dad], I broke them. I was like, 'I don't believe in this. I shouldn't have these.' My friends thought I was insane or something. They were

like, 'You paid like 20 bucks for those things. You could've given them to me,' and I'm like, 'I'd rather not spread it. I'd rather it be thrown in the garbage and no one be affected by it.'

Thus, in a time of experimentation, Jasmine turned to her family and religion for guidance. She ended up heeding her father's words and even broke the CDs she bought from the hypnotist so as not to "spread it." Here we see a clear example of the perceived "danger" of the outside world. Jasmine even wanted to protect her non fundamentalist friends from these dangers by destroying the possible source of "pollution."

As our conversation continued, Jasmine spoke about what it was like to live out her faith at CMU on a more practical level, including following church guidelines for women such as wearing skirts, not cutting her hair, and leaving hair and nails their natural color. She did, in fact, paint her toenails a light color at her roommate's urging. Although she enjoyed it and thought it looked nice, she felt guilty and embarrassed afterward. In her words, the fact that she painted her toenails "just really like scared the heck out of me. I [was] like, 'Oh my goodness, look at me.'" She explained further in a subsequent interview:

I know when I came here I wanted to paint my nails a different color. Now I'm like, 'I don't wanna do that.' That's like throwing 18 years of something down the toilet. It's kinda like me just keeping what I've been doing all this time anyway. That's who I am now. My roommate's like, 'Your hair is so long. I would just cut it off.' I'm like, 'No I couldn't do that.'

Jasmine's decision-making process, based on her authoritarian understanding of the hierarchy in her life, reflects Berliner's (1997) argument that for many fundamentalist children, there is a direct line from God to their parents. That is, learning to submit to God starts with learning to submit to one's parents. Thus, after taking small excursions—albeit unknowingly in the case of the hypnotist—away from what her church dictates and into a world of shades of grey and ambiguity, Jasmine decided to return to her original way of being and "who she is." In essence, she briefly found herself on the outside of the "wall of virtue" and quickly scrambled to get back on the inside (Sivan, 1995).

Intersections

We have seen that it is through her faith that Jasmine principally defines herself and that the role of religion in her life is profound and far reaching. For

example, the lack of academic preparation for college that Jasmine noted—
and I noticed as well—can, in part, be linked to the interaction of her family's
religious worldview (which includes beliefs about public schooling) and the
ways in which the schools were equipped (or not) to work with and support
Jasmine.

I would be remiss, however, if I were to paint Jasmine as a one-dimensional
person, someone for whom religion is the *single* defining feature. Indeed, religion intersected race and class for Jasmine during her first year in college
in important ways. For example, Jasmine had been participating in a Bible
study group on campus, which she hoped would provide a safe space for her
and that through this group she would find her "niche" at CMU. However,
when one of her peers made hurtful comments about Mexicans during a meeting, the group became unwelcoming and racist for Jasmine and something in
which she stopped participating. (See Chapter 5 for a detailed account of this
incident).

Finding a "niche" at CMU that simultaneously fit with the religious,
racial, *and* socioeconomic elements of Jasmine's identity proved to be an unattainable goal. Indeed, when I asked Jasmine in November what should be
changed at CMU to make the transition easier for her, she highlighted the
intersection of race and class for her at CMU by responding, "[CMU needs]
more diversity. I know a lot of [Students of Color at CMU] who are like, 'I feel
so out of place here.'"

She then shared that she, too, felt "out of place" because her peers were
wealthier than she:

> A lot of times, I feel like I'm surrounded by people that are richer than me. They
> never had to struggle or anything, you know? They can go to a store and spend $200
> no problem, mommy and daddy are gonna pay for it, you know? Me, I didn't have a
> laptop. My parents couldn't afford it…. So, sometimes I feel like I'm fitting in, but
> not *exactly*, 'cause everyone here is from suburbia or something, and they're lucky if
> they've seen someone of another color. Sometimes I just feel out of place.

Thus, the interrelated issues of race, class, and religion were salient for Jasmine
in terms of fitting in on campus. Indeed, while it is helpful and sometimes necessary to separate these categories, it is crucial to recognize the ways in which
they come together in the formation of one's identity. Significantly, these three
facets of her identity (Student of Color, working class, and Christian fundamentalist), taken individually, can each pose challenges for students as they
transition to college, particularly a public, predominantly White institution

(PWI). Thus, Jasmine faced a unique challenge; indeed, one can imagine that had she been a White fundamentalist with at least some disposable income, her transition to CMU would have been different in some meaningful ways.

Conclusions and Implications

... [A]s institutions within a liberal state, schools must treat young people as emerging moral agents and help them develop the capacity for autonomous thinking. (McAvoy, 2008, p. 16)

Toward the end of her first year at CMU, Jasmine was making arrangements to leave CMU and move back home with her family. Although her GPA was a 2.8—far from failing out of school—Jasmine, who did not have a strong "school-kid" identity, reasoned that it did not make sense to continue at CMU if she was unsure of what she wanted to study, especially given the financial burden her college tuition placed on her family. When Jasmine faced challenges during her first year at CMU, she turned to her family for support and for reinforcement of the worldview in which she had been raised. Indeed, her family ties provided her with a safety net, and her connection to her church was upheld. CMU was not a place at which she felt comfortable, and she was very tempted to return to what was safe, familiar, and comfortable.

What Jasmine's family provided her was not readily accepted or recognized at CMU. As we have seen, Jasmine was "used to being told what to think"; her fundamentalist upbringing instilled in her an authoritarian way of thinking and viewing the world. This mode of thought, emblematic of authoritarian populism (Apple, 2006), is in conflict with the democratic, exploratory nature of public universities. In other words, Jasmine experienced "irreconcilable conflicts" between her worlds of family and school (Flores-Gonzaléz, 2002).

Jasmine's story, then, begs the question: What is to be done when a student's background does not provide access to, in McAvoy's words, "the capacity for autonomous thinking"? Given that the very purpose of liberal arts higher education, as stated by the AAC&U, is to prepare students for "engagement with big questions," as well as "critical and creative thinking," what happens when a student arrives with knowledge and experiences that cannot be used to one's advantage in the liberal arts college environment?

If we are to address these questions on a practical level, we must first examine the theoretical notions of "familial capital." Indeed, it is not sufficient to say that all families provide their children with various forms of capital and that Students of Color come to school with under recognized forms of familial capital. While this is true, it is incomplete. As we have seen here, when theory is applied to real life, things get complicated. The notion of familial capital, rooted in CRT and thus focused on Students of Color, has done much to push our thinking forward.

However, Jasmine's story reminds us of the intersecting and multiple "categories" of one's identity. Jasmine's identity is composed of various foundational "categories" in addition to race. She is Latina, a fundamentalist Christian, and is of a working-class background, to name a few. *Each* of these facets of her identity was set in relief against the backdrop of CMU's campus. For Jasmine, raised in a fundamentalist paradigm, her worldview is no more a choice than race, class, gender, or physical ability. Yet, tellingly, the "diversity page" on CMU's website makes no mention of religious differences whatsoever. As Schweber and Irwin (2003) assert, we must include religion as a "category" within "multicultural education frameworks" (p. 1693).

Thus, when we attempt to view Jasmine's experiences in school as they relate to her religion through the lens of familial capital, we come up short. Jasmine is part of a tight-knit community that takes care of its members; she has a faith that provides her with a specific meaning for her life; and, it can be argued, her faith contributes to her happiness. However, can these aspects of what her family provided her with be converted into advantages for Jasmine within the environment at CMU? In other words, do these aspects constitute "familial capital"? As we have seen, the answer is no. The norms of her home community are at odds with the academic expectations of the university. In other words, that which makes Jasmine happy and comfortable runs contrary to her academic success at CMU. Were Jasmine to have attended a fundamentalist Christian college, however, we can imagine that she would have indeed possessed familial capital.

Specifically, there are central aspects of Jasmine's worldview (e.g., black-and-white thinking and the perception of the non fundamentalist, secular "outside" as a threat) that are in direct opposition with the goals and purposes of a liberal arts education. While other religious beliefs can act as a support system (and can indeed be familial capital), Jasmine's fundamentalism is in conflict with her education. Because her belief system includes Sivan's (1995) "wall of virtue," attending CMU seemed to place Jasmine at a crossroads: *either* climb the wall, risk hell, and have a greater chance at succeeding at CMU *or* remain within the wall, know that her soul will be saved, and not finish college.

This case begs the question, then: Is fundamentalism, writ large, a fund of knowledge and something that could be considered "familial capital," or is it a deficit? On the one hand, if religious fundamentalism is a fund of knowledge, then it should be a celebrated aspect of diversity. If, on the other hand, it is a deficit, it follows that it would be recognized as cause for providing specific sorts of support to a student, much like various forms of support are provided to students who come from a significantly low SES. While the comparison between being born into a fundamentalist family and being born into a family living in poverty may at first blush seem brash and offensive, a closer examination proves otherwise. Both groups do not have access to key prerequisites for academic success in mainstream settings. While of course members of these groups can possess strengths and skills, they are not often assets that are recognized or useful in school settings. Because of this, members of these groups essentially start out "behind the starting line" on an uneven playing field.

While schools, including institutions of higher education, have clearly addressed how to support students living in poverty and those who are from working-class backgrounds, they have not figured out how to interact with fundamentalist students. Although sorting out the specifics of the university's obligations in cases like Jasmine's is beyond the scope of this work, increased awareness of a virtually invisible category of identity and multiculturalism is a necessary start. Higher education needs to include the category of religion within the paradigm of "multiculturalism." But, as we have seen, the "category of religion" is vast and varied; and what's more, many consider fundamentalism to be a "movement" and a set of "religious phenomena" as opposed to a religion (Almond et al., 1995b).

Thus, campuses might do well to increase awareness of fundamentalism and the ways in which it differs from mainstream religions. Were this to happen, it is possible that Jasmine's conversation with her instructor about her English "debatable paper" might have looked different. The instructor may have had an inkling that the student might be of a worldview that has not included thinking critically, and he may have been able to help her understand the assignment by being aware that the "language" she was speaking was based on a specific worldview. Further, increased awareness of fundamentalism might make it possible to offer support, for example, in the form of a group tailored toward fundamentalist students who may be struggling at CMU. The facilitators of such a group might make the "rules of the game" (see Delpit, 1995) explicit to these students and clarify what is expected of them from within a supportive environment. To be sure, these are not simple suggestions. We have seen that the path to figuring out how to support and educate fundamentalist students is not a clear or easily navigable one.

This case, then, is also a call for further examination and research: We need to learn more about what it looks like, for example, when fundamentalist students succeed in a liberal arts higher education setting. Is it possible, for example, for these students to "accommodate without assimilating" (Gibson, 1998), thereby becoming "fluent" in the culture of the college for the purposes of graduating without altering their fundamentalist worldview and lifestyle? If so, to what end? Indeed, if public institutions, specifically institutions of liberal arts higher education, are committed to providing students with the tools to "see the whole tree" and "develop the capacity for autonomous thinking," we must commit ourselves to learning more about the interaction of public education and fundamentalism, especially in the face of the increasing trend toward fundamentalism worldwide.

· 7 ·

"YOU'RE GETTING A LITTLE TOO KNOWLEDGEABLE"

School Kids and Changing Family Relationships

In Chapter 6, we saw the ways in which Jasmine's parents played a role in her schooling and the ways in which she felt their support. Her family was the foundation and the source of her Christian fundamentalist perspective and lifestyle; and, after Jasmine experienced significant conflict between the two worlds of her family (and the beliefs they raised her with) and her life at CMU, Jasmine ultimately chose to align herself with her family and her upbringing. In this chapter, I explore Engracia's transition to CMU, paying specific attention to the role of her family in her schooling and her new life at CMU.

In notable ways, these two young women have much in common. Jasmine and Engracia are both young Latina women who grew up in large urban centers in the Midwest, and they are both from working-class families. Both are first-generation college students living away from home to attend prestigious, competitive CMU. Both women have lighter skin than many of their Latin@ peers and thus are not subjected to alienating stares from White students at CMU, as are, for example, Antonio and Moriah.

When it comes to academics, however, Jasmine and Engracia have virtually nothing in common. And, when it comes to the role of family in each woman's schooling and transition to CMU, we see significant differences.

The absence of a "school kid" identity that we saw in Jasmine in Chapter 6 stands in stark contrast to Engracia's robust, well-developed school kid identity. Indeed, we saw in Chapter 6 that Jasmine's struggles at CMU ultimately pushed her closer to her family and away from CMU, and her reliance on her family and Christian Fundamentalism deepened. Engracia, on the other hand, enjoyed a seamless transition to CMU as far as her sense of belonging, her adjustment to college life in general, and her engagement and success with academics. Enrgacia's struggle came, however, when her relationships with her family in Center City began to change as a result of her living away from home and becoming a college student.

Family and Critical Race Theory

As discussed in earlier chapters, Critical Race Theory (CRT) moves us away from a deficit model of perceiving the educational experiences of People of Color and toward a vision that allows for understanding and honoring the gifts and experiences that People of Color possess. It also *centers* the experiences and voices of People of Color, which have historically been in the periphery of academic literature. Yosso's model of community cultural wealth, her alternative to the traditional notion of cultural capital, meets these goals of CRT. Yosso (2005) defines *familial capital*, one of the six forms of community cultural wealth, as "those cultural knowledges nurtured among *familia* (kin) that carry a sense of community history, memory, and cultural intuition" (p. 79). The thoughts of a Chicana mother, quoted in Yosso's (2006) counterstory, are helpful in clarifying this concept. As she contemplates familial capital, this mother explains that in part it means "how our families model lessons of caring, coping, and providing" (p. 46). She goes on to point out that, "Family lessons help shape us emotionally and give us moral guidance" (p. 46). We will see here, however, that just as one's identity shifts and changes across time and contexts, the role of one's family does as well.

The Formation of School Identities

Flores-González (2002) explores how and why some Latin@ high school students take on "school identities" and others do not, as discussed briefly in Chapter 6. Using role-identity theory, she argues that schools either foster or hinder the development of a "school kid" identity and that one's "school kid" or "street kid" identity ultimately has an effect on school success and gradua-tion. More than an identity solely bound to school, her "school kid" identity is an all-encompassing and cumulative identity that "represents an image of how these youths view themselves and how they want to be viewed by oth-ers—as good kids" (p. 11). This cumulative identity includes family, school, and community identities, "such as the obedient and dutiful daughter, the all-American school athlete, and the church-boys and -girls" (p. 11).

Significantly, Flores-González (2002) argues that when students' multiple worlds are congruent or similar, their multiple roles are also similar and inter-related. This congruence allows for the all-encompassing school kid identity that is expressed in their different worlds (such as school, sports, community activities, and family). She found that while those students who persisted in school "flourished in the presence of multiple non-conflicting identities," those who left school as well as those who left and later returned "experi-enced role strain brought about by the irreconcilable conflicts that emerged among their multiple, and conflicting, identities" (p. 23). School, she argues, can either "make or break" the school kid identity depending on the types of experiences it offers for the students to become engaged in school (p. 12). Further, students become engaged in school when they feel successful and academically competent, and to achieve competence and success, "they must develop a sense of membership or belonging to school through meaningful interactions with teachers and peers" (p. 12).

The Family Role in Student Transition to College

Echoing Flores-Gonzaléz's (2002) above notion of "congruence" is the widely read work of Tinto (1993, originally published in 1987), in which he explores persistence in college and develops his theory on the same. Tinto bases his work on the idea that a lack of congruence between a student and his or her college context will impede a student's progress in and commitment to col-lege and will lead to eventual withdrawal. Recall that Tinto argues that there are three stages one must pass through in order to successfully enter college life: (1) separation from communities of the past, (2) transition between high school and college, and (3) incorporation into the society of college.

Specifically, Tinto (1993) argues that first students must "disassociate" themselves, to varying degrees, from their families and home communities. He states that "Such communities differ from college not only in composition but also in the values, norms, and behavioral and intellectual styles that char-acterize their everyday life" (p. 95). Although this separation causes stress for almost all college students, the degree of stress and isolation varies—particu-larly when we consider the family background of students. Tinto claims that for students from disadvantaged backgrounds and those from families who have not gone to college themselves, this separation is often more painful.

Recall, however, from Chapter 6 that Tinto's "foundational" theory is not without criticism (Goldrick-Rab, Carter, & Wagner, 2007, p. 2463). Indeed, his tangential consideration of minorities is at the root of most of this criticism (see, for example, Stanton-Salazar, 2001; Cabrera, Amaury, Terenzini, Pascarella, & Hagedorn, 1999; Tierney, 1992, 1999; Nora, 1987; Nora & Rendon, 1990; Yosso, 2006). As Goldrick-Rab (2007) explains, "The experience of minorities in higher education is thought to differ from the experience of majority students—and these different experiences are said to account for some of the racial variation in degree completion rates" (p. 2464).

Specifically, Stanton-Salazar (2001) criticizes the work of Tinto and others for containing "fairly typical Anglo middle-class and functionalist undercurrents" (p. 13). He explains that functionalist thought is commonly linked to "Anglo-Protestant utilitarian individualism" and that frameworks based on this school of thought are concerned with preserving the status quo in society and have generated "simplistic and extremely ethnocentric accounts of social inequality" (p. 288). Further, he explains that these per-spectives focus on "socialization processes that function to socially integrate the individual by conferring a new identity and facilitating adherence to the educational system's moral order and ideological functions" (p. 13). In other words, he views Tinto's theory as one based on White, middle-class experi-ences of transitioning to college, and he claims that it marches in lockstep with a traditional function of schooling, namely to assimilate all students into the inherently racist hierarchy of schools and universities in order to preserve the status quo.

Recall, also, that Yosso (2006) offers an alternative to Tinto's stages. Although Yosso notes that Tinto's theory is valuable in analyzing undergrad-uate experiences, she, too, argues that it is based on the experiences of middle-class White students. Chican@ college students in her counterstory offer their insights into Tinto's ideas as they relate to their transition to college. As one student explained, Tinto's (1993) ideas seem to claim that in order "'to suc-ceed in college you must melt into the pot'" (p. 111). Another student adds, drawing on the work of Delgado Bernal (2002):

Tinto's... model would assume that I wouldn't draw on the lessons I've learned from my family to get through this place. But actually, I couldn't sustain myself here if I didn't have the support of my family, emotionally, spiritually, culturally, in so many ways. (p. 119)

Yosso explains that instead of assimilating, Chican@ students acculturate; that is, they do not abandon their own culture and "some of who they are" in order to "conform to the new situation"; rather, they add the new culture to their own (p. 110). In other words, instead of simply incorporating themselves into the college culture, students are able to critically navigate *among* the multiple worlds of family, home communities, and college—without giving up their identities and cultures.

Giving Back to Family and Changing Family Relationships

Various scholars have studied the desire to "give back" or "help" one's family and/or community with financial gifts (Stack, 1974; Edin and Lein, 1997; Yang, 2011), and others have studied the ways in which this desire plays a role in one's schooling (see, for example, Fuligini & Pedersen, 2002; Fuligini, Tseng, & Lam, 1999; Danziger & Ratner, 2010; Goldrick-Rab & Han, 2011; Minikel-Lacocque, Goldrick-Rab, & Kinsley, 2011; Perna, 2010; Suarez-Orozco & Suarez-Orozco, 1995).

Specifically, Fuligini and Pedersen (2002) have studied what they term "family obligation," which they define as "the extent to which family members feel a sense of duty to assist one another and to take into account the needs and wishes of the family when making decisions" (p. 856). What's more, Fuligini, Tseng and Lam (1999) found that secondary students in the U.S. from Asian and Latin American backgrounds consistently reported a stronger sense of family obligation than did their peers from European backgrounds. Fuligini and Pedersen (2002) studied young adults' sense of family obligation over time and found that it increases during the transition to adulthood—even among Whites—with slight variations according to ethic and socioeconomic backgrounds. Additionally, they found that a sense of family obligation was associated with more positive emotional well-being.

This desire to "give back" to one's family, however, can be more complex than its presence or absence or its correlation to emotional well-being. Scholars have found that young adults with a strong sense of family obligation often feel "torn" between choosing a major and subsequent career path that they are interested in and something that will, on the other hand, make enough money to help support their parents (Fuligini, Rivera, & Leininger, 2007; Minikel-Lacocque, Goldrick-Rab, & Kinsley, 2011). Paying specific attention to low-income Latin@ adolescents, Suárez-Orozco and Suárez-Orozco (1995) found that these students feel a duty to support their families financially. Their work also shows that while family obligation is related to increased academic motivation, the responsibilities associated with family obligation can have negative consequences for school performance.

In addition to creating stress within families, college attendance can generate distance between students and their families, thus straining the families' sense of obligation (Gofen, 2009). We also know that relationships between college students and their families undergo changes (Tinto, 1993; Gofen, 2009; Yosso, 2006) upon college enrollment. More specifically, and as Lubrano (2004) discusses, parents of first-generation college students can feel as if their children perceive themselves to be "better than" their parents as a result of receiving a higher education (p. 65). Lubrano also points out that these parents often worry that their children will abandon them and become "strangers" (p. 33).

Engracia's Experiences: The Data

In this section, I explore Engracia's experiences with her family, paying specific attention to her family's role in the formation of her "school kid identity," the ways in which her family served as motivation for Engracia to do well in school and to someday "give back" to them financially. Finally, I examine the challenges that Engracia faced in terms of her relationship with her parents.

Engracia, School Kid

Within minutes of meeting Engracia, I had the strong impression that she possessed a strong "school kid" identity. During the summer before her first year at CMU, I attended the Amigos orientation to recruit participants for my study. Immediately after I presented my project to the group, Engracia approached me. Her large smile belied the all-business nature of her comments; she quickly said, "I'll do it. I researched Latino drop out rates in high school, so I know a bit about your topic. I'll be in your study." And, during our first interview in September, she was eager to tell me how much she liked school and how involved she was in school, listing activities ranging from sports to student council to math club. She also made her academic successes clear: "I was always an honor student, a good student. I have perfect attendance, everything." Further, she stated that she felt prepared for CMU and that she felt "lucky" to have attended the public high school she did because it provided her with strong college preparation. When I asked if her high school should have done anything else to prepare her for CMU, she answered "no" and explained that anything her high school didn't do, Amigos did do in terms of preparation.

Regarding her parents' role in her education and her success in school, Engracia paints a very supportive, albeit limited and somewhat conflicted, picture of her parents' involvement in her schooling. She explains that her parents, who have limited formal education (recall that her father completed third grade in Mexico, and Engracia is fairly certain that her mom completed high school), did everything they could to help her with school, even after they were unable to help her with her homework. In our first interview, she said, "My parents would help me with my homework, but after maybe fourth grade, they couldn't help anymore. But, you know, they tried." When I asked her to tell me about her parents' influence on her education, Engracia pointed to their involvement in her schooling:

> They always went to my report card pick-ups. They did everything that they could. Yeah, at some point they couldn't [help with homework], but if I needed help with something, they would take me early to school so I could go to tutoring.

Engracia's mother continued to encourage the development of her daughter's "school self" even in the face of family conflict. Engracia remembers:

> When I was young, my parents used to fight because my father used to drink more. The first thing [my mom] would always say every day when she took me to school was, 'Do *not* let this interfere with your studies.' It was more like an *order*. I was like, 'Okay, I'll do all my homework, *right now* [laughter]!'

Reflecting on her mother's highlighting the importance of education, Engracia continued, "You know, I feel as though I can do anything I want.... She told me every day, 'Get an education.'"

While her parents' influence on Engracia's commitment to school is central to the development of her "school self," her *familia* also played a significant role. For example, when I asked Engracia to talk about why she thinks that she, in essence, has such a strong school kid identity and has been extremely successful in school, she pointed to her godmother Tina's influence on her. A childhood friend of her mother's, who is also Puerto Rican, Tina has a college degree and was someone Engracia went to for help with homework while in high school. When it came to Tina's influence on her, however, it was much more salient for Engracia that Tina enjoyed a comfortable, middle-class life-style than it was that Tina had the ability to help Engracia with homework after the point at which her parents could not.

When I asked her to tell me more about Tina's role in her schooling, Engracia explained that Tina would wake up at 6:00 a.m., take the train downtown at 7:00 a.m. when "most people on the train are reading stuff," and get out of work at 5:00 p.m., thus having time to spend with her kids. Engracia went on to contrast Tina's desirable lifestyle of working one steady job with regular hours, being surrounded by people reading on the way to work, and having time for one's children, with her parents' lifestyle of working multiple jobs and long, irregular hours. Witnessing the lifestyle Tina was able to attain with a college degree—coupled with her parents' regular encouragement for her to go to college precisely in order to avoid having *their* lifestyle—made a significant impact on Engracia as she progressed through her K-12 schooling.

In sum, then, Engracia's *familial capital* provided her with three important types of support, which in turn helped cultivate her school self: (1) Her parents supported and were involved in her K-12 schooling in ways such as going to parent-teacher conferences, helping her with homework when possible, and driving her to school early to get tutoring. (2) Her parents encouraged Engracia's education and saw it as a means for her to *get out of* their lifestyle. (3) Her *familia* provided her with a role model to aspire to. Through her god-mother, Engracia had direct access to a lifestyle she wanted for herself.

"I want to get my dad a Rolex"

As the first in her family to attend college, Engracia not only wanted to avoid the difficult lifestyle she saw her parents lead, but she also wanted to help her parents *escape* that lifestyle. In other words, she had a strong sense of "family obligation," discussed above. Recall from Chapter 1 that in her neighborhood in Center City, Engracia was known as "the girl with the rabid dad" and that her dad stood up to—and even intimidated—local gang members to get them to leave Engracia alone. She credits her dad's protection as well as the fact that she had grown up with the boys who were now involved in gangs as the reasons she did not feel threatened by gang members in her neighborhood.

And, as we have seen, Engracia cites the support of her parents—both in the ways they protected her and encouraged her to succeed in school—with some of her success. Now she wanted to be able to give back. It was clear on multiple occasions that she saw college, in part, as a path to a career that would enable her to help her parents financially. This commitment to help her parents affected the choices she made regarding her future. Specifically, when it came to choosing a major and possible career, Engracia explained that although she would love to major in dance, she was worried that such a major would not provide a job with enough income to support her parents. After reflecting on being drawn to dance, she commented, "But I want to help my parents." So, she concluded, she planned to be involved in campus dance activities, including the student dance team, but not major in dance.

After securing a job in which her income would allow her to help her parents financially, she was determined, she explained, to fulfil her dad's long-standing dream of owning a Rolex watch. Thus, we see Engracia's experiences reflected in the research discussed above, both in terms of the desire to give back to her family as well as her sense of family obligation extending to her choice of major and eventual career path. Next, we examine the ways in which her relationship with her family undergoes changes as a result of her becoming a college student.

Changing Family Relationships

Recall that Engracia did not feel unwelcome at CMU, as did others in the study. She did not receive the "stares" from White students that others described. As discussed above, she came to CMU with a strong school kid identity as well as with excellent college preparation. Thus, while some of her peers struggled with the transition to CMU in terms of their lives on campus, Engracia's struggles during her transition to college were in relation to her family members at home—particularly her parents. Upon arriving at CMU, Yosso's (2006) first phase of *culture shock* was all but absent for Engracia, due in part to her college prep-oriented high school, the social and cultural preparation she received through the Amigos program, and her access to Tina, a middle-class member of her *familia*. As the first semester at CMU progressed, however, tension did arise for Engracia, tension that was caused by her parents perceiving changes in her.

At the end of October, Engracia and I met in a bustling Collegeville café for our third interview. By that point in the study, we were very comfortable with one another; Engracia chatted easily about topics ranging from her dance team competitions to her broken braces to her pet snake. However, the tone of our conversation changed suddenly after I asked how her expectations of college compared to the reality of CMU. Engracia explained that she expected to be independent at CMU and that she liked the independence she now felt. Part of her newfound independence, however, meant that she was considering not going home to Center City (roughly a three- to four-hour bus ride) for Thanksgiving weekend, which upset her mother very much. It was soon very clear that Engracia's upcoming Thanksgiving weekend and all it entailed involved significant conflict for her. Indeed, it was a topic we revisited in our interviews throughout the rest of the study. Parts of our conversations follow:

Julie: Is CMU what you expected it to be? What did you think it was going to be like?

Engracia: I have a lot of independence. I like it a lot. My mom's kind of upset 'cause I don't wanna go home for Thanksgiving. I told her to come over here. And she's like, 'Why don't you want to come home?'

Julie: And why don't you want to go home?

Engracia: I have papers to write. It's better for me for them to come here and then leave, and I can just work on my stuff, than for me to spend time over there.

Julie: Have you gone back at all?

Engracia: No, I haven't gone. 'Cause I mean, I can show you my planner right now. My mom thinks I'm over here, like, hanging out. Then I got kind of upset because she asked me about my [recent belly-button piercing] and then she asked me about Thanksgiving, and then she was like, 'Oh you're forgetting who you are.' She started like, 'You're turning so White, blah, blah, blah. You're forgetting who you are.' All this stuff, and I'm like, 'Mom, I'm not doing anything.' She was like, 'You're acting like those White girls.' My mom has always said White people are more open-minded. Like they don't see virginity as such an important thing. Stuff like that, like they are too liberal. They let their kids do whatever they want.

As Engracia continued, her anger and upset over the assumptions her mother was making about her became more evident:

Engracia: Like, [growing up] I was never allowed to sleep over [at friends' houses]. I was never allowed to go to other people's houses. And like now, [my mom is] like, 'Don't start being like White girls and Americanizing yourself. You have to remember where you came from, blah, blah, blah.' All this stuff. I got so upset because that's *not true!*

...

It's not true. Like, I got so upset, I'm like, 'Hold up. I'm over here going to church every week and before I came here, I didn't go to church as much.' I missed a week of church because I was *so* busy and I went to [a neighboring state] for my dance competition, and I, like, apologized to God. I honestly was like, 'I seriously have to do my homework.' And I told my mom I only missed one week, and she was like, 'Oh that's how it starts.' And I got *upset.* I was like, 'Mom, when I lived in Center City, I didn't even go to church. Now I'm over here by myself and I'm choosing to go by myself to church. Don't yell at me for not going one week.' And I was like, 'Why are you doing this? You are really upsetting me. Like as it is, I'm stressed out about school. I don't need you complaining about how I'm changing, and all this stuff.'

Julie: Did her comment about becoming White and that you were chang-ing—know it made you mad obviously, understandably. But did it make you doubt anything about yourself? Like, 'Oh no, what if I *am* changing?'

Engracia: No, no. No, it didn't. It upset me. It didn't make me doubt at all. It's just these little comments [she makes]. She was like, 'That's where me and your father are gonna end up one day, in an old people home.' [She's] trying to say we don't care about her so we're just gonna throw them into [a home].

Julie: Do you think part of her is kind of freaked out because you're in college?

Engracia: I think part of her is freaked out at the fact that I've assimilated so well. I think she would like me to call her every day and be like, 'Oh I miss you, come here, blah, blah, blah.' You know?

When I asked her if she got homesick at all, Engracia explained, "I'm not homesick. I mean, I miss them, but I like it here. I'm happy here."

In the end, Engracia decided to surprise her family and went home for Thanksgiving weekend. Her family was ecstatic to see her, and she enjoyed being home. The conflict with her mother had dissipated by the time Engracia went home for the holiday and was partly resolved for her mother precisely *because* she chose to go home. However, while at home in Center City for the long weekend, Engracia faced a different kind of challenge in relation to the ways she was changing—this time with her father. Engracia was eager to discuss what she was learning in college but was surprised by her father's resistance and caution during their conversation. She explained:

Engracia:	I did my research paper on whorism—on the death of women and whores and stuff. And I told him about all these investigations I read about. And…he was like, 'Don't write about stuff like that.' And I was like, 'Why?' He was like, 'Because people can get hurt like that, like'—
Julie:	Hurt from?
Engracia:	Not like *hurt*, but [he meant] don't always speak your mind. Don't always speak your mind 'cause it's not good for you. And I was like, 'What are you talking about?'
	And then were talking about [Hurricane] Katrina and Iraq and all these issues. I guess he didn't know that I was like—I guess he thought that I was really ignorant. And I guess I kind of surprised him 'cause every time we argued, I knew all the responses. I knew everything. And he was like, 'You're getting a little too knowledgeable, that can be bad.'
	See, I bought this shirt [in Collegeville] that said, 'Who's the Illegal Alien, Pilgrim?' He got mad at me 'cause I bought that shirt. He's like, 'You can't go around wearing that. There are people in charge here. How are you gonna wear that?' He was saying, like, 'Be careful, don't upset people'…. My uncle was like, 'Looks like she's kinda smart if she knows all this. Why is that bad?' And my dad is like, 'No, sometimes if someone doesn't agree with you, they can hurt you.' He's always talking about how the White people are in charge in this country.

In these conversations with Engracia, we see that her mother fears that, as a result of leaving home and attending CMU, Engracia is becoming too "Americanized" or "White" (see Chapter 4 for a discussion on "acting White"). It is important to note that Engracia's mother is not referring to the popular rhetoric of academically successful Students of Color "acting White." She is not speaking of academic success; rather, she is speaking of what she fears is a transformation (read: deterioration) of Engracia's values, steeped in Latin@ traditions, into what she considers "White" values. And, her father warns her against becoming "too knowledgeable" and tells her that people can "get hurt" if they challenge those (Whites) "in charge."

These fears on the part of Engracia's parents, coupled with her close familial ties and her family's significant impact on her educational path, are consistent with Stanton-Salazar's (2001) findings from interviews with immigrant parents. He writes:

> Prominent in the achievement views of these parents was the primacy of parenting and family processes, manifested in part by *orgullo* or pride in the family's unity and cohesiveness, and coupled with a belief that such an environment provides a strong foundation for success in school and in life. We also found parents distressed when

they saw their family's cohesion and stability threatened by such things as … the rapid and unbalanced acculturation of their children to American values and *vicios* (vices). (p. 99)

In Engracia's parents' comments, we can see their distress regarding how they see their daughter changing. The perceived threat to the family's stability is clear in her mother's fear that, as a result of the changes she perceives in Engracia, she and Engracia's father would one day end up in a home for the elderly instead of being cared for by her children.

As Lubrano (2004) explains, perhaps her parents feared that Engracia was becoming a "stranger" to them because of her success in and engagement with college, and would eventually abandon them and have no need for them. Thus, although Engracia's strong school identity allows her to fit in and enjoy her life and studies at CMU, her challenge came in fitting in at home once she started college. It is ironic, perhaps, that the very people who, in so many ways, helped her form such a strong school-based identity—her parents—are the ones she is most alienated from during the initial months of transitioning to college.

Conclusions

We saw that, in Engracia's struggle with her family relationship during her first semester at CMU, she travelled through something akin to Tinto's first phase of the transition to college, separation from communities of the past. However, as in most cases, theory gets complicated and messy when applied to real life. To be sure, Engracia repeatedly asserted over the course of the study—an example of which is seen above—that she did not feel like being at CMU was changing who she was or causing her to "doubt" anything. And, even throughout her struggles with her parents, she made it clear that she relied on their support—especially her mother's—to get her through the stress of college. Indeed, she spoke to her mother at least once daily on the phone during her first year at CMU. Thus, instead of separating from them, she began to modify and redefine how she interacted with them, given her new experiences and knowledge.

It is also clear that Engracia, whose family helped foster her robust school kid identity, was motivated to give back to her family once she secured a career after her education at CMU. It was not simply that Engracia wanted to one day earn enough money to avoid the lifestyle her parents had; indeed, she also wanted to help her parents financially so they could escape their low-income lifestyle, which included working long and unpredictable hours at labor-focused jobs and regularly experiencing financial stress. Engracia's exposure to Tina's middle-class lifestyle, which included a job with regular hours and the ability to live comfortably in a safe neighborhood, gave her direct access to the kind of life she wanted for herself *and* for her parents. In essence, Engracia possessed significant familial capital (Yosso, 2005) from which she indeed reaped benefits.

Importantly, we also saw that Engracia experienced an emotional struggle in terms of her relationship with her parents once she started at CMU. She felt as if her parents did not understand her life as a college student; she worried that her parents thought she was "like, hanging out" in Collegeville instead of working hard. She was proud of her work ethic, her discipline that allowed her to attend church more often than she did while living at home, and her ability to remain efficient and productive within an extremely busy schedule of classes, extracurricular activities, and required meetings for Amigos.

Significantly, Engracia was also succeeding academically in her classes, and she was experiencing a smooth transition to CMU—she was, by all accounts, happy in her newfound life as a college student at a prestigious PWI. While her parents no doubt wanted her to succeed at CMU, they were also afraid of the changes brought about by her education at CMU. They wondered, was she "becoming White" and "forgetting who she was"? Were they, her parents, somehow less important to her now, to eventually be abandoned by her? And, finally, was Engracia in danger by "becoming too knowledgeable" through her courses at CMU?

Given that campuses like CMU are dominated by White, middle-class students and faculty, it follows that the majority of people that first-generation college students encounter on campus may not be aware of the conflicts, worries, and stresses discussed above. Thus, campuses could go a long way toward easing these parental fears, as well as helping first-generation students navigate changing relationships with their home community, by providing specific support to first-generation students and their families. This support could come in various forms, including campus-based support groups that address these issues, facilitated by staff members; programs to increase faculty members' awareness of the particular challenges first-generation students can face regarding their families; and, importantly, workshops geared toward parents of first-generation students. These workshops and other services could fit easily into the orientation program that colleges and universities provide before the start of the students' first year in college.

Partnerships between campus counseling centers, the various support organizations responsible for planning student orientation programs, and faculty members who may have personal and/or academic knowledge of the lived experiences of first-generation college students would be fruitful in creating effective support structures for students and their families. Indeed, as the numbers of first-generation students increase on campuses across the U.S., colleges and universities must do their part to recognize and address the painful changes and conflict that can arise within families as a result of sending a child to college for the first time.

· 8 ·

IS COLLEGE READY?

Fostering Relationships and a Sense of Belonging

We argue that how Midwest University and many other large state schools currently organize the college experience systematically disadvantages all but the most affluent—and even some of these students.
—Armstrong and Hamilton, 2013, p. 3

[*Author's Note*: "Midwestern University" is the pseudonym given to a Midwestern flagship university that served as Armstrong and Hamilton's research site. The similar name is a coincidence only.]

The Students

It's now April of the students' first year, and the study has just officially ended. Antonio, Crystal, Engracia, Jasmine, Mario, Moriah, and I have finished our celebratory dinner and have cleaned up the CMU classroom that served as our dining room. As we make our way out of the campus building, there is constant chatter among the group; it sounds as if the students have known each other for much longer than a matter of hours. The plans they had made to walk each other home are quashed as we step outside and are met with a hefty downpour—it is, after all, spring in the Midwest. We clamber into my minivan, and the jokes and banter continue. I am at once grateful to these young men and women for generously allowing me into their lives, nostalgic for the myriad hours we've spent together over the past ten months, and curious as to what the future holds for each of them. I linger for a moment after they, one by one, climb out of the minivan and step into the rain and reflect on what I've learned from them and their unique stories.

Antonio

Antonio finished his first semester with a 2.07 GPA. He was happy at CMU, he involved himself in various Latin@ student organizations, and he had an active social life. He had discovered the joy and purpose in organizing with fellow Latin@s at CMU and helping grade-school Latin@ students through his volunteer work. He, by all accounts, had found his niche on campus.

Antonio's story, especially when juxtaposed with Mario's, demonstrates how phenotype, biology, and self-identification interact to help form identities, which are multiple and complex. Antonio's mother is White and his father is Mexican, and he identifies as Mexican-American/Chicano/Latino. His racial identity is uncontested at CMU, and he enjoys unquestioned membership in CMU's Latin@ community. His "very Mexican" phenotype, combined with his choice of dress, allows his self-identification to be unchallenged at CMU.

He experienced racial microaggressions at CMU, and his claim that they were "no big deal" seemed to me to be an understatement. We talked openly and frequently about these incidents, and he had clearly spent time and energy evaluating them. While I cannot be sure of the cause, it was clear that his explanations of the microaggressions, in both tone and frequency, did not match his stated claim that they were "no big deal." Indeed, the microaggressions he faced at CMU and no doubt for years prior to college appear to have had a negative effect on his perceptions of Whites.

While his GPA was lower than he had hoped for, he was confident he would improve it in the coming semesters. He had plans to apply to the elementary education program but was concerned he might not have the grades to gain acceptance into the program. Prior to starting CMU, his involvement in Pre-College and SBS had a significant impact on his college preparation and his confidence in his ability to succeed. Although he attends periodic events required by the Pre-College program, for all intents and purposes, this program's support ended when Antonio started college. He is part of the ASA program but does not use it outside of meeting with an advisor to plan for registration. His tuition is paid by the Pre-College Program.

Crystal

Crystal ended her first semester with a 3.7 GPA. By the study's end in April, she was undecided as to her future major and was very much looking forward to going home to Center City and "not do much of anything." Crystal felt successful at CMU, was very grateful to be a part of the Amigos program, and was looking for ways to "branch out" and meet people outside her Amigos cohort. She felt prepared for CMU both by her rigorous K-12 schooling and by the college preparation supplied by Amigos. Crystal did not experience significant stress related to finances—Amigos paid her tuition. Although Crystal certainly experienced racism and isolation at CMU, she always had her "Amigos family" to lean on for support. As she told me more than once, were it not for her Amigos peers and the support of the program, she would have had a significantly harder time making it through her first year at CMU.

Engracia

Engracia finished her first semester with a 3.6 GPA. Although she was proud of this accomplishment, she had really wanted a 4.0. She was busy with a heavy credit load, her campus job, her dance group, and her Amigos meetings. She spent much of her time studying but had a close group of friends to rely on. Her relationships with her parents, who have always been a reliable source of support for her in terms of her schooling, experienced strain as she transitioned to CMU. Her mother feared Engracia was "becoming White" as she delved deep into her studies, enjoyed a newfound independence, and had less time for visits to Center City or for long, frequent talks on the phone. Her father was leery of all she was learning, and warned her not to become "too knowledgeable" and upset those "in power." While these issues with her parents represented a significant struggle for Engracia, the struggle was relatively short lived and was resolved by the end of the study.

She was undecided as to a major but was considering Mandarin, Portuguese, Spanish, and international relations as possibilities. Amigos was a big part of her life on campus, and although she automatically had a "spot" in the EFAS program due to being a part of Amigos, she did not use it. She had a full scholarship through Amigos, which caused her financial situation to be virtually stress free.

Jasmine

Jasmine finished with a 2.83 GPA. Academics at CMU were a near-constant struggle for her, and she often felt lonely. She was extremely homesick but tried to limit her trips home to Lakeside in the hopes of becoming more "independent." She knew she was surrounded by peers who had much stronger college preparation than she did, and this chipped away at her already shaky confidence in her academic abilities. Her Christian fundamentalist worldview added to the isolation she already felt due to her lack of academic skills and college preparation. As a fundamentalist Christian on a very liberal campus, she was met with worldviews and ways of thinking that were unfamiliar to her. She was often asked to explain—and sometimes defend—her beliefs, which she was unprepared to do. In brief, she was unable to find her place at CMU as a fundamentalist Latina from a working-class background.

Although she came to CMU because of its pharmacy program, Jasmine soon realized that admission to this program was out of her reach, and by April of her first year, she had decided not to return to CMU for her sophomore year. She reasoned that if she was not going to major in pharmacy, staying at CMU—the most expensive university in the state—did not make sense. Having received minimal scholarships, she struggled to pay in-state tuition, and the loans she took out weighed heavily on her mind. She planned to move back home with her family and enroll at Lakeside's state university. Although she was a part of the EFAS program, she did not find it helpful and used it sparingly.

Mario

Mario came to CMU with plans to become a psychiatrist. By April, he was still steadfast in his goal of becoming a doctor but was considering other specialties. His first semester GPA of 2.5 was bolstered by the college credits earned through the SBS program, resulting in a cumulative GPA of 2.9. He knew he needed to improve his GPA in order to be accepted to medical school, and he was confident he could do so. His membership in the marching band, a highly respected group at CMU, kept him extremely busy. Although he very much enjoyed the marching band, which provided him with an instant set of friends, he wanted to "branch out" and meet new people.

Mario arrived at CMU with significant social capital. His father's friends, also CMU employees, had alerted him to the SBS and ATC programs while he was in high school, which helped him prepare for CMU. While at CMU, these men took Mario under their collective wing and supported him in various ways, including being available for informal chats, sharing meals, and helping connect him to campus resources. Significantly, his connections resulted in his being awarded in-state tuition, which greatly relieved his financial stress. He received financial help from his parents and did not have a job. Together, SBS and ATC had a significant impact on helping him feel prepared for CMU. He was part of ASA, and although he took part in the required advising meetings to plan for class registration, he did not use it for academic support.

Although Mario enjoyed the benefits of being well connected as he transitioned to CMU, he struggled to feel like he fit in. At CMU, it was as if Mario was not allowed to be who he is: a Mexican-American. Most often people assume Mario is White or "half-White" due to his light skin, choice of dress, and way of talking. Mario feels as if others—both Whites and Latin@s—deny him the right to self-identify as Mexican-American, resulting in his not fully fitting in with either group. Simply put, he feels that he is "too White" for some and "not quite White enough" for others. Through the (virtually all-White) marching band, he faced a racial microaggression run wild. As his protests of the incident went unheeded and were even denied, his attempts at reclaiming and exerting his own power to name and reject the offense were shattered. He was left, alone, to pick up the pieces and figure out how to move forward. As do all the study participants, Mario reminds us of the complexity of real-life stories: Despite the racial struggles Mario experiences at CMU as well as his relatively low first-semester GPA, he reports being happy at CMU and has a full social life. He feels successful and plans to stay for the duration of his college career, with the hope of staying on campus after graduation to attend CMU's medical school.

Moriah

Moriah, the valedictorian of her urban, trades-focused Lakeside high school, had considered dropping out of CMU almost as soon as she started courses in the fall. With a first-semester GPA of 3.65, she flew under the radar of the only support program she was in, EFAS. The support staff of this program couldn't have known that she was miserable at CMU and that not wanting to "end up on welfare" had prevented her from dropping out thus far. They could not have known this because her high GPA did not flag her as someone in need of support; thus, they did not pursue her to come in for check-in meetings. As far as they knew, she was doing just fine.

In reality, Moriah felt extremely isolated and was having a difficult time adjusting to being a student of color at CMU; indeed, her whole life until this point had been spent in a racially diverse urban neighborhood in which Whites were all but absent. She rarely saw anyone at CMU that looked like her or who seemed to share her low-income background; she couldn't relate to her peers at CMU, and she was sure they could not relate to her. Moriah came to CMU with very little social capital. Although her brother's friend worked at CMU's law school and had offered support, this man was not active in seeking Moriah out and offering his help, unlike Mario's family connections. The support program she was in, EFAS, was not helpful to her, mostly because it felt "impersonal" and the staff did not take the time to know her. Her lack of connections is sharply contrasted with Mario's multiple, helpful connections. Her financial situation was dire; she struggled to pay her tuition in spite of her relatively long work hours. Her family was unable to support her financially.

Rethinking Programs

They have their dog and pony show every year. They have this "diversity plan," but what have they really done? I don't see much of a change here.
—CMU Minority Programs Coordinator

The common cornerstones of campus improvement plans with regard to diversity are redoubled efforts at increasing diversity in the student and faculty/staff population, and offering support programs for underrepresented students. While both of these initiatives certainly are important, they are simply insufficient. Indeed, "diversity plans" can end up being perceived as nothing more than a "show," as we see in the words of the CMU staff member quoted above. We must rethink the traditional models of addressing "diversity" and "campus climate"; below, I offer ways in which we can "rethink" the current approach to "getting college ready" by going above and beyond the existing efforts to recruit and retain underrepresented students. Significantly, the following suggestions have the potential to attract underrepresented students to campuses and support these students after college admittance, thereby increasing campus diversity.

Early, Sustained Contact with University

As Gándara and Contreras (2009) argue, K-12 school reform is necessary if all students are to have similar access to college. The revamping of schools, so that college preparation becomes a right and not the privilege of a chosen few, is crucial if we are to come closer to leveling the playing field and thus providing better access to and chances for success in college. If this reform were to become a reality, many college access and support programs would become obsolete.

Part of this reform must be the early, sustained contact with college personnel for all (and perhaps especially underrepresented) students that Vásquez (2003) calls for. If all students—urban, rural, and suburban—had equally rigorous college preparation, including explicit access to the "rules of the game" of college, we can imagine how the experiences of the students in this study might be different. It's possible that Jasmine, through her K-12 education and exposure to college, would have had a better understanding of what it means to be a college student at CMU. Had she chosen CMU in that scenario, it's conceivable she might still be there, perhaps fulfilling her goal of becoming a pharmacist. Moriah would not be struggling as much financially, as she would have had helpful precollege guidance pointing her in the direction of scholarships and other awards. She would also be more confident in her academic skills. And, significantly, she would not feel as racially isolated because there would simply be more Students of Color at CMU. Further, if such school reform were implemented, expensive programs like Pre-College and Amigos would be unnecessary and money used for them could be directed toward other, farther-reaching support efforts.

Not only would early, regular contact with university personnel (instructors and students alike) help K-12 students become comfortable with and conversant in the culture of college, but it would also help undergraduate students in their transition to college. Vásquez (2003) argues, for example, that college students volunteering in K-12 community schools—the very kind of volunteer work Antonio did through CMU's Latin@ organizations—can help students like Antonio adjust to college and find a purpose in "giving back." While the sweeping type of school reform needed to increase college access is admittedly daunting, there would potentially be a significant impact if every public university required its undergraduates (or even a portion of them) to volunteer in the community's K-12 schools, thus making college visible for all K-12 students—as well as possibly helping the college students' transition.

Expanded Understandings of "Success"

Grades and test scores are the most commonly used indicators of school success and resulting eligibility for college admission. Too often, however, these indicators are used devoid of the larger context. For example, a student who "looks good" on paper might not have the knowledge of how college works and thus might be dangerously under prepared. Indeed, college should be recognized as the specific cultural system that it is so that we may more effectively prepare all students (Vásquez, 2003). Similarly, a college student from an underrepresented group who is earning top-notch grades in college is automatically considered successful; a strong GPA effectively halts the need for any further examination of that student's college experience.

Due to the nature of large, federally funded college support programs, there is little time with which staff members can make meaningful, lasting connections with students in their charge. Indeed, Moriah craved these relationships, and Mario noted the significant positive impact these types of relationships had on his transition to CMU. Were we to undertake the sweeping changes in our approach to college access and support discussed above, it is conceivable that the caring relationships that Valenzuela (1999) and Gándara and Contreras (2009) argue for could become a reality. Instead of limiting our approach to systematic checks of grades and test scores, we could expand this approach to include exploring questions such as, "How does this student feel with regard to fitting in on campus? Does this student feel emotionally and/or racially comfortable here? Has anyone taken the time to get to know this student?"

Recognition of Identities beyond Fixed Categories

Race, gender, socioeconomic status, and physical ability are commonly considered the "categories" within a multiculture (Schweber & Irwin, 2003). I have argued, as have Schweber and Irwin (2003), that religion needs to be incorporated into the common understanding of multiculture and multicultural education. Indeed, religion belongs in the deepest, defining category that affects how people see the world. Scholars tend to treat religion as a category analogous to appearance and dress: It is often considered a choice, as something one can take or leave depending on the circumstances. As we saw in Jasmine's case, however, Christian Fundamentalism—which is commonly categorized as a religion—is most often not a choice. Jasmine could not "turn off" her fundamentalist worldview and beliefs when they clashed with the culture and mode of thought represented at CMU. Put simply, she could no more easily choose—or change—her worldview than could a CMU student who, for example, grew up in poverty. A deeper understanding of fundamentalism, as well as of the experiences of fundamentalist students, on the part of university personnel would go a long way toward helping students like Jasmine understand what is expected of them if they are to undertake a liberal arts education.

Too often, identities are conceptually treated as singular and cleanly edged. In reality, identities are multiple and layered, with messy edges—and they need to be considered as such. Jasmine, for example, is a Latina, a fundamentalist, and someone who feels out of place when surrounded by middle-class peers. Jasmine claims Latina, Christian fundamentalist, and member of the working class as facets of her identity. Is there one of these groups to which she belongs "more"? Mario is a light-skinned Texan who feels he is not fully accepted by Whites or Latin@s; he is a Mexican-American in the virtually all-White marching band; and he is a former football player who has lived in predominantly Mexican trailer parks *and* the White suburbs. Does he "belong" to one of these groups more than another? University personnel charged with supporting students must realize that there is no single, simple answer to these questions, and the answers indeed change across time and context. In our work to support underrepresented students, we must honor this complexity, or, in other words, "the multiplicity of identities" (Carter, 2005, p. 162).

When considering this complexity of identities, we must also recognize the role of phenotype in one's identity formation. For example, we saw that for Mario, having lighter skin and stereotypically "White" features can play a significant role in the ways which students at predominantly White CMU interacted with him. Further, we saw that the ways in which lighter-skinned Students of Color may be treated by White students—such as *not* receiving "unwelcoming stares," when their peers of color do—can cause pain, anger, and confusion. For Mario, who explained that he did not fully belong with either Mexican-Americans or Whites, he felt as if others were deciding *for* him, based on his phenotype, to which group he most "belongs."

Explicit Emphasis on Racism

I have argued for open, direct conversations about race and racism on college campuses. I have also argued that, in order to do this, we need to have an understanding of the most common form of racism today—racial microaggressions—as well as have a clear language with which to guide these conversations. Part of this clarity involves the changes in terms I argued for in Chapter 4 as well as the addition of the concept "contested microaggression." While this call for many more conversations about racism is a sweeping one and one that reaches across existing programs, classes, and various employee-student interactions, there remains a specific need that can be targeted in explicit ways that are above and beyond existing efforts at "diversity education."

Indeed, although most campuses today have "diversity" course requirements for all students, they are often considered "meaningless," in the words of the assistant dean of CMU's School of Education. In their efforts to support diversity and conversations on the same, campuses place underrepresented students and their experiences in the spotlight and direct mainstream (read: middle-class White) students to learn about "them" and "their" experiences. This learning about the "other" comes at the expense of self-reflection for mainstream students. Thus, as Lee (2005) and others have argued, the study of Whiteness must be included within the paradigm of multicultural education. That is, Whites must "reflect on their own racial privilege in order to challenge inequality" (Lee, 2005, p. 127). The very notion of "White privilege," however, continues to be controversial; and the notion of reflecting on one's privilege is commonly met with resistance. For example, Sue, Capodilupo, Nadal, and Torino (2008a) echo Lee's argument and explain that many Whites are unwilling to engage in this reflection:

> Many White Americans have difficulty acknowledging race-related issues because they elicit guilt about their privileged status, threaten their self-image as fair, moral, and decent human beings, and more important, suggest that their 'unawareness' allows for the perpetuation of inequities and harm to people of color. To accept the racial realities of people of color inevitably means confronting one's own unintentional complicity in the perpetuation of racism. (p. 277)

The invisibility of White privilege and power is at the root of many, if not all, of the racial microaggressions discussed in this book, and is indeed at work when the perpetrators in Mario's "Nickname Story" refuse to acknowledge Mario's claims of racism. Currently, White middle-class students at CMU are allowed to be unaware of and at the very least unchallenging of their privilege and thus contribute to racial inequities and injuries. In the excerpt below, the assistant dean of CMU's School of Education, pseudonym

Alex, acknowledges this glaring oversight within CMU's efforts to improve campus climate:

Julie: Is there anything else that you can think of that could be done to make that transition [for Latin@ students] better or easier?

Alex: We need to do more with [White] students rather than Students of Color. We have quite a bit of services [for Students of Color]. We do have specialized services for Students of Color, but I think a larger issue is what are we going to do about the majority of the [White] students who come here? And we don't seem to do a good job of— actually, I'm not aware that we are doing *anything* [with the White students]. I know we have an ethnic study requirement, but it's so broad that it's a meaningless kind of requirement. ... More has to be done, and I think by [working with White students] we can change the climate on this campus.

Thus, race and racism must be explicitly addressed for *everyone* on college campuses, so that Students of Color no longer shoulder the burden exclusively. There are relatively inexpensive ways to begin this task. First, perhaps the least daunting change to undertake involves the summer orientations that most universities require entering first-year students to attend. These summer orientations for rising first-year students should be modified to be the first step in encouraging awareness of racism *and* White privilege. For example, the type of information regarding CMU's campus climate and the racial and socioeconomic backgrounds of CMU's student body that is currently given to underrepresented students at these orientations also needs to be given to White, middle-class students. Second, explicit dialogues about race, racism, and White privilege need to be included in these orientations and must be structured for students by experienced, skilled staff. Once these initial steps are taken and established as practice, the summer orientation sessions could prove to be rich contexts in which meaningful work can be done in terms of racial awareness and sensitivity.

Finally, the existing "ethnic studies" course requirements at CMU— and, arguably, like many similar "diversity" course requirements on campuses nationwide—must be improved so that the courses students take are not "meaningless." All students need to be guided by skilled and sensitive instructors to explore the nature and history of race and racism, and, significantly, *all* students must be guided to recognize themselves as racial beings and as having a place in race relations writ large. Expanding the requirement to courses or guided experiences (such as volunteering in the community) beyond the first year of college is also something to consider.

The Call for Border Crossing

In the end, each student in this study is being asked by CMU to be a skil-ful "border crosser." Border crossing, defined as "the movement and adap-tation youth must make to cope with incongruities in expectations, values and beliefs, and actions across worlds" (Lewis-Charp, Yu, & Friedlaender, 2004, p. 109), requires these students to successfully navigate the multiple and varied worlds they face. Specifically, then, CMU expected the students in this study to easily cross the border between the world of their home culture (including its racial, ethnic, socioeconomic, and religious contexts) and the world of CMU. Importantly, the institution expected these students to cross these borders, or "critically navigate" (Yosso, 2006) their multiple worlds, suc-cessfully—but provided little or no explicit support to do so.

While crossing the border from pre college life to the culture of college is no doubt an expectation of *all* college students, the young women and men in this study had multiple borders to cross. In contrast, "mainstream" (read: White, middle-class) students are not asked to cross borders associated with socioeconomics, race, ethnicity, religion, and schooling simultaneously upon arriving at CMU, as were Antonio, Crystal, Engracia, Jasmine, Mario, and Moriah. Importantly, neither are "mainstream" students asked to cross the border between their world and the worlds of their Peers of Color; rather, it is expected that Students of Color will travel into the "mainstream" world instead.

Focusing on students from subordinated racial/ethnic groups, Carter (2005) develops a concept closely related to border crossing. She explains that "multicultural navigators" are able to:

> ...draw on skills and knowledge from the repertoire of the culture of power, which is linked to mobility in mainstream society and to draw on one or more nondominant cultural repertoires, which are linked to status and position in within marginalized or subordinate cultural communities. Multicultural navigators know how and why members of nondominant ethno-racial groups might want to 'keep it real' and main-tain a commitment to their group and self-identities. They also fully grasp how things work in dominant and mainstream social institutions, organizations, places and cul-tural spheres. (p. 173)

Attaining the ability outlined in Carter's concept, then, can be seen as a goal for the students in this study. If all of six of them had been able to be "mul-ticultural navigators," it seems as though some of their struggles would have been ameliorated. But, importantly, it is not enough for Students of Color, already required to cross multiple borders just by attending a PWI, to be skilful border crossers and multicultural navigators. "Mainstream" students also need to make the effort to cross borders and must have skills and awareness comparable to those that their Peers of Color are expected to possess. In order for members of underrepresented groups to become skilful "multicultural navigators" and for mainstream students to learn how to share in the work of border crossing, we need to rethink the ways in which we support college students. Indeed, as this chapter's epigraph suggests, the current structure of many universities runs the risk of placing "all but the most affluent" students at a disadvantage.

Relationships and a Sense of Belonging

Latino students who are the first in their families to go to college need sensitive counselors and friends who can give them the support and encouragement they need not just to survive, but to excel. (Gándara and Contreras, 2009, p. 325)

The student border crossing discussed in the previous section inherently requires the navigation of their relationships with others. And, as we look across the experiences of the students in this research, as well as across the central themes of race, family, and religion and supporting the transition to college, it becomes clear that meaningful, human relationships are at the core of it all. For example, Antonio faces microaggressions that threaten and damage his relationships with Whites, and he finds a comfortable niche (or "counterspace") on campus that is based on his close relationships with other Latin@s. Despite his relatively low first-semester GPA, he was comfortable at CMU and felt prepared for the challenges of college; indeed, he attributed this confidence to the Pre-College Program and the Summer Bridge Program he attended. These programs provided Antonio with relationships with university staff and with his peers. These relationships, in turn, gave Antonio access to the capital (cultural, social, and economic) that made it possible for him to persist at CMU—capital he very well may not have had otherwise.

Engracia's parents could not provide her with the school know-how that middle-class parents provide their children (e.g., help with homework and applying to college, passing on an understanding of the culture of college), but she benefited greatly from a close familial-type relationship with her godmother, Tina. Tina had gone to college and could provide forms of capital her parents could not. Once at CMU, the intimate relationships she had with her Amigos cohort provided her with invaluable support.

Crystal, also part of Amigos, cited the family-type relationships she enjoyed with her Amigos peers as "the reason [she] survived her first semester" at CMU. Jasmine, in part due to the numerous moves among Lakeside schools, lacked close relationships with school staff and fellow students during her K-12 career. In essence, a connection to school never formed for her. At CMU, she was lonely and longed for close relationships on campus and was unable to find them. In the absence of acceptance and understanding in her relational life at CMU, she ultimately returned to the familiar, strong bonds of her family.

Mario also longed for belonging. Although he was easily accepted on a superficial level by his White peers at CMU, he did not feel fully accepted by either Whites or Latin@s on campus. He did, however, have close, meaningful relationships with Latino male staff members. These relationships afforded him much, including a deep sense of support and financial relief. Moriah's academic success was overshadowed by her sense of isolation at CMU. She could not find a niche in which to feel accepted and thus returned home to Lakeside as often as possible. She explicitly noted the importance—and absence—of caring relationships with CMU support staff.

Indeed, a sense of belonging—or the lack thereof—is at the foundation of the ways in which each student experienced the transition to college. Understanding how to foster the relationships necessary to create a sense of belonging for underrepresented students must become a central facet of how we conceive of getting college ready for all students. Once we succeed in expanding the near-exclusive focus on traditional benchmarks of success to include the types of relationships argued for here, we pave the way for students to excel instead of merely survive.

EPILOGUE

It's now March of the students' third year in college. That rainy April evening was in fact not a "goodbye"; most of the students and I still meet frequently to catch up and are in regular touch via email. Although I was not able to get in touch with Crystal, the other students shared with me that she is still enrolled at CMU. As the students wrap up their junior years at CMU, it is clear that their journeys into early adulthood have taken them in various directions, some expected and some surprising, some hopeful, and some tenuous.

Engracia

I most recently caught up with Engracia as she rushed from class to her campus job, apologizing profusely for not having more time and suggesting times we could meet for lunch after spring break. She is currently triple-majoring in women's studies, Portuguese, and Latin American Studies, and minoring in LGBTQ studies and Chicana/Latina studies. She continues to dance through CMU student groups and is active in a sorority. She plans to travel to Turkey this summer for a women's studies course and to Brazil next year for a study-abroad program. Engracia is unsure of her career plans and is considering doing Teach for America while she decides on a career path.

Antonio

Antonio was accepted into the elementary education major at CMU and has started coursework in that area. He has a minor in Chicana/Latina studies. He has brought up his cumulative GPA to approximately a 3.0 and was on the Dean's List for a semester due to the 3.5 GPA he earned. He plans on pursuing a master's degree in education administration and working as a counselor or advisor on a college campus. His goal is to eventually earn a Ph.D. and work in the public schools as a vice principal or principal.

He has worked for CMU's college access program for high school students, *Access to College,* the previous two summers and plans to work for the bridge program he attended, Summer Bridge Semester, this summer. He currently works for the Pre-College program tutoring high school students. For the past three semesters, he has served as the president of CMU's Latin@ student organization and continues to be active on campus and in the community.

Antonio's father was laid off from his factory job and is now collecting unemployment. His younger brother, who also participates in the Pre-College program, will be coming to CMU in the fall and will be on campus over the summer as a student in the Summer Bridge Semester program.

When I recently asked Antonio how he has changed since the start of the study, he replied, "I'm more sure of who I am, I'm older," and with a chuckle added, "wiser." He thought for a moment and continued, "I'm more prepared for classes."

I asked him how he was feeling in terms of racial issues at CMU, and he said not much has changed. He recounted how he felt singled out during a recent discussion in his history class on the topic of the traditional Latina coming-of age-celebration for girls, the *quinceañera.* As the only Latina student in the room, he felt that all "eyes were on [him]." He did not want to be the "representative" for Latinas, so he chose not to speak at all during that discussion.

Not long after that, however, he found himself in a similar situation in one of his education classes during a discussion of the various terms used to refer to Latin@s. In this case, he spoke up. He explained that he gave an impromptu presentation on which terms people prefer and why, because he felt more comfortable with his fellow education majors, he believed they genuinely wanted to know this information, and he trusted the knowledge would help their future work with schoolchildren He explained, "I was the only Latino in the room, except for my friend who wasn't going to talk, and I realized, Shit I'm gonna be the one to talk right now.' But I was okay doing it, because if nobody else tells them, how else are they gonna learn?

Moriah

After "clashing" with her science classes, Moriah changed her career goal from becoming a forensic scientist to a lawyer, with the intention of practicing family law. She has seen many broken families, she explained, and wants to have the power to affect change for them. She is currently waiting to find out if she has been accepted into CMU's human development and family studies major, which she has decided is the best fit for her intended career. She maintains a 3.0 GPA, which she is proud of considering her earlier struggle with science courses. She now works in the ticket booth of various campus parking garages, which she likes because "it's easy" and she can get her homework done.

Her boyfriend from Lakeside has moved in with her and attends the local technical college. He has also joined the military. He and Moriah are awaiting news as to where he will go for basic training this summer. They plan to marry when he returns from training.

While we were having coffee a few months ago, Moriah mentioned that Collegeville was now her "home." I recently asked her, over email, to explain that comment.

She started, "How do I feel about Collegeville? Well, I guess it has become home; a home away from home. I mean, I have my own apartment and it's my own space. After going home to visit my family it's nice to get home to my own personal space. Collegeville is my home in that sense, but my real home is still Lakeside."

> In terms of school, I couldn't imagine myself anywhere else. I am still out of my element, but after three years I have become accustomed to it a little bit. Sometimes as I walk around campus I think about how blessed I am to be here after everything I struggled with (and how lucky the university is to have me as a student…lol). I am extremely proud of myself because I could have easily given up. I guess that confidence we talked about really helped me! I still struggle with juggling work, school, family, and everything else, which can get overwhelming but I manage. After all I am a year and a half away from graduation. Can you believe it?!

Jasmine

Although Jasmine had planned to transfer to the state university in Lakeside after leaving CMU at the end of her first year, she has not continued her schooling. Jasmine's family decided to leave Lakeside and move to a smaller town about an hour away because of their commitment to church activities in that area. Jasmine moved with her family and now works full time as an optometrist's assistant. She recently sent me an update over email:

> Jasmine: I started as a Pre-Pharmacy student at CMU, but by the end of the second semester wasn't sure of what major I really wanted. At the end of the year I decided I would wait until I knew what I wanted then go to school instead of just taking classes for the credits. I have since moved to Southtown. I started out as a waitress and then a cashier at a grocery store. I had very good customer service skills at the grocery store, leading to pins that you receive when you are recognized by customers as doing a good job. My manager received a card on my behalf and a secret shopper landed me with a perfect score. When I first moved to Southtown I had applications in everywhere and State Vision decided that I might be a good candidate for their needs. I still work there and average 40 hours a week.

Mario

Mario still plans on going to medical school. Although he knows his 2.6 cumulative grade-point average is not typically what medical schools look for, he is hoping his involvement in extra curricular activities, such as CMU's marching band and high school sports, as well as his recent volunteer work in a Collegeville hospital, will offset his less-than-stellar GPA. He is double-majoring in psychology and Spanish, minoring in Chicana/Latina studies, and fulfilling all the pre-med requirements. He plans on getting involved in research in the psychology department, as it interests him and will bolster his medical school application. To fulfill his goal of becoming a fluent Spanish speaker, he plans on studying in Argentina for the spring semester of his junior year. This summer, he will stay in Collegeville and work for the Summer Bridge Semester program, volunteer in the hospital, and play baseball.

Soon after the study ended, the majority of his fellow band members had stopped calling him Burro. His protests of the nickname, discussed in

Chapter 5, were eventually heeded by all but the few upperclassmen responsible for the name, with whom he did not have much contact.

When we sat down to catch up recently, I expected him to tell me that because the involved upperclassmen have since graduated, *Burro* was a thing of the past. I was wrong.

Mario:	Now only the brand-new freshmen call me Burro—they are the only ones. The other members were around when it all went down, so they don't call me that. My good friends broke the taboo of calling me by my given name.

He went on to explain that the initial decrease in people calling him Burro had a ripple effect: His close friends refused to follow the time-honored tradition of never using one's given name, and called him Mario. Eventually other members caught on and followed suit. When the incoming first-year students arrived in the fall and were inducted into the lore of the marching band, they obeyed the "rules"; three first-year students now call him Burro.

Mario:	I don't say anything to the young ones because they don't know any better. They don't know what was involved in the whole thing, so why get mad at them for it? [He then grabbed his trumpet case, which was propped up against our café table.] Look at this.

He pulled something from the clear plastic window on the instrument case and handing to me. It was a professionally printed nametag, sporting CMU's colors. It read, "BURRO."

Julie:	Wow. [shocked] How do you feel about that?
Mario:	I don't know how to feel about it. It's part of who I am now. Some people still know me by that, so personally I am already past the point of caring. It doesn't affect me anymore. It's not as controversial for me as it was initially. I have bigger issues to worry about. [He paused for a moment and went on, as if he were thinking out loud.]
	It's interesting, because I'm still digesting all of it and how it went down. I don't really think about it anymore, but talking about it with you is bringing it up again for me, making me think about it. I'll probably be in band one more year. I'm focusing on the future now. I'm not gonna be looking back on this name, I'm gonna be hopefully focusing on med school and my accomplishments.
	I won the argument initially, and that's all I care about. Proving my point was more important than the aftermath. I've already moved on,

I feel like I won. But in the end who really did? [I nodded silently, giving him the space to continue.]

Yeah, I proved my point, but it's still lingering [pointing to the nametag on his trumpet case]. Does that mean they won? Who really won here?

Postscript

Years later, as this book is being prepared for publication, I still often think of Antonio, Crystal, Engracia, Jasmine, Mario, and Moriah. My time with them and the lessons I learned through their generous openness with me no doubt inform all of the work I do today in the areas of social justice advocacy, anti-racism education, and much more. Put simply, my work with these students has compelled me to consistently remember that relationships really are at the core of it all. My hope is that this book, made possible by them, can help spark many more relationships and conversations toward a more just future.

NOTE

1. All names of people, programs, and places are pseudonyms. The pseudonym "Midwestern University" has been used in other studies referenced in this book; this similarity is a coincidence and does not reflect any similarities across research sites.

BIBLIOGRAPHY

Adelman, C. (2001). Putting on the glitz: How tales from a few elite institutions form America's impressions about higher education. *Connection: New England's Journal of Higher Education and Economic Development, 15*(3), 24–30.

Almond, G. A., Sivan, E., & Appleby, R. S. (1995a). Fundamentalism: Genus and species. In M. E. Marty & R. S. Appleby (Eds.), *Fundamentalisms comprehended* (pp. 399–424). Chicago, IL: University of Chicago Press.

Almond, G. A., Sivan, E., & Appleby, R. S. (1995b). Explaining fundamentalisms. In M. E. Marty & R. S. Appleby (Eds.), *Fundamentalisms comprehended* (pp. 425–444). Chicago, IL: University of Chicago Press.

Antrop-González, R., Vélez, W., & Garrett, T. (2005). ¿Dónde están los estudiantes puertorriqueños exitosos? [Where are the academically successful Puerto Rican students?]: Success factors of high-achieving Puerto Rican high school students. *Journal of Latinos and Education, 4*(2), 77–94.

Anzaldúa, G. (1987). *Borderlands, la frontera: The new mestiza*. San Francisco, CA: Aunt Lute Books.

Apple, M. (2006). Educating the "right" way: Markets, standards, God, and inequality (2nd ed.). New York, NY: Routledge.

Armstrong, E. A., & Hamilton, L. T. (2013). *Paying for the party: How college maintains inequality*. Cambridge, MA: Harvard University Press.

Arrellano, A., & Padilla, A. (1996). Academic invulnerability among a select group of Latino university students. *Hispanic Journal of Behavioral Sciences, 18*(4), 485–507.

Associated Press. (2013, March 17). Fast growth of Latino population blurs traditional US racial lines. *New York Daily News*. Retrieved from http://www.nydailynews. com/news/national/fast-growth-latino-population-blurs-traditional-u-s-racial-lines-article-1.1291138

Association of American Colleges and Universities. (2011). *The LEAP vision for learning: Outcomes, practices, impact, and employers' views*. Washington, DC: Association of American Colleges and Universities.

Auerbach, S. (2002). "Why do they give the good classes to some and not others?" Latino parent narratives of struggle in a college access program. *Teachers College Record, 104*(7), 1369–1392.

Barrow, L., & Rouse, C. E. (2005). Does college still pay? *The Economists' Voice, 2*(4), 1–8.

Belluck, P. 1999, August 12. Board for Kansas deletes evolution from the curriculum. *New York Times*, p. A1–A13.

Bergin, D., & Cooks, H. (2002). High school students of color talk about accusations of "acting white." *The Urban Review, 34*(2), 113–134.

Berliner, D. (1997). Educational psychology meets the Christian right: Differing views of children, schooling, teaching, and learning. *Teachers College Record, 98*(3), 381–416.

Boudreau, S. (2009). Diversity education and the marginalization of religion. In S. R. Steinberg (Ed.), *Diversity and multiculturalism: A reader* (pp. 297–306). New York, NY: Peter Lang Publishing.

Bourdieu, P. (1977). *Outline of a theory of practice*. Cambridge, UK: Cambridge University Press.

Bourdieu, P. (1986). The forms of capital. In J. G. Richardson (Ed.), *Handbook of theory and research for the sociology of education* (pp. 241–258). Westport, CT: Greenwood.

Bourdieu, P. (1991). *Language and symbolic power*. Cambridge, MA: Harvard University Press.

Bourdieu, P., & Passeron, J. C. (1977). *Reproduction in education, society and culture*. Beverly Hills, CA: Sage.

Bourdieu, P., & Passeron, J. C. (1979). *The inheritors: French students and their relation to culture*. Chicago, IL: University of Chicago Press.

Bowen, W. G., Chingos, M. M., & McPherson, M. S. (2009). *Crossing the finish line: Completing college at America's public universities*. Princeton, NJ: Princeton University Press.

Brighouse, H., & McAvoy, P. (2009). Liberal education, privilege, and higher education. In Y. Raley & G. Preyer (Eds.), *Philosophy of education in the era of globalization* (pp. 165–180). New York, NY: Routledge.

Cabrera, A. F., Amaury, N., Terenzini, P., Pascarella, E., & Hagedorn, L. S. (1999). Campus racial climate and the adjustment of students to college: A comparison between White students and African-American students. *The Journal of Higher Education, 70*(2), 134–160.

Carter, P. (2005). *Keepin' it real: School success beyond black and white*. New York, NY: Oxford University Press.

Camille, C. Z., Fischer, M. J., Mooney, M. A., & Massey, D. S. (2009). *Taming the river: Negotiating the academic, financial, and social currents in selective colleges and universities*. Princeton, NJ: Princeton University Press.

Coleman, J. (1988). Social capital in the creation of human capital. *American Journal of Sociology, 94*, Supplement. S95–S120.

Conchas, G. (2001). Structuring failure and success: Understanding the variability in Latino school engagement. *Harvard Educational Review, 71*(3), 475–504.

Danziger, S., & Ratner, D. (2010). Labor market outcomes and the transition to adulthood. *The Future of Children, 20*(1), 133–158.

Davis, P. (1989). Law as microaggression. *Yale Law Journal, 98,* 1559–1577.

Deil-Amen, R., & López Turley, R. (2007). A review of the transition to college literature in sociology. *Teachers College Record, 109*(10), 2324–2366.

Delgado Bernal, D. (2002). Critical race theory, LatCrit theory, and critical raced-gendered epistemologies: Recognizing students of color as holders and creators of knowledge. *Qualitative Inquiry, 8*(1), 105–126.

Delpit, L. (1995). Other people's children: Cultural conflict in the classroom. New York, NY: New Press.

Dias, E. (2013, April 15). The *Evangélicos. Time, 181,* 20–28.

Dobson, James. (1985). *The strong-willed child.* Wheaton, IL: Tyndale House Publishers.

Dovidio, J. F., & Gaertner, S. L. (2000). Aversive racism and selective decisions: 1989–1999. *Psychological Science, 11,* 315–319.

Edin, K., & Lein, L. (1997). *Making ends meet.* New York, NY: Russell Sage Foundation.

Espenshade, T. J., & Radford, A. W. (2009). No longer separate, not yet equal: Race and class in elite college admissions and campus life. Princeton, NJ: Princeton University Press.

Everett-Haynes, L., & Deil-Amen, R. (2009). Converging Realities and Identities: A Case Study of African American and Latino(a) Students Negotiating Self-actualized Duality. Paper presented at the annual meeting of the American Sociological Association Annual Meeting, San Francisco, CA. Retrieved from http://www.allacademic.com/meta/p308917_index.html

Feagin, J., Vera, H., & Imani, N. (1996). The agony of education: Black students at White colleges and universities. New York, NY: Routledge.

Flores-González, N. (2002). *School kids/street kids: Identity development in Latino students.* New York, NY: Teachers College Press.

Fordham, S., & Ogbu, J. (1986). Black students' school success: Coping with the 'burden of acting white.' *The Urban Review, 18*(3), 176–206.

Foucault, M. (1980). *Power/Knowledge: Selected interviews and other writings 1972–1977.* Brighton, UK: Harvester Press.

Fuligini, A.J., Rivera, G.J., & Leininger, A. (2007). Family identity and the educational progress of adolescents from Asian and Latin American backgrounds. In A.J. Fuligini (Ed.), *Contesting stereotypes and creating identities: Social categories, social identities, and educational participation* (239-264). New York, NY: Russell Sage Foundation Press.

Fuligini, A.J., & Pedersen, S. (2002). Family obligation and the transition to young adulthood. *Developmental Psychology, 38*(5), 856–868.

Fuligini, A.J., Tseng, V., & Lam, M. (1999). Attitudes toward family obligations among American adolescents with Asian, Latin American, and European backgrounds. *Child Development, 70*(4), 1030–1044.

Gándara, P. (1995). *Over the ivy walls: The educational mobility of low-income Chicanos.* Albany, NY: State University of New York Press.

Gándara, P. (2002). A study of high school Puente: What we have learned about preparing Latino youth for postsecondary education. *Educational Policy, 16*(4), 474–495.

Gándara, P., & Contreras, F. (2009). *The Latino education crisis: The consequences of failed social policies.* Cambridge, MA: Harvard University Press.

Geertz, C. (1973). *The interpretation of cultures: Selected essays.* New York, NY: Basic Books.

Geis, S. (2006, April 30). Latino Catholics increasingly drawn to Pentecostalism: Shift among immigrants could affect politics. *The Washington Post,* A03.

Gibson, M. (1998.) Accommodation without assimilation: Sikh immigrants in an American high school. Ithaca, NY: Cornell University.

Gibson, M., Gándara, P., & Koyama, J. P. (2004). The role of peers in the schooling of U.S. Mexican youth. In M. Gibson, P. Gándara, & J. P. Koyama (Eds.), *School connections: U.S. Mexican youth, peers, and school achievement* (pp. 1–17). New York, NY: Teachers College Press.

Glense, C. & Peshkin, A. (1992). *Becoming qualitative researchers: An introduction.* White Plains, NY: Longman.

Gofen, A. (2009). Family capital: How first-generation higher education students break the intergenerational cycle. *Family Relations, 58*(1), 104–120.

Goldrick-Rab, S., & Han, S. (2011). Accounting for the socioeconomic differences in delaying the transition to college. *Review of Higher Education, 34*(3), 423–445.

Goldrick-Rab, S., Carter, D. F., & Wagner, R. W. (2007). What higher education has to say about the transition to college, *Teachers College Record, 109*(10), 2444–2481.

Hawkins, M. R. (2005). ESL in elementary education. In E. Hinkel (Ed.), *Handbook of research on second language learning and teaching* (pp. 25–43). Mahwah, NJ: Lawrence Erlbaum.

Heath, S.B. (1983). *Ways with words: Language, life, and work in communities and classrooms.* Cambridge, UK: Cambridge University Press.

Hunter, M. (2002). If you're light you're alright: Light skin color as social capital for women of color. *Gender and Society, 16*(2), 175–193.

Hurd, C. (2004). "Acting out" and being a "Schoolboy": Performance in an ELD classroom. In M. Gibson, P. Gándara, & J. Petereson Koyama, (Eds.), *School Connections: U.S. Mexican youth, peers, and school achievement* (pp. 63–86). New York, NY: Teachers College Press.

Hurtado, S., Milem, J., Clayton-Pedersen, A., & Allen, W. (1998). Enhancing campus climates for racial/ethnic diversity: Educational policy and practice. *Review of Higher Education, 21*(3), 279–302.

Ladson-Billings, G. (1998). Preparing teachers for diverse student populations: A critical race theory perspective. *Review of Research in Education, 24*(1999), 211–247.

Ladson-Billings, G., & Donnor, J. (2005). The moral activist role of critical race theory scholarship. In N. K. Denzin & Y. S. Lincoln (Eds.), *Handbook of qualitative research* (pp. 279–301). Thousand Oaks, CA: Sage.

Ladson-Billings, G., & Tate, W. F. IV. (1995). Toward a critical race theory of education. *Teachers College Record, 97*(1), 47–68.

Lareau, A. (2003). *Unequal childhoods: Class, race, and family life.* Berkeley, CA: University of California Press.

Lareau, A., & Conley, D. (Eds.). (2008). *Social class: How does it work?* New York, NY: Russell Sage Foundation.

Lareau, A., & Weininger, E. (2008). Class and the transition to adulthood. In A. Lareau & D. Conley (Eds.), *Social class: How does it work?* (pp. 118–151). New York, NY: Russell Sage Foundation.

Lawrence-Lightfoot, S. (1997). A view of the whole: Origins and purposes. In S. Lawrence-Lightfoot & J. Hoffmann Davis (Eds.), *The art and science of portraiture* (pp. 3–16). San Francisco, CA: Jossey-Bass.

Lawrence-Lightfoot, S., & Hoffmann Davis, J. (Eds.). (1997). *The art and science of portraiture.* San Francisco, CA: Jossey-Bass.

Lee, S. (2005). *Up against whiteness: Race, school, and immigrant youth.* New York, NY: Teachers College Press.

Lemke, J. (1995). *Textual politics: Discourses and social dynamics.* Bristol, PA: Taylor & Francis.

Lewis-Charp, H., Yu, H. C., & Friedlaender, D. (2004). The influence of intergroup relations on school engagement: Two cases. In M. A. Gibson, P. Gándara, & J. P. Koyama (Eds.), *School connections: U.S. Mexican youth, peers, and school achievement* (pp. 107–128). New York, NY: Teachers College Press.

Loza, P.P. (2003). A system at risk: College outreach programs and the educational neglect of underachieving Latino high school students. *The Urban Review, 35*(1), 43–57.

Lubrano, A. (2004). *Limbo: Blue-collar roots, white-collar dreams.* Hoboken, NJ: John Wiley & Sons.

Matsuda, M., Lawrence, C., Delgado, R., & Crenshaw, K. (Eds.). (1993). *Words that wound: Critical race theory, assaultive speech, and the First Amendment.* Boulder, CO: Westview Press.

McAvoy, P. (2008). Should arranged marriages for teenage girls be allowed? How public schools should respond to illiberal cultural practices. *Theory and Research in Education, 6*(1), 5–20.

Minikel-Lacocque, J. (2015). "You see the whole tree, not just the stump": Religious fundamentalism, capital, and public schooling. *Curriculum Inquiry,* forthcoming.

Minikel-Lacocque, J. (2013). Racism, college, and the power of words: Racial microaggressions reconsidered. *American Educational Research Journal, 50*(3), 432–465.

Minikel-Lacocque, J., Goldrick-Rab, S., & Kinsley, P. (2011). Working paper. "You're supposed to help family:" How financial reciprocity affects the use of college financial aid. Presented at the annual meeting of *American Educational Research Association,* New Orleans, LA.

Morfin, O. J., Perez, V. H., Parker, L., Lynn, M., & Arrona, J. (2006). Hiding the politically obvious: A critical race theory preview of diversity as racial neutrality in higher education. *Educational Policy, 20*(1), 249–270.

Muñoz, D. (1986). Identifying areas of stress for Chicano undergraduates. In M.A. Olivas (Ed.), *Latino College Students* (pp. 131–156). New York, NY: Teachers College Press.

Nora, A. (1987). Determinants of retention among Chicano college students: A structural model. *Research in Higher Education, 26*(1), 31–59.

Nora, A., & Rendon, L. (1990). Determinants of predisposition to transfer among community college students: A structural model. *Research in Higher Education, 31*(3), 235–255.

O'Connor, C. (1997). Dispositions toward (collective) struggle and educational resilience in the inner city: A case analysis of six African-American high school students. *American Educational Research Journal, 34*(4), 593–629.

Ogbu, J. (1978). *Minority education and caste*. New York, NY: Academic Press.

Ogbu, J. (1987). Variability in minority school performance: A problem in search of an explanation. *Anthropology & Education Quarterly, 18*(4), 312–334.

Ogbu, J. (1991). Involuntary minorities. In M.A. Gibson & J.U. Ogbu (Eds.), *Minority status and schooling* (pp. 3–32). New York: Garland.

Ogbu, J., & Matute-Bianchi, M.E. (1986). Understanding sociocultural factors: Knowledge, identity and school adjustment. In D.D. Holt (Ed.), *Beyond language: Social and cultural factors in language minority students* (pp. 73–142). Sacramento: California State Department of Education, Bilingual Education Office.

Oliver, M., & Shapiro, T. (1995). Black wealth/White wealth: A new perspective on racial inequality. New York, NY: Routledge.

Orfield, G., Marin, P., & Horn, C. (Eds.). (2005). *Higher education and the color line: College access, racial equity, and social change*. Cambridge, MA: Harvard Education Press.

Patton, L. (2006). The voice of reason: A qualitative examination of Black student perceptions of Black culture centers. *Journal of College Student Development, 47*(6): 628–646.

Pennycook, A. (2001). *Critical applied linguistics: A critical introduction*. Mahwah, NJ: Lawrence Erlbaum Associates.

Perna, L. (Ed.). (2010). *Understanding the working college student: New research and its implications for policy and practice*. Sterling, VA: Stylus Publishing.

Peshkin, A. (1987). The truth and consequences of fundamentalist Christian schooling. *Free Inquiry*, Fall, 5–10.

Pierce, C. (1974). Psychiatric problems of the Black minority. In S. Arieti (Ed.), *American handbook of psychiatry* (pp. 512–523). New York, NY: Basic Books.

Pierce, C. (1995). Stress analogs of racism and sexism: Terrorism, torture, and disaster. In C. Willie, P. Reiker, B. Kramer, & B. Brown (Eds.), *Mental health, racism, and sexism* (pp. 277–293). Pittsburgh, PA: University of Pittsburgh Press.

Pierce, C., Carew, J., Pierce-Gonzalez, D., & Wills, D. (1978). An experiment in racism: TV commercials. In C. Pierce (Ed.), *Television and education* (pp. 62–88). Beverly Hills, CA: Sage.

Rueda, R. (2005). Making sense of what we know: From nine propositions to future research and interventions. In W. G. Tierney, Z. B. Corwin, & J. E. Colyar (Eds.), *Preparing for college: Nine elements of effective outreach* (pp. 189–200). Albany, NY: State University of New York Press.

Saunders, M., & Serna, I. (2004). Making college happen: The college experiences of first-generation Latino students. *Journal of Hispanic Higher Education, 3*(2), 146–163.

Schweber, S., & Irwin, R. (2003). "Especially special": Learning about Jews in a fundamentalist Christian school. *Teachers College Record, 105*(9), 1693–1719.

Sensoy, Ö. (2009). Kill Santa: Religious diversity and the winter holiday problem. In S. R. Steinberg (Ed.), *Diversity and multiculturalism: A reader* (pp321–332). New York, NY: Peter Lang Publishers.

Sivan, E. (1995). The enclave culture. In M. E. Marty & R. S. Appleby (Eds.), *Fundamentalisms comprehended* (pp. 11–68). Chicago, IL: The University of Chicago Press.

Solórzano, D. G. (1998). Critical race theory, racial and gender microaggressions, and the experiences of Chicana and Chicano scholars. *International Journal of Qualitative Studies in Education, 11*(1), 121–136.

Solórzano, D. G., Ceja, M., & Yosso, T. (2000). Critical race theory, racial microaggressions, and campus racial climate: The experiences of African American college students. *Journal of Negro Education, 69*(1/2), 60–73.

Solórzano, D. G., Villalpando, O., & Oseguera, L. (2005). Educational inequities and Latina/o undergraduate students in the United States: A critical race analysis of their educational progress. *Journal of Hispanic Higher Education, 4*(3), 272–294.

Solórzano, D. G., & Yosso, T. (2000). Toward a critical race theory of Chicana and Chicano education. In C. Tejada, C. Carillo, & Z. Leonardo (Eds.), *Charting terrains of Chicana(o)/Latina(o) education* (pp. 35–65). Cresskill, NJ: Hampton Press.

Stack, C. (1974). *All our kin*. New York, NY: Basic Books.

Stanton-Salazar, R. (2001). Manufacturing hope and despair: The school and kin networks of U.S.-Mexican youth. New York, NY: Teachers College Press.

Stonebanks, C. D., & Stonebanks, M. (2009). Religion and diversity in our classrooms. In S. R. Steinberg (Ed.), *Diversity and multiculturalism: A reader* (pp.307–320). New York, NY: Peter Lang Publishers.

Strange, C. C., & Banning, J. H. (2001). *Educating by design: Creating campus learning environments that work*. San Francisco, CA: Jossey-Bass.

Suárez-Orozco, C., & Suárez-Orozco, M. M. (1995). Transformations: Immigration, family life, and achievement motivation among Latino adolescents. Stanford, CA: Stanford University Press.

Sue, D. W. (2010). Microaggressions in everyday life: Race, gender, and sexual orientation. Hoboken, NJ: John Wiley & Sons, Inc.

Sue, D. W., Bucceri, J. M., Lin, A. I., Nadal, K. L., & Torino, G. C. (2007). Racial microaggressions and the Asian American experience. *Cultural Diversity and Ethnic Minority Psychology, 13*(1), 72–81.

Sue, D. W., & Capodilupo, C. M. (2008). Racial, gender, and sexual orientation microaggressions: Implications for counseling and psychotherapy. In D. W. Sue (Ed.), *Counseling the culturally diverse: Theory & practice*. Hoboken, NJ: John Wiley & Sons.

Sue, D. W., Capodilupo, C. M., Nadal, K. L., & Torino, G. C. (2008). Racial microaggressions and the power to define reality. *The American Psychologist, 63*(4), 277–279.

Sue, D. W., Capodilupo, C. M., Torino, G. C., Bucceri, J. M., Holder, A.M.B., Nadal, K. L., & Esquín, M. (2007). Racial microaggressions in everyday life: Implications for clinical practice. *American Psychologist, 62*(4), 271–286.

Sue, D. W., Lin, A. I., Torino, G. C., Capodilupo, C. M., & Rivera, D. P. (2009). Racial microaggressions and difficult dialogues on race in the classroom. *Cultural Diversity and Ethnic Minority Psychology, 15*(2), 183–190.

Sue, D. W., Nadal, K. L., Capodilupo, C. M., Lin, A. I., Rivera, D. P., & Torino, G. C. (2008). Racial microaggressions against Black Americans: Implications for counseling. *Journal of Counseling and Development, 86*(3), 330–338.

Taylor, E. (2000). Critical race theory and interest convergence in the backlash against affirmative action: Washington state and initiative 200. *Teachers College Record, 102*(3), 539–561.

Teranishi, R. T., Behringer, L. B., Grey, E. A., Parker, & T. L. (2009). Critical race theory and research on Asian Americans and Pacific Islanders in higher education. *New Directions for Institutional Research, 2009*(142), 57–68.

Thelin, J. R. (2004). *A history of American higher education.* Baltimore, MD: The Johns Hopkins University Press.

Tierney, W. G. (1992). An anthropological analysis of student participation in college. *Journal of Higher Education, 63*(6), 603–618.

Tierney, W. G. (1999). Models of minority college-going and retention: Cultural integrity versus cultural suicide. *Journal of Negro Education, 68*(1), 80–91.

Tierney, W. G., & Serra Hagedorn, L. S. (Eds.). (2002). *Increasing access to college: Extending possibilities for all students.* Albany, NY: State University of New York Press.

Tinto, V. (1993). *Leaving college: Rethinking the causes and cures of student attrition* (2nd ed.). Chicago, IL: University of Chicago Press.

Tobin, E. (2009). The modern evolution of America's flagship universities. In W. G., Bowen, M. M. Chingos, & M. S. McPherson (2009). *Crossing the finish line: Completing college at America's public universities* (pp. 239–264). Princeton, NJ: Princeton University Press.

U.S. Census Bureau (2012). The 2012 statistical abstract: The national databook. Retrieved from http://www.census.gov/compendia/statab/cats/education/educational_attainment.html

U.S. Department of Education. (2006). The Condition of Education, 2005 (NCES 2005-094). Washington, DC: U.S. Government Printing Office.

U.S. Department of Education. (2007). *The Nation's Report Card, 2007.* http://NCES.ed.gov/nationsreportcard/nies/nies_2007/n0029.asp.

Valdés, G. (1996). Con respeto: Bridging the distances between culturally diverse families and schools: An ethnographic portrait. New York, NY: Teachers College Press.

Valdés, G. (2001). Learning and not learning English: Latino students in American schools. New York, NY: Teachers College Press.

Valenzuela, A. (1999). *Subtractive schooling: U.S.–Mexican youth and the politics of caring.* Albany, NY: State University of New York Press.

Vásquez, O. (2003). La Clase Mágica: Imagining optimal possibilities in a bilingual *classroom.* Mahwah, NJ: Lawrence Erlbaum.

Villalpando, O., & Delgado Bernal, D. (2002). A critical race theory analysis of barriers that impede the success of faculty of color. In W. A. Smith, P. G. Altbach, & K. Lomotey (Eds.), *The racial crisis in American higher education: Continuing challenges for the twenty-first century* (pp. 243–269). Albany, NY: State University of New York Press.

Yang, D. (2011). "Migrant Remittances." *Journal of Economic Perspectives, 25*(3), 129–151.

Yosso, T. J. (2005). Whose culture has capital? A critical race theory discussion of community cultural wealth. *Race, Ethnicity and Education, 8*(1), 69–91.

Yosso, T. J. (2006). Critical race counterstories along the Chicana/Chicano educational pipeline. New York, NY: Routledge.

Yosso, T. J., Smith, W. A., Ceja, M., & Solórzano, D. G. (2009). Critical race theory, racial microaggressions, and campus racial climate for Latino/a undergraduates. *Harvard Educational Review, 79*(4), 659–690.

INDEX

N

ABOUT THE AUTHOR

Julie Minikel-Lacocque is an assistant professor in the Department of Curriculum and Instruction in the College of Education and Professional Studies at the University of Wisconsin-Whitewater. She teaches courses on bilingual education, race and racism in schools, and critical approaches to teaching, and she directs the university's bilingual education licensure program. Julie is also the founder of a "Saturday College" program that brings Latin@ K-12 students and their families to campus. The program, Latin@s Logrando Altas Visiones Educativas (LLAVE), is aimed at increasing college access for Latin@s as well as increasing diversity in Wisconsin's public universities. Julie holds a Ph.D. from the School of Education at the University of Wisconsin-Madison and a Masters of Arts in Teaching from the School for International Training in Brattleboro, Vermont. Before earning her doctorate, she taught high school and college in both urban and rural settings. Her research interests include college access, race and racism in schooling, critical approaches to multicultural education, and peer-based sociocultural processes experienced by K-12 students in dual-language education programs in the United States. Contact: minikelj@uww.edu.

A BOOK SERIES FOR EQUITY SCHOLARS & ACTIVISTS

Virginia Stead, H.B.A., B.Ed., M.Ed., Ed.D., *General Editor*

Globalization increasingly challenges higher education researchers, administrators, faculty members, and graduate students to address urgent and complex issues of equitable policy design and implementation. This book series provides an inclusive platform for discourse about—though not limited to—diversity, social justice, administrative accountability, faculty accreditation, student recruitment, admissions, curriculum, pedagogy, online teaching and learning, completion rates, program evaluation, cross-cultural relationship-building, and community leadership at all levels of society. Ten broad themes lay the foundation for this series but potential editors and authors are invited to develop proposals that will broaden and deepen its power to transform higher education:

(1) Theoretical books that examine higher education policy implementation,
(2) Activist books that explore equity, diversity, and indigenous initiatives,
(3) Community-focused books that explore partnerships in higher education,
(4) Technological books that examine online programs in higher education,
(5) Financial books that focus on the economic challenges of higher education,
(6) Comparative books that contrast national perspectives on a common theme,
(7) Sector-specific books that examine higher education in the professions,
(8) Educator books that explore higher education curriculum and pedagogy,
(9) Implementation books for front line higher education administrators, and
(10) Historical books that trace changes in higher education theory, policy, and praxis.

Expressions of interest for authored or edited books will be considered on a first come basis. A Book Proposal Guideline is available on request. For individual or group inquiries please contact:

Dr. Virginia Stead, General Editor | *virginia.stead@alum.utoronto.ca*
Christopher S. Myers, Acquisitions Editor | *chrism@plang.com*

To order other books in this series, please contact our Customer Service Department at:

(800) 770-LANG (within the U.S.)
(212) 647-7706 (outside the U.S.)
(212) 647-7707 FAX

Or browse online by series at www.peterlang.com